BALANCING THE SCALES OF JUSTICE

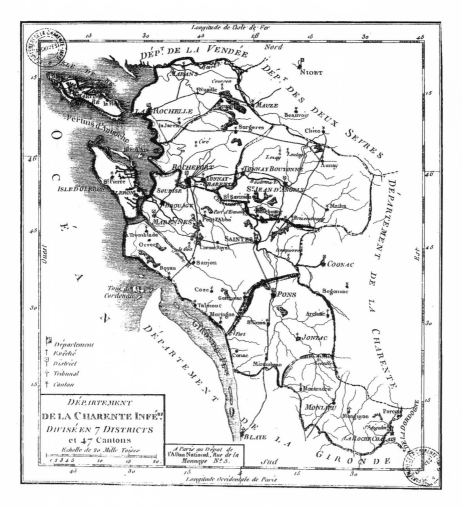

Revolutionary Charente-Inférieure

BALANCING THE SCALES OF JUSTICE

Local Courts and Rural Society
in Southwest France,
1750–1800

ANTHONY CRUBAUGH

KJV
3758
.C78
2001
West

The Pennsylvania State University Press ■ University Park, Pennsylvania

Library of Congress Cataloging-in-Publication Data

Crubaugh, Anthony, 1962–
    Balancing the scales of justice : local courts and
rural society in southwest France, 1750–1800 /
Anthony Crubaugh.
        p.   cm.
    Includes bibliographical references and index.
    ISBN 0-271-02077-6 (cloth : alk. paper)
    ISBN 0-271-02078-4 (paper : alk. paper)
    1. Justice, Administration of—France,
Southwest—History.   2. Manorial courts—France,
Southwest—History.   3. Justices of the
peace—France, Southwest—History.   I. Title.

KJV3758.C78   2001
347.44′7—dc21   00-035684

Copyright © 2001 The Pennsylvania State University
All rights reserved
Printed in the United States of America
Published by The Pennsylvania State University Press,
University Park, PA 16802–1003

It is the policy of The Pennsylvania State University
Press to use acid-free paper for the first printing of all
clothbound books. Publications on uncoated stock
satisfy the minimum requirements of American National
Standard for Information Sciences—Permanence of
Paper for Printed Library Materials, ANSI Z39.48–1992.

WE WILL NO LONGER SEE THE SCALES OF JUSTICE

BEND IN FAVOR OF THE POWERFUL MAN WHO

SIMULTANEOUSLY PRESSES HIS SWORD AGAINST THE WEAK.

—M. Boucherit, mayor of Port d'Envaux,
at a ceremony for swearing in a justice of the peace,
23 DECEMBER 1790

LIST OF MAPS AND TABLES

A project begun nearly a decade ago, in a different millennium, even, cannot but result in the accumulation of enormous personal and professional debts. I have no adequate means to repay those debts or to express satisfactorily my sincere gratitude.

In France, the kind and professional staff at the departmental archives in La Rochelle first tolerated the presence of a clueless American graduate student and then proved enormously helpful when I did know what I was doing. A fellow researcher, Pauline Arsenault, gave me language and paleography lessons and introduced me to the beauty of La Rochelle as well as the *douceur* of life in *la France profonde*. My baseball teammates on the La Rochelle Cubs allowed me to witness first hand what anthropologists refer to as the "opacity" of another culture. Finally, I am sincerely grateful for the friendship of Xavier Martin and his family. Their generosity, without which this book could never have been completed, included several summers of free room and board in La Rochelle, and I hope that it is not too presumptuous to consider them my French family.

In New York, Karthik Sankaran was an impressive cook, a perfect roommate, an intellectual companion, and a valued friend, while David Cannadine provided crucial guidance at times. My intellectual development and teaching career owe a great debt to Deborah Valenze; she assumed the roles of advisor and friend despite no obligation to do so. To Isser Woloch, whose insightful criticism, skillful editing, and timely cajoling are responsible for anything of merit in this book, all I can say is "thank you."

At Connecticut College, the emotional and professional support of Lisa Wilson and Fred Paxton went far beyond the call of administrative duty. As chairs of the history department they made prodigious efforts to keep me employed in a nearly ideal position as visiting professor during a tough academic job market. Alexis Dudden was the consummate colleague and inspired me with her intelligence and infectious love of learning. Special thanks go to Marc Forster, who not only made me a better teacher and historian but also offered valuable criticism and encouragement of my research.

As this project progressed from dissertation to book stage, Robert

Forster graciously read an unsolicited manuscript sent by a (then) stranger and was subsequently instrumental in getting this book published. Kathleen Kete and Cynthia Bouton commented insightfully on parts of the manuscript, while Mel Edelstein shared the fruits of his research as well as his knowledge of secondary sources. Steven Reinhardt and John Markoff read the entire manuscript with extreme care and intelligence and offered countless and excellent suggestions for improvement. My appreciation of their professionalism is matched by my admiration of their expertise. It has been a pleasure and an honor to work with Peter Potter at the Penn State Press. Needless to say, this book would not exist without his love and knowledge of French history. My friend and brother-in-law, Alan Hill, generously volunteered his talents to produce the cover art and maps.

My parents, John and Jane Crubaugh, provided financial support and emotional encouragement for this project long beyond the time frame established by natural law or common sense. For periods of three consecutive years they allowed me to retreat to their home in the bucolic splendor of rural Wisconsin, during which time I wrote nearly the entire manuscript. Riding bicycles with my father through rolling farmland and walking with my mother along the shore of Lake Michigan constituted great sources of peace, and joyful memories of our shared time will linger long after I have forgotten the content of this work. Finally, my wife, Polly Bedford, and our children, Floréal and Ressa, have magnanimously accepted the disruptions to family life that such a project necessarily entails. I happily close this chapter in my life just as I look forward to the next one with them. This book is dedicated to Polly.

During my period of research in La Rochelle, it was a Friday custom to end a week of work in the departmental archives by meeting friends for an aperitif at La Cave de la Guignette. The route to the wineshop meandered from the Atlantic coast, past the enormous and malodorous fish market, along the famous towers that once rendered La Rochelle impregnable to everyone but Cardinal Richelieu's Catholic armies, and finally into the charm of the arcaded streets. La Guignette, situated at the end of the twisting, hidden pedestrian rue St. Nicolas, was an establishment catering to local mariners, *chômeurs,* and students. Inside, once your eyes became accustomed to the poorly lit room and the haze from the smoke of strong tobacco, you could take in your surroundings: bottles of wine stacked from floor to ceiling and barrels serving as tables around which sailors and fishermen traded stories and students chain-smoked Marlboros and consumed pastis and the charentais specialty, pineau. A glass of wine cost around three francs and a *demi* of Kronenbourg around six, making it the cheapest drinking establishment in town. La Guignette is one of those places that a francophile foreigner will inevitably, albeit understandably, feel snobbish about, having "discovered" a wineshop beloved by locals but never destined to appear in *Let's Go* or a Frommer's guide.

One evening after I had wedged my way to the counter to place an order, my accent must have piqued the curiosity of an elderly Rochelois. We chatted for several moments, and then he asked in a boozy voice about the subject of my research at the archives. With exaggerated self-importance, I answered, "I'm studying justice during the French Revolution." "Justice during the Revolution?" he repeated, but as an interrogative. "Il n'y en avait pas" (There wasn't any). A visceral laugh exposed brown teeth and hinted that the putative lack of justice during the French Revolution did not disturb his sleep.

The idea that there was no justice during the French Revolution reflects the degree to which the extraordinary and political adjudication of the Revolutionary Tribunals has entered popular consciousness. Everyone knows how these courts supposedly offered a steady diet of victims to the insatiable guillotine. Scholars, too, have focused their energies on the political nature of much adjudication from 1789 to 1815, so much so that Robert

Badinter laments that the Revolutionary Tribunal has been confounded with justice during the Revolution.[1] This study of eighteenth-century French local justice originated, in part, from Badinter's plea for historians to examine the revolutionary institutions and practices of ordinary justice, of those courts mostly (or potentially) immune to the vicissitudes of political upheaval.[2]

On the other hand, this book's genesis was influenced by the research project of my graduate advisor, Isser Woloch. In his recent work, *The New Regime: Transformations of the French Civic Order, 1789–1820s,* Woloch fills a void in Tocqueville's argument (that the revolutionary divide of 1789 disguised the continuity of the growth of the central authority) by examining the policies and institutions of the French state from 1789 to 1820.[3] Through his research on local government, policing, the judiciary, charitable institutions, and military conscription, Woloch explains how revolutionary regimes attempted to fulfill their goal of penetrating rural areas and establishing a new civic order.[4] By researching the institution of the justice of the peace (*justice de paix*), one of the most crucial yet unstudied intersections where the French state encountered the mass of rural dwellers, I hope to contribute to Woloch's agenda by illuminating the dynamics of the central authority's desire to reach denizens of the countryside. What policies did the state enact to gain legitimacy in the eyes of French people? What did revolutionary changes in the system of local justice mean to members of rural society?

Although a study of revolutionary justices of the peace would itself be justified, in this project I also examine local justice prior to 1789; in other words, I have also researched the institution of seigneurial justice. The juxtaposition of the conception and practice of seigneurial justice with the

1. See the introduction, "Naissance d'une justice," to R. Badinter, ed., *Une autre justice: Contributions à l'histoire de la justice sous la Révolution française* (Paris, 1989).

2. So extensive is the neglect of ordinary justice that there appears to be only one study of a departmental district court during the Revolution, even though this was the basic civil court in France. See A. Vincenti, *Le Tribunal du département du Vaucluse, de l'an IV à l'an VIII* (Aix-en-Provence, 1928). And, of course, the paucity of studies on justices of the peace, the other pillar of the revolutionary reorganization of justice, justifies this study.

3. A. de Tocqueville, in *The Old Regime and the French Revolution,* trans. S. Gilbert (Garden City, N.Y., 1955), describes the centralization of the French state in the Old Regime but not after 1789.

4. Woloch defines the civic order as the values, policies, and institutions at the juncture of state and civil society. *The New Regime: Transformations of the French CIvic Order, 1989–1820s* (New York, 1994), 14.

institution of the justice of the peace—or the crossing of the 1789 chronological boundary—highlights how revolutionary changes in the system of
dispute resolution affected rural French society. Despite the myriad view-
points contained in the *cahiers de doléance* of 1789, they exhibited near una-
nimity in their dissatisfaction with the French system of justice at the local
level. Did the Revolution, then, actually fulfill its promises of providing fair
and inexpensive justice, of mitigating the litigious passions of French people, of restoring calm to the countryside, and of protecting peasants from
the avaricious practices of seigneurs and lawyers? If so, could this not have
paved the way for the acceptance of the intrusion of the French state in the
countryside?

Unlike rural justices of the peace, whom most historians have relegated
to the realm of inconsequentiality,[5] seigneurial justice has received the attention of several scholars.[6] However admirable the studies of seigneurial

5. Among the few studies on rural justices of the peace are J. Bart, "La justice de paix du canton
de Fontaine-Française à l'époque révolutionnaire," *Mémoires de la société pour l'histoire du droit et des
institutions des anciens pays bourguignons* 26 (1965): 193–216; D. Bouguet, "La sociabilité conflictuelle
dans le canton de Loches d'après les archives de la justice de paix (1790–an III)," *Histoire moderne et
contemporaine* 1, no. 2 (1986): 159–70; A. Bleton-Ruget, "L'infrajudiciaire institutionalisée: Les justices
de paix des cantons ruraux du district de Dijon pendant la Révolution," in B. Garnot, ed., *L'infrajudiciaire du Moyen Age à l'époque contemporaine. Actes du colloque de Dijon, 5–6 octobre, 1995* (Dijon, 1996);
and C. Coquard and C. Durand-Coquard, "Société rurale et Révolution: L'apport des actes de deux
justices de paix de l'Allier (1791–fin de l'an VI)," (thèse de doctorat, Université de Bourgogne, 1998).
The latter is essentially a "total history" of a small region derived from the records of justices of the
peace. See also J.-L. Debauve, *La justice révolutionnaire dans le Morbihan, 1790–1795* (Paris, 1965).
Woloch recognizes the importance of the institution in his work but has few in-depth studies from
which to draw. On Parisian justices of the peace, see R. Andrews, "The Justices of the Peace of
Revolutionary Paris, September 1792–November 1794 (Frimaire Year III)," *Past and Present* 52 (August
1971): 56–105 and G. Métairie, *Le monde des juges de paix de Paris, 1790–1838* (Paris, 1994).
6. The most important works on seigneurial justice are A. Giffard, *La justice seigneuriale en
Bretagne aux XVIIe et XVIIIe siècles* (Paris, 1902); H. Bataillon, *Les justices seigneuriales du bailliage de
Pontoise à la fin de l'ancien régime* (Paris, 1942); P. Lemercier, *Les justices seigneuriales de la région
Parisienne de 1580 à 1789* (Paris, 1933); A. Combier, *Les justices seigneuriales du bailliage de Vermandois
sous l'ancien régime* (Paris, 1897); P. Villard, *Les justices seigneuriales dans la Marche* (Paris, 1969); and
A. Poitrineau, "Aspects de la crise des justices seigneuriales dans l'Auvergne du XVIIIe siècle," *Revue
historique du droit français et étranger* 39 (1961): 552–70. Z. Schneider's recent work on justice in
Normandy is also very important, especially for showing the limits of absolutism in Old Regime
France. See "The Village and the State: Justice and the Local Courts in Normandy, 1670–1740"
(Ph.D. diss., Georgetown University, 1997). Jeremy Hayhoe has conducted as yet unpublished re-
search on seigneurial courts in Burgundy. Finally, the study by E. Guillaume, although weighted
towards the genealogical interests of the amateur historian, is also interesting and informative. See
his *Justice seigneuriale et vie quotidienne dans la vallée du Mont-Dore au XVIIIe siècle* (Clermont-
Ferrand, 1992). J. Markoff surveys the literature on seigneurial justice in *The Abolition of Feudalism:
Peasants, Lords, and Legislators in the French Revolution* (University Park, Pa., 1996), 111–18.

tribunals may be, they largely focus on legal doctrine and jurisprudence; questions about the origins, theory, and jurisdiction of seigneurial justices and their relation to royal courts dominate the works of these authors. Because scholars have approached seigneurial justice from the angle of jurisprudence, the role that lords' courts played in rural French society is not well known, and some historians have assumed that the institution was moribund on the eve of the French Revolution.[7]

In contrast to the approach of legal scholars, I treat law as an aspect of social practice and am most interested in how the operation of an institution affects society. Thus, in this book I will examine the implications for French society of a seigneurial system in which justice was an amalgam of the public and the private—considered the exercise of a public service in civil and criminal cases *and* as one's patrimony to be exploited as a source of power, honor, and profit in feudal cases and the right to police. I will then investigate the implications of revolutionary local justice for French society. Since Parisian legislators conceived of justices of the peace more as mediating nonspecialists armed with equity than as judges armed with statutes and because these lawmakers linked the new state's legitimacy to its ability to assure the fair and expeditious resolution of conflicts, it is necessary to witness the revolutionary creation in action. What did an informal setting, the emphasis on conciliation without the input of lawyers, the prohibition of written evidence, and the election of salaried officials without legal training mean to the practice of local justice? What impact did these changes have on rural inhabitants, their relations with one another, and their interaction with the French state?

Understandably, I have divided my study into two parts, the first of which treats the institution of seigneurial justice. The opening chapter provides an overview of the theory, geographical organization, personnel, jurisdiction, and activity of seigneurial justice. I demonstrate how the exercise of the right of justice by private persons and the proliferation of jurisdictions resulted in problems in the administration of local justice. Chapter 2 treats civil justice in seigneurial tribunals. In particular, I illuminate the inadequacies of these courts in the resolution of disputes: civil justice was slow, expensive, and therefore inaccessible to many rural justiciables. In Chapter 3 I examine how lords used their right of justice to protect their

---

7. For example, P. Bois justifies ignoring seigneurial justice altogether in his study of the eighteenth-century Sarthe, *Paysans de l'Ouest: Des structures économiques et sociales aux options politiques depuis l'époque révolutionnaire dans la Sarthe*, abridged ed. (Paris, 1971), 178.

social and economic status and explore the significance of rural inhabitants' belief that the system of justice primarily enforced a social hierarchy. Chapter 4 exposes how the high costs of criminal justice borne by lords left seigneurial agents wary of pursuing disruptions of local law and order. I then speculate on the implications of the absence of an effective repressive force for rural society.

Part II sees the focus shift to the justice of the peace (JP), commencing with a chapter on the principles that guided this revolutionary creation. An examination of its conception, jurisdiction, geographical organization, and personnel places the justice of the peace in clear contrast to the institution of seigneurial justice. The remaining chapters then follow the new institution in practice. In Chapter 6 I study civil cases under the justice of the peace and assess the impact of the revolutionary style of justice on the length and cost of trials and the accessibility of justice. I offer in Chapter 7 an in-depth study of rural *bureaux de paix,* in which justices of the peace mediated between quarreling parties. How successful was the revolutionary emphasis on conciliation as a form of dispute resolution, and what repercussions did it have for rural social relations? Finally, in dealing with the JPs' role as local police officers, in Chapter 8 I point out the ambivalence of rural dwellers toward the more effective but intrusive maintenance of law and order.

The location for this examination of eighteenth-century local justice is the department of Charente-Maritime, which roughly comprises the historical regions of Aunis and Saintonge. The creation of Charente-Inférieure (as the department was known at its inception) in 1789 reflected administrative expediency rather than any historical, sociological, or geographical reality, since Aunis and Saintonge, each too small to constitute a department of its own, were distinct regions even though both belonged to the *généralité* of La Rochelle.[8] Aunis, with its poor soil and numerous mars-

---

8. J-N. Luc, ed., *La Charente-Maritime: L'Aunis et la Saintonge des origines à nos jours* (St. Jean d'Angély, 1981). Among the very few studies of the countryside of Aunis are R. Jousmet, "Fermiers et métayers d'Aunis, 1750–1789" (thèse de doctorat, Université de Rennes II, 1989); C. Laveau's valuable "Le monde rochelais de l'ancien régime au Consulat," (thèse de doctorat, Université de Paris, 1972); and C. Valin, "Recherches sur La Rochelle, ville frontière, au cours de la crise révolutionnaire, 1790–an III," 2 vols. (thèse de doctorat, Université de Rouen, 1994). See also R. Forster's *Merchants, Landlords, Magistrates: The Depont Family in Eighteenth-Century France* (Baltimore, 1980). The history of rural Saintonge is even less well known. See the introduction by J.-N. Luc to his *Paysans et droits féodaux en Charente-Inférieure pendant la Révolution française* (Paris, 1984) and also J.-M. Augustin, *La Révolution française en Haut-Poitou et pays charentais* (Toulouse, 1989).

hes, was agriculturally unproductive, and contemporaries cited a paucity of both livestock and rural workers in the region. Despite the physiocrats' apotheosis of monoculture, overreliance on viticulture to the neglect of grain production left Aunis perilously close to dearth in years with poor harvests in other parts of France or when harsh winters hindered the traffic in foodstuffs. Not even the salt industry thrived, as the exploiters of salt marshes faced much competition from other parts of the kingdom. Economically and socially, the region was dominated by the great *négociant* families of La Rochelle, whose wealth rested on trade with Saint-Domingue, and Aunis was noted for the weakness of its nobility. But even this once dynamic mercantile element of Aunisian society appeared in decline on the eve of the French Revolution, since La Rochelle never recovered from the Seven Years War's disastrous effects on trade in the Western hemisphere. Unproductive agriculturally, cut off from its once lucrative trade routes, outside the population explosion experienced by the rest of France, Aunis in the eighteenth century seemed as stagnant as its marshy waters.[9]

By contrast, while not exceptionally fertile, the soil of the Saintonge supported the subsistence agriculture of a fairly dense rural population. Since the Saintonge bordered the Cognac region, the production of eau-de-vie existed alongside subsistence agriculture, and vine growers floated their goods down the lazy Charente River toward the ultimate destination of Bordeaux. In addition, the Saintonge had an important textile industry. Unlike Aunis, the countryside of the Saintonge still experienced the presence of a strong nobility who, along with the bourgeois purchasers of *seigneuries,* actively enforced the rights and dues that were the privileges of proprietors of fiefs. That enforcement would later precipitate a wave of antiseigneurial activity—alternately violent and passive—in the early years of the French Revolution. Although rural society in the eighteenth-century Saintonge still awaits its historian, one has the impression of a traditional region: subsistence agriculture, an entrenched nobility, a peasantry burdened by pressures on the land as well as seigneurial and royal fiscal agents, and only a limited influence of outside markets and ideas. Like its main town, Saintes, once an important administrative seat in the Roman Empire but subsequently having few advantages save its presidial court and its loca-

---

9. The grim description of eighteenth-century Aunis is not meant to impugn the present-day region. Indeed, La Rochelle is a beautiful city, and the charentais coast attracts hordes of vacationers to its sunny beaches.

tion on the road from Paris to Bordeaux, the entire Saintonge struck Arthur Young as a mediocre region.

The heterogeneity of Aunis and Saintonge was juridical as well, since the regions fell under different legal systems. Aunis was an area of custom law, and the appeals from its courts were under the jurisdiction of the Parlement of Paris, whereas the Saintonge was a region of written law under the Parlement of Bordeaux. The heterogeneity of the new department of Charente-Inférieure immediately revealed itself in a bitter struggle between its principal towns, La Rochelle and Saintes, each vying for the advantages of becoming the *chef-lieu*. Ultimately, the Constituent Assembly selected Saintes on a temporary basis because of its centrality to the department's other towns and hamlets.

The justification for choosing Charente-Maritime as the source of this study, then, comes from the quality of its archives rather than its existence as a recognizable historical, social, geographical, or juridical entity.[10] The paucity of works on eighteenth-century French local justice reflects, to a significant degree, the nature of the archival records, since seigneurial records are in a notoriously poor state and because the records of justices of the peace are famously reticent (the emphasis on minimizing paperwork having rendered them not very fruitful to work with). Thus, it was important to find a location where sufficient records have survived for both seigneurial tribunals and justices of the peace, and the department of Charente-Maritime met this crucial criterion. Originally, I had intended to limit my study to only one district in Aunis or Saintonge; in other words, I had hoped to do research on perhaps six justices of the peace in a relatively small territory and compare the workings of the justice system there to the operations of the thirty or forty seigneurial courts that would have corresponded to that territory. But even in the departmental archives of Charente-Maritime I encountered so many lacunae in the records, both geographical and chronological, that I was forced to cast a much wider net across the entire department in order to attain an accurate picture of the institutions of local justice.

The reader may object that, in its encompassing a diverse region, this study loses sight of the fine gradations in rural society, that it lumps "rural dwellers," "rural inhabitants," or "rural society" together without exhibiting an awareness of the varied interests and concerns of different groups in

10. I thank Robert Schwartz of Mount Holyoke College for directing me to the rich records of local justice in La Rochelle.

rural society. Although keenly aware of the socioeconomic, psychological, religious, regional, and gender fault lines along which groups can organize themselves, I treat rural society as that group of people requiring the services of justice and as an entity distinct from the state. It is the intersection and relationship between the state and rural society—or the providers and consumers of the service of justice, to use a modern, if somewhat anachronistic, conceptualization—that constitute the focus of this study. Hence the benefits of expanding its geographical boundaries in order to attain a more detailed picture of the operation of local justice outweigh the drawbacks of losing sight of a detailed portrait of rural society in eighteenth-century France.

To recapitulate, my research will contribute to our growing knowledge of Old Regime justice and society,[11] just as its focus on the *justice de paix* will offer the first in-depth study of an institution deemed essential by revolutionaries but essentially ignored by historians. In addition, it illuminates one of the few areas of France that a paucity of scholarly works has rendered relatively obscure. Most important, as a rare study crossing the chronological divide of 1789, it will contribute to the ongoing debate on the effects and meaning of the French Revolution.

---

11. Much of this work is in English and focuses on criminal justice. See R. Andrews, *Law, Magistracy, and Crime in Old Regime Paris*, vol. 1, *The System of Criminal Justice* (Cambridge, 1994); J. Ruff, *Crime, Justice, and Public Order in Old Regime France: The Sénéchaussées of Libourne and Bazas, 1696–1789* (London, 1984); I. Cameron, *Crime and Repression in the Auvergne and the Guyenne, 1729–1790* (Cambridge, 1981); S. Reinhardt, *Justice in the Sarladais, 1770–1790* (Baton Rouge, 1991); M. Greenshield, *An Economy of Violence in Early Modern France: Crime and Justice in the Haute-Auvergne, 1587–1664* (University Park, Pa., 1994). Perhaps the most comprehensive study of Old Regime justice is N. Castan, *Justice et répression en Languedoc à l'époque des Lumières* (Paris, 1980).

PART I

Old Regime Seigneurial Justice

CHAPTER I

Public Power, Private Persons

The Organization of Seigneurial Justice in Aunis and Saintonge

On 5 August 1790, the honorable Jean Louis Viaud convened the court of the baronnie de St. Seurin d'Uzet in the cabaret of the widow Cochain.[1] Besides the obvious affront to the majesty of justice posed by such a setting, the presence of Viaud as presiding judge might have raised questions. He normally served the court as an attorney, signaling that in all likelihood he did not hold a law degree and was unqualified to fulfill the role of magistrate. A surviving list of legal expenses enumerated on the front of a nine of spades likewise does little to inspire confidence in the quality of justice in the barony. Now imagine that a peasant had a civil case over an inheritance pending before the court, the resolution of which was of supreme economic importance to his or her family. Given the setting—its association with drinking and gambling—and personnel, what guarantees existed to convince the litigant that the case would be adjudicated fairly or knowledgeably?

Had the regular judge been present that day in 1790, the peasant would have been assured of the adjudication of the case by a law graduate whose qualifications for the position had been confirmed by the royal court at Saintes. Still, royal approval notwithstanding, the lord of St. Seurin d'Uzet would have made the original *choice* of the judge and would have been responsible for the payment of the latter's salary. Indeed, the judge would have retained his position only with the consent of the lord of St. Seurin d'Uzet, who, as a private person, had inherited or purchased the right of justice—the very essence of public power.

Consider another hypothetical peasant, this time summoned to appear before the court for nonpayment of seigneurial dues. The case dealing with

1. Archives Départementales de Charente-Maritime (hereafter ADCM), B 2437, Baronnie de St. Seurin d'Uzet.

the peasant's putative failure to fulfill obligations to his lord would be heard in that very same lord's court. The lord's fiscal agent, the *procureur fiscal*, would represent the "public" party, and a judge chosen by, paid by, and responsible to the lord would render a decision. In this example, what could dissuade the peasant from his conviction that justice, rather than constituting a public function for the unbiased resolution of disputes, had degenerated into a forum for the administration of the lord's private business?

These examples of the bastardization of justice in ancien régime France would have surprised no one less than the indefatigable apologist of royal power Charles de Loyseau. In a famous treatise of 1604, Loyseau denounced the proliferation of petty seigneurial justices, which he considered an unadulterated usurpation of the king's prerogative of justice. "Justice belongs only to the king, who holds the property as a fief from God . . . and is in no way communicable to subjects, especially to private persons."[2] To be sure, French monarchs had recruited many great lords to help administer justice in the realm, but this act merely constituted the appointment of magistrates and was not an alienation of *imperium*—the king's right of sword, justice, and the power to command. According to Loyseau, the great mistake was to think that by conferring a fief upon a vassal and by appointing him a judicial magistrate as well, the king had somehow rendered justice a kind of property tied to the fief. Thus, during periods of feudal anarchy, vassals of the king granted fiefs, including the right of justice, to their own vassals, or the latter simply usurped this prerogative, resulting in a judicial system largely in private hands and free of royal control. "Is it possible to imagine a greater absurdity, than to have communicated to private persons—to the vassals of vassals and the subjects of subjects—justice, the right of the sword, and the power to command?"[3] Loyseau's juridical challenge, then, was to convince the French that the possession of a fief or *seigneurie* did not entail the right of justice, and by the eighteenth century his efforts had largely succeeded. Most of France adhered to the maxim that "fief and justice have nothing in common,"[4] that all justice, in theory at least, emanated from the king.

Despite Loyseau's efforts, the confusion over the nature of seigneurial

2. Loyseau, *Discours de l'abus des justices de villages* (Paris, 1604), 2. All of the literature critical of seigneurial justice in the seventeenth and eighteenth centuries borrows heavily from Loyseau. Indeed, most authors were even content to cite the same examples of abuse.

3. Loyseau, *Discours de l'abus*, 35.

4. "Fief et justice n'ont rien de commun." Its competing, antithetical doctrine that "fief et justice sont tous un" remained strong in such regions as Brittany. See Giffard, *Les justices seigneuriales en Bretagne*, 3–33.

justice appears justified, for a *seigneurie* remained an amalgam of the public—the right to exercise justice—and the private—enjoyment of the real ownership (to use a thing, to collect its fruits, and to alienate it) of land.[5] In fact, a *seigneurie* was usually referred to as *terre, fief, et seigneurie,* where *terre* signified the lord's demesne, *fief* the property leased or granted in return for "faith and homage" (to nobles) or for acts of fealty and payment of certain dues (to commoners), and *seigneurie* the right of justice. Fiefs existed without powers of justice, and lords called themselves *seigneurs* of those fiefs (for example, Seigneur de l'Etoile for the proprietor of the fief of l'Etoile), but only a lord in possession of *terre, fief, et seigneurie* could call him- or herself *seigneur* without appending the name of the territory.

Public and private overlapped in the cognizance that lords had over cases arising from a system of seigneurial land tenure; in other words, lords invoked their public power of the right of justice during disputes over leases, payments of dues, and recognition of rights stemming from their ownership of property, a private concern. To complicate matters further, lords treated the right of justice as their patrimony, subject to alienation (but not division) and inheritance like the rest of their property.

Besides addressing the issues of public law raised by the existence of seigneurial justice, Loyseau animadverted on the practical problems of the institution as well. He abhorred the confusion of petty jurisdictions and the myriad levels of justice, in some instances up to six, that a case had to go through before its definitive resolution. Such protracted litigation was not only financially ruinous for individuals but also weakened all of France economically by diverting people from the proper spheres of attention: commerce and cultivation. In addition, Loyseau argued that lords often abused justice in pursuit of their feudal rights, sometimes by coercing seigneurial notaries to backdate documents, resulting in the easy oppression of the poor and defenseless members of society.[6]

Loyseau reserved his most vehement vituperations, however, for the judges of the small seigneurial jurisdictions, whom he portrayed as ignorant country yokels. Not only were they "people of little means [*gens de peu*], without honor and conscience," but they were also fixtures of the local tavern and frequent participants in its debaucheries. A later critic of sei-

---

5. This discussion of the jurisprudential status of the *seigneurie* follows closely that of R. Mousnier, *The Institutions of France Under the Absolute Monarchy (1598–1789),* vol. 1, *Society and the State* (Chicago, 1979), chap. 11, 477–513. See also R. Robin, "Fief et seigneurie dans le droit et l'idéologie juridique à la fin du XVIIIe siècle," *Annales historiques de la Révolution française* 43 (1971): 554–602.

6. Loyseau, *Discours de l'abus,* 56–57. He claimed to write the treatise "out of pity for the poor people."

gneurial justice, in an attempt at one-upmanship over Loyseau, told a probably apocryphal tale of a judge in Sologne who was also a *cardeur de laine,*
with his shop in a cave. When someone requested his services by ringing a
bell, he would call out, "Est-ce pour carderre, ou pour jugerre?"[7] Devoid of
material, intellectual, and moral merit, these men obviously lacked the
judge's essential quality of independence, the integrity of which was crucial
for the proper functioning of the judicial system. "These petty judges depend entirely on the power of their gentleman, who can divest them at his
will."[8] For Loyseau, the sole remedy for such abuses was the immediate
abolition of seigneurial justice where a lord did not possess a title documenting a royal concession of this right: "This would be the healthiest
edict relative to justice, the most honorable for the conservation of his [the
king's] authority, the most useful for the poor people; briefly, the most
necessary for the reform of justice that has ever been made."[9]

How accurately do the strictures of Loyseau, a formidable royalist the-
orist, and the example of St. Seurin d'Uzet, taken from a period a few
months prior to the death of seigneurial justice in 1790, reflect the actual
operation of the institution in eighteenth-century Aunis and Saintonge?
After all, one need look no further than Montesquieu or the barristers of
the Parlement of Paris to find powerful and persuasive advocates of the
lords' rights of justice.[10] Was St. Seurin merely an aberration in a judicial
system that normally worked rather smoothly and according to accepted
procedure? By the eve of the French Revolution, had the system eradicated
the abuses specified by Loyseau almost two centuries earlier? Indeed, was
seigneurial justice, although a functioning component of the French judicial system in the eighteenth century, still a thriving institution, or had the
encroachment of the royal courts succeeded in rendering it meaningless
except for the most insignificant cases of petty justice? Answers to fundamental questions about the organization and activity of seigneurial justice
will clarify its role in, and highlight some problems of, local justice in ancien régime Aunis and Saintonge.

---

7. Fouqueau de Pussy, *Idées sur l'administration de la justice dans les petites villes et bourgs de
France pour déterminer la supression des juridictions seigneuriales* (Paris, 1789), 51.
    8. Loyseau, *Discours de l'abus,* 55.
    9. Loyseau, *Discours de l'abus,* 61.
    10. Montesquieu considered seigneurial justice part of France's original constitution; *De l'esprit
des lois* (bk. 2, chap. 4). For an example of a barrister's defense of the institution, see Pierre Jacquet,
Traité des justices de seigneur, et des droits en dépendent conformément à la Jurisprudence actuelle . . .
(Paris, 1764).

The Geographical Organization of Lords' Justice

Although an understanding of the origins of seigneurial justice remains obscured by a paucity of documents, the crown's own inability to determine the number of subaltern courts hints strongly at the prevalence of usurpation and suggests the confusion surrounding the entire institution.[11] An attempt by the intendant of La Rochelle in 1775 to ascertain the prevalence of subordinate tribunals has survived, however, and allows for an estimate of the number of seigneurial justices in the region. Since the report is especially thorough for St. Jean d'Angély, I will focus on that area to determine the institution's geographical organization.[12]

The royal *sénéchaussée* at St. Jean d'Angély covered an area of roughly 127 square *lieues* and served the 152,000 inhabitants of its 146 parishes. Within the territory of the *sénéchaussée* existed an astounding 171 seigneurial justices, or one justice for every 889 inhabitants. For the larger presidial court at Saintes, the figure must be less exact, because the report identifies only those 107 courts whose appeals went directly to the presidial court and fails to account for the approximately ninety subaltern tribunals whose appeals were directed to other seigneurial courts such as the *sirerie* of Pons. These 197 jurisdictions under the *présidial* of Saintes covered 332 parishes, and gave the Saintonge (St. Jean d'Angély and Saintes) a total of 368 justices for 478 parishes, or one justice for every 1.3 parishes and nine hundred inhabitants. No report exists for the more urban and less densely populated Aunis, but if we accept the figure of 1.3 justices per parish, the region would have included approximately 125 seigneurial justices. Thus, the royal courts at La Rochelle, Saintes, and St. Jean d'Angély oversaw and heard the appeals from almost five hundred subordinate tribunals. The figures render the region fairly typical, since most studies of seigneurial justice depict territories possessing one to two courts per parish.[13]

11. For a good essay on the creation of seigneurial justices, see P. Villard, *Les justices seigneuriales dans la Marche*, chap. 1, sec. 1, "Essai sur la création des justices seigneuriales," 30–48. Villard concentrates on these courts mainly from the thirteenth through the seventeenth centuries.

12. The following material is based on ADCM C 179 (B3).

13. P. Villard discovered 350 seigneurial courts for the Marche, S. Reinhardt found 109 in the Sarladais (for 205 parishes), and P. Lemercier notes that 460 operated in the *généralité* of Paris. A region such as Brittany, where the maxim "fief and justice are one and the same" resulted in roughly thirty-five hundred tribunals, is the exception. The figures are cited in N. Castan, *Justice et répression en Languedoc*, 104; S. Reinhardt, *Justice in the Sarladais*, 56–60; and Giffard, *Les justices seigneuriales en Bretagne*, 69–70.

Regions of Old Regime France

The high number of seigneurial courts is significant, on the one hand, because it suggests that they admirably fulfilled one qualification of local justice: proximity to those people requiring its services. On the other hand, the plethora of tribunals raises questions about their viability, about the clarity of jurisdictional boundaries, and about the ability of the royal bureaucracy to control the justice meted out in the king's name and to limit chicanery, whose ubiquity rural dwellers denounced incessantly.

The majority of seigneurial jurisdictions were exceedingly diminutive; of the 171 courts from St. Jean d'Angély, the territory of 78 (46 percent) covered less than one parish, and another 39 (23 percent) were coextensive

Principal Towns of Aunis and Saintonge

with a single parish.[14] Most undoubtedly lacked the workload capable of justifying their existence, and the report from Saintes indicates that 67 seigneurial courts rarely adjudicated more than two or three cases per year. The proliferation of jurisdictions approached absurdity in the parish of Torxé, where the justices of la Bertinière et le fief de l'Etoile, le Cochet, le haut

14. ADCM C 179 (B3).

Champagné, le grand Champagné, l'Isle, l'Houmée et le fief de St. Mamert, Perai et Hérissou, Pourcay, and the Prieuré de Torxé all operated. It is inconceivable that a single parish required nine courts to handle its legal business despite the litigious reputation of the eighteenth-century French.

The excessive number of seigneurial justices in Aunis and Saintonge implies a certain amount of inefficiency but is not, in itself, an indictment of the judicial system. Problems arise, however, when the numbers lead to confusion over jurisdictions and therefore the proper functioning of justice. Eighteenth-century ledgers for recovering the costs of justice, maintained by the intendants, document the crown's inability to determine who was responsible for justice in various *seigneuries* and the territory contained therein. One letter from the comptroller general of France requested the intendant of La Rochelle, Barentin, to locate the boundaries between the royal domain and the jurisdiction of the bishopric of Saintes in order to allocate properly the costs of supporting abandoned children, one of the responsibilities of *seigneurs justiciers*.[15] In another entry, the seigneur of high justice of Fouras refused to reimburse the treasury 113 livres for the transfer of a suspect from the prison of Paris to that of La Rochelle. "This *seigneur haut justicier* maintains that the infraction was not committed in his justice of Fouras but rather in that of St. Laurent of the Field belonging to Charon d'Obonière."[16] Similarly, the priests of the Oratoire de La Rochelle, as seigneurs of St. Jean dehors, contested the cost of prosecuting a break-in committed in the village of La Fond. Although the hamlet was located on their fief, the fief did not carry with it the right of justice. In any case, the priests wondered if the crime occurred at the outside door; such a circumstance, because the door faced a royal road, would have rendered the case the responsibility of the crown instead of the seigneur.[17] These examples of the bickering between royal and seigneurial courts are but a few of the many that demonstrate how the confusion over the geography and possession of jurisdictions impeded the fulfillment of the duties—especially the costlier ones—incumbent on the holders of the rights of justice.

Nor was the proximity of the seigneurial courts, resulting from their proliferation, an unqualified advantage for rural dwellers, for the augmentation of subaltern justices often simply translated into an increase in the

---

15. ADCM C 179 (107–9), January–February 1744.

16. ADCM C 179 (31), 1739. The jurisdiction of seigneurial justices did not extend to the policing of royal roads.

17. ADCM C 179 (29, 34), 1737.

stages of appeals a case had to undergo before reaching even a royal tribunal. Many seigneurial courts in Aunis and Saintonge depended on other seigneurial courts to hear appeals; as noted, 90 out of 197 fell into this category for the *présidial* of Saintes. Theoretically, because of the multiplicity of positions among judges, this could give rise to a situation where the same judge decided the same case in the first instance and on appeal.[18] In any case, by adding another degree of justice it rendered litigation needlessly expensive, time-consuming, and frustrating, especially for the poor. The *cahier de doléance* of St. Pierre près Surgères, in entreating Louis XVI to enact a law sending all appeals from subaltern courts directly to a royal seat, lamented the predicament of litigants from La Gravelle, whose wild goose chase in search of justice took them from La Gravelle to Ciré, from Ciré to Surgères, then on to Benon, and finally to the royal *présidial* of La Rochelle, from where it might proceed to the Parlement of Paris. "In such a case among two competing parties," the inhabitants of St. Pierre asked rhetorically, "Which of the two will succeed in quieting the other? Will it be the most just or the most contentious?"[19]

The benefits that seigneurial justice offered by being close to the rural denizens it served, then, must be qualified by the increasing degrees of justice and by the distance of the *justiciables* from the royal court, which often decided cases definitively. In the regions of Saintes and St. Jean d'Angély, the journey from 55 of 178 subaltern courts to royal courts of appeals was at least five *lieues*. Although most distances did not require extended journeys, any voyage of more than six *lieues* necessitated an entire day of travel with the subsequent loss of work time and the additional expenses of eating and staying at inns. A journey of twelve *lieues* from Montlieu to Saintes was extremely grueling, and the National Assembly in 1789 predicated its new judicial organization on, among other things, bringing appeals courts closer to the litigants.

Personnel

The personnel of every seigneurial tribunal included at least three essential members: a judge (called the *bailli* or *sénéchal*), a *procureur fiscal,* and a clerk

---

18. For example, the judge of the sirerie de Pons might also be the judge for the High Justice of Mônac, whose appeals went to Pons. Such arrangements were admittedly very rare in practice. However, the multiplicity of offices was not and is treated below.

19. ADCM C 267 (73).

(*greffier*), although attorneys (*procureurs*) and auxiliaries often supplemented the list, especially in larger *seigneuries*. For example, the court of the seigneuries de l'île de Ré contained a judge, a fiscal procurator, seven attorneys, two clerks, and three sergeants—all indicative of a litigious jurisdiction capable of sustaining a significant workforce.[20] Perhaps only the position of *procureur fiscal* is unfamiliar to modern readers and requires an explanation of its nature. This position combined the duties of a public party responsible for the community's interests, such as prosecuting criminals and protecting the interests of minors by appointing guardians, with those of a seigneurial fiscal agent. In the latter capacity the *procureur fiscal* ensured that inhabitants paid their seigneurial dues and generally respected the rights and honors to which the lord laid claim. That the public interest and the lord's private interests were confused by the investiture of one officer to oversee them both embodies the very essence of the institution of seigneurial justice.

Among the personnel of Ré, two members of the Ventijol family acted as attorneys and another was the head clerk, signifying that the business of justice was often a family affair. Some forty years later, in 1791, a Ventijol became the justice of the peace for Ars-en-Ré. In theory, royal ordinances had prohibited brothers or a father and son from exercising the functions of judge and public party in the same jurisdiction, but as even the *procureur général* Joly de Fleury realized, they failed to prevent the practice in many seigneurial courts where families sometimes monopolized positions. "It must be admitted that the rigor of the ordinances prohibiting relatives of certain degrees from possessing offices in the same seat has never extended to the subordinate justices."[21]

Although the lower positions of clerk and sergeant were often farmed out to the holders, higher court positions were rarely venal. Instead, the lord carefully chose his or her own judge and paid close attention to the selection of *procureur fiscal*, for this official was crucial to the proper financial administration of the lord's property. By avoiding the venality of offices, seigneurs maintained the right to nominate or fire judges "at their pleasure" (*à nôtre plaisir*), giving lords more control over their officers of justice than the king had himself—one of the many paradoxes of Old Re-

20. ADCM B 2134, Seigneuries de l'île de Ré, 1749.
21. Bibliothèque Nationale, MSS Joly de Fleury 2423 (n.d.).

gime France. Of course, this high degree of control ensured that the lord's affairs were properly looked after in his or her court.[22]

By law, lords were required to attain the approval of a royal court for their judicial nominees, thereby granting some semblance of truth to the jurisprudential doctrine that the monarch was the source of all justice. Hence, one finds the count of Bourdeilles and Mastas "sufficiently convinced of the upright life and morals of Master Jean Petit, substitute fiscal procurator of our county of Mastas, and of the profession that he makes of the Roman Catholic and Apostolic religion," supplicating the judges of the *sénéchaussée* of St. Jean d'Angély to confirm the nomination of Petit.[23] Catholicism was only one of the qualifications for a seigneurial judge, the others being male and twenty-five years of age or older and possessing a law degree, as well as the impractical requirement of living within the jurisdiction, to which judges almost never adhered.

Requiring that a judge be a university law graduate was the best means of filling the subaltern courts with competent personnel, and a majority of judges apparently possessed the necessary degree. Table 1 lists how forty-four seigneurial judges in Aunis and Saintonge from 1750 to 1790 identified themselves, and for at least thirty the possession of a degree cannot be doubted. Furthermore, the number of judges who were also *avocats en Parlement* is striking.[24] Of course, a law degree is not ipso facto a certificate of competence, but the frequency of university graduates seems to belie the claims of Loyseau that benighted morons monopolized the position of seigneurial judge. On the other hand, it was not altogether unknown for a court to have attorneys serve as judges, as was the case in the *seigneuries* of Tesson and la Chapelle.

22. The manner in which seigneurial courts served as forums for the administration of the lords' affairs constitutes the theme of Chapter 3.

23. ADCM B 2468, Comté de Mastas, 6 September 1785. How seriously royal judges took this nomination procedure is another matter. The *cahier* for the clergy of Saintes complained that seigneurial judges were "too easily received." Cited in A. Proust, *Archives de l'Ouest, réceuil de documents concernant la Révolution, 1789–1800. Série A: Opérations électorales de 1789* (Poitiers, 1867), 153.

24. M. Gresset suggests that a stint as a seigneurial official might have been a normal part of a legal career, though L. Berlanstein found that no more than 10 percent of Toulousain barristers served as seigneurial judges. See M. Gresset, *Gens de justice à Besançon: De la conquête par Louis XIV à la Révolution française, 1674–1789* (Paris, 1978), 100, and L. Berlanstein, *The Barristers of Toulouse in the Eighteenth Century (1740–1793)* (Baltimore, 1975), 24. Berlanstein argues that some barristers used their positions as seigneurial judges to encourage litigants to appeal to royal courts in order to drum up business and that several *cahiers* complained about it.

TABLE I   The Professions of Seigneurial Judges

Position	Number of Justices
Avocat au présidial	7
Avocat en parlement	13
Avocat au présidial et parlement	3
Avocat	5
Avocat au siège royal	1
Licencié en lois	1
	30 with law degrees (68%)
Juge seigneurial	2
Conseiller du roi	1
	3 likely degree holders (7%)
Notaire royale	8
Procureur/justice seigneuriale	1
Procureur/siège royal	1
Procureur fiscal	1
	11 unlikely degree holders (25%)
Total	44

SOURCE: *Inventaire sommaire des Archives départementales de Charente-Inférieure*, Série B: *Justice*.

Much more common than having *procureurs* as judges and more damning to the quality of the lords' justice, however, was the absenteeism among regular judges, which left courts nominally headed by educated magistrates frequently in the hands of attorneys. The archives for seigneurial justice in Charente-Maritime are full of registers indicating court sessions held before attorneys, and the practice was so common that lords often dictated procedures to be followed during the expected absence of their judges: "In the event of the absence or recusation of the *juge sénéchal,* the *procureur postulant* [head attorney] will replace him in all cases, including the exercise of police, and will possess all the rights and honors attached to the functions of the *juge sénéchal.* He will be free to preside over the case . . . and he will consult the opinion of the judge, without being obliged to follow it."[25] The pronounced dissatisfaction among rural dwellers with attorneys

25. ADCM B 2064 (letter of Camille-Louis de Lorraine, prince de Marsan, sire de Pons), 1 October 1766.

as judges practically guaranteed prolonged and expensive appeals, and many *cahiers* demanded that judges "never let themselves be represented by *procureurs postulants* unless the latter are graduates."[26] In still other jurisdictions, the lack or absence of judges resulted in sessions presided over by the *procureur fiscal*—in other words, with the public party and the lord's fiscal administrator fulfilling the functions of magistrate. For example, during a five-year period in the register of the seigneurie des Trappes, there is no sign of a regular *sénéchal;* instead, Jean Robert, the *procureur fiscal,* performed this function. In cases prosecuted by Robert in his role as fiscal procurator, the attorney Guesdon served as the substitute of the substitute judge.[27]

It is difficult to determine the salaries of seigneurial officials, but they almost certainly varied according to the size of a jurisdiction.[28] A judge's nomination for a small jurisdiction giving rise to but a handful of judicial matters per year might stipulate that he would not receive wages (*pas de gages*), while the *procureur fiscal* for the baronnie de Montguyon earned a mere fifteen livres for his services in 1708.[29] In 1787 the lessee of the large seigneurie de Ars, Loix, et Portes en Ré agreed to pay the salaries of the judicial officials, including fifty livres to the *sénéchal,* thirty livres to the *procureur fiscal,* and twenty-five livres to the clerk.[30] In general, the salaries of the personnel of subaltern justices failed to constitute a sufficient source of income.

Exacting *épices* for services rendered in cases was one means by which court officials could supplement their incomes. Originating from a distant period in which financially independent magistrates dispensed justice out of a concern for justice itself and without regard to material gain (although they might accept an *épice* from litigants), *épices* had become fixed costs that every litigant expected to pay and probably accounted for a significant portion of the incomes of officials, especially judges. Indeed, why else would a nonsalaried judge accept a position in a diminutive jurisdiction? Pierre Villard correctly mentions that *épices* appear only exceptionally in

26. ADCM C 263bis, Soubise ville.

27. ADCM B 2350 (registre 1751–56), Seigneuries des Trappes et St. Fort.

28. For a description of the wages of seigneurial officials in the South, see J. Bastier, *La féodalité au siècle des lumières dans la région de Toulouse (1730–1790)* (Paris, 1975), 108–12.

29. ADCM 4 J 1514 (livret de recettes et de dépens, 1708), Baronnie de Montguyon.

30. ADCM B 2153 (bail, 28 March 1787). Pierre Sangrain, entrepreneur, leased from the Collège Mazarin, lords of the seigneuries de Ré, all revenues and rights for nine years at a cost of forty-two thousand livres per year.

the registers of seigneurial courts, but if that is because they were rarely collected in the Marche, the same does not hold true for Aunis and Saintonge.[31] Lists of court expenses usually ended with the phrase "not including our *épices,*" signifying that the amount was off the books and thus free of royal scrutiny. When specified, *épices* could be quite high, as was the case in a 1774 lawsuit between a priest and a *négociant;* of the 292 livres in court costs, 60 were for *épices.*[32] A disputed inheritance from des Breuils grand et petit generated a hefty twenty-five livres in *épices* for the judge.[33] In the comté de Marans, a register of *épices* was kept for its jurisdiction in which it was indicated that people paid twelve livres for noncontentious civil matters and eighteen livres for contentious litigation.[34]

In addition to *épices,* court personnel received payment for various judicial procedures for which they were responsible. Thus, a judge earned ten sols for every witness whose depositions he took; a *procureur fiscal* received eighteen livres per brief offering his conclusions in a case; a clerk charged a fixed rate per page for copies of various documents. When Jeanne Roche appeared before the court of Marennes in order to be appointed the guardian of her son, she paid the judge four livres sixteen sols for his services, three-quarters that amount (three livres twelve sols) to the *procureur fiscal,* half that amount to the clerk, and one-quarter to the sergeant.[35] The issue of the costs of justice will be treated more thoroughly in Chapter 2; suffice it to say here that insufficient wages for court personnel often forced them to favor lengthy and complicated procedures and sometimes to implement dishonest practices in order to earn a living. Of course, the repercussions for rural inhabitants who desired expeditious and inexpensive justice were manifest.

The Parlement of Bordeaux constantly harangued the seigneurial justices in its jurisdiction, including Saintes and St. Jean d'Angély, for their abuses of justice and the resultant escalation of costs. The magistrates of Bordeaux especially distrusted the lords' *greffiers,* who, for a price, communicated confidential proceedings to parties and who ignored decrees mandating twelve syllables per line and twelve lines per page for writs; by using small sheets of paper and writing in large script, clerks could increase the

---

31. According to Villard, royal courts had suppressed or sharply reduced the collection of *épices. Les justices seigneuriales dans la Marche,* 228.

32. ADCM B 3333, Marennes, 2 August 1776.

33. ADCM B3347. The case lasted from 1784 to 1790 and cost more than 413 livres.

34. ADCM B 3254, Comté de Marans.

35. ADCM B 3342, Marennes, 22 December 1788.

costs of a document many times over.[36] More seriously, the Parlement discovered abuses in the amount of money that judges charged litigants, casting a dark shadow on the honesty of the court personnel and corroborating the complaints of peasants about the high costs of justice:

> Today the *procureur du roi* entered and said that he can no longer dissimulate that the majority of subaltern justices are in contravention of Article 33 Title 31 of the Ordonnance of 1667. . . . This article compels them in writing to enumerate the expenses charged to parties involved in a trial. . . . Nevertheless we commonly see that the expenses fixed by the judgments or sentences of these judges contain no enumeration of the articles that make up their totality and always exceed the just rights fixed by the law.[37]

In an attempt to rectify this abuse and to ensure that parties paid only legitimate court costs, the parlement required all judges to maintain a ledger detailing every legal expense. According to the documents in the judicial archives, the rarity of full lists of expenses demonstrates that few judges complied with the orders from Bordeaux in this matter.

A more honest, but still potentially problematic, manner in which judges augmented their meager incomes was to hold multiple seigneurial offices. Hence, one learns that around 1785 Jean Perrinet was the *sénéchal* for the *seigneuries* of Breuil d'Arces, Théon, Sorlut, Conteneuil-Cozes, and Thomeville, all of which contained the right of justice. Similarly, in 1768 Madame de Parabère, dame abbesse of the Royal Abbey of Notre Dame, named Antoine Bazin to nine judgeships of small fiefs and *seigneuries* for which she was lord. Nicolas-Simon-Marie Billaud, an attorney at the *présidial* of La Rochelle, moonlighted as the judge of the baronnie de Chataillon, of Chagnollet, of Grois, and of the chatellénie d'Esnades throughout the 1770s.[38] In fact, it is much less common to come across a judge whose sole position was with a single seigneurial tribunal than to discover judges who operated within several jurisdictions.

Without a doubt, this practice proved mutually beneficial to lord and

---

36. ADCM B 3073, Jonzac, 26 August 1768. In comparison, the clerks' handwriting for judicial registers, kept at the lords' cost, was miniscule. The formula was always the same: maximize revenues for officials, minimize costs for lords.

37. ADCM B 2275 (Arrêt de parlement), Comté de Cosnac, 17 April 1765.

38. For the example of Mme de Parabère, see ADCM B 3327, Marennes, 21 May 1786. For the others, consult the *Inventaire sommaire des archives départementales de Charente-Inférieure,* Série B, *Justice.*

magistrate, for it is unlikely that Madame de Parabère paid Bazin nine salaries for the positions he held from her, whereas Bazin might have succeeded in making a satisfactory albeit modest living from the accumulated activity of nine minor courts. It also benefited the *justiciables* of Aunis and Saintonge insofar as it obviated an unreasonable number of qualified judges to fill the approximately five hundred seigneurial seats in the region. But the ostensible benefits for the rural inhabitants were probably chimerical, since the ambulatory nature of the magistrates was largely responsible for the absenteeism that led to infrequent court sessions or sessions presided over by unqualified attorneys. Of course, the amount of judicial activity in a lilliputian seigneurial jurisdiction did not require a sitting judge who convened his tribunal every other week. What was important for the inhabitants, however, was that they have immediate access to the services of the court and a quick resolution of the problem when a legal issue *did* arise. And it was this need that seigneurial justice, with its absentee personnel and procedural gouging, often failed to satisfy. To remedy the problems caused by the infrequency of sessions in small jurisdictions, many *cahiers,* including that of the parish of Conlonge, requested their suppression: "We demand the unification of the small jurisdictions with those on which they depend. In them one never sees the end of trials because sessions are held only every two or three months and sometimes less frequently, which puts us in the state of never peacefully possessing what is ours."[39]

JURISDICTION

All seigneurial justices fell into the categories of high, middle, or low justice, which conferred different competencies, rights and obligations on *seigneurs justiciers.*[40] According to the customs of Aunis, for example, a lord with the right of high justice could erect a pillory, a scaffold, and a gibbet, effective symbols of the powers of repression, although the number of uprights on the gibbet depended upon the title of the seigneur: a duke could

---

39. ADCM C 26obis, Conlonge parish.
40. This discussion of the juridical powers of seigneurial courts is based largely on J.-H. Bataillon, *Les justices seigneuriales du bailliage de Pontoise à la fin de l'ancien régime* (Paris, 1942), 23, and especially follows closely Mousnier, *The Institutions of France,* vol. I, chap. II, "The Territorial Communities: The *Seigneuries.*" For the rights of justice in Aunis, see R.-J. Valin, *Nouveau commentaire sur la coutume de La Rochelle et du pays d'Aunis* (La Rochelle, 1756).

maintain eight, a count six, but a mere lord of high justice could erect only two. A nonspecialist in feudal matters quickly gets lost in such minutiae, but the contours of the most important aspects of the competence of seigneurial justices can be readily discerned.

In civil matters the courts of high justice exercised important powers, having full cognizance of contentious litigation except for cases concerning the royal domain and *bénéfices*.[41] Hence, lawsuits concerning personal, real, or mixed matters, such as marriages, successions, and so on fell within their jurisdiction. Their powers extended to all voluntary affairs as well, including the naming of guardians and the emancipation of minors from them, affixing seals, compiling inventories, opening closed wills, alienating the property of minors, and separations.

Furthermore, the lords' courts had cognizance of feudal matters; that is to say, a judge appointed by a seigneur heard disputes between that very seigneur and those under his power if they pertained to the fief, demesne, payment of dues, leases, or honorific rights.[42] Simply put, a seigneurial court was a forum for the administration of the *terrier*, all the lands within a fief leased on the condition of homage or fealty and payment of certain rights to the lord. If a lord happened to be a party to a proceeding unrelated to the fief—for example, in a case over an ordinary debt—he or she was required to seek out a higher seigneurial or a royal court. Otherwise the lord would be judge and party in the same case!

In order to keep possession of the rights of high justice it was incumbent on lords to fulfill certain obligations, including the maintenance of a courthouse outside of the demesne and a prison, both of which were burdensome expenses to petty lords. Obviously a lord had to keep court positions filled so that inhabitants had access to civil legal services. In addition, lords shared the costs of nourishing abandoned children and paid for such miscellaneous services as investigations into the deaths of people whose

41. In theory, a case was adjudicated in the defendant's jurisdiction. However, imprecise territorial boundaries, questions over the nature of a case, and the invocation of the right of *prévention* (see below), sometimes led to arguments over the proper jurisdiction. One party's insistence that a dispute be resolved before a (distant) royal court might be an attempt at intimidation, since the expenses and time involved would be greater than those before a seigneurial tribunal. On the other hand, a decision by a royal court in the first instance could obviate an appeal from a subaltern jurisdiction. On the jurisdiction of Old Regime courts, see P. Dawson, *Provincial Magistrates and Revolutionary Politics in France, 1789–1795* (Cambridge, Mass., 1972), 30–34.

42. Lords could not render decisions in their court. They "merely" controlled the right to appoint judges, who decided matters in the lord's name.

corpses were discovered on the *seigneurie*. The powers of high justice included the right, or responsibility, of "police." By public proclamation, lords issued decrees (*règlements*) covering a wide range of activity—from the dates opening the wine harvest to the enforcement of cabaret hours, from permission to practice a trade to proper weights and measures—and heard disputes arising from those decrees. Finally, lords exercised important repressive functions, being responsible for the investigation, prosecution, and punishment of certain crimes committed in their territories.

In return for often burdensome responsibilities, the powers of high justice conferred significant honorific rights upon the lord, not the least of which was the exclusive right to hunt on the fief. *Seigneurs hauts justiciers* were also considered the proprietors of nonnavigable rivers and solely possessed the right to take fish from them. In regions of custom law, they received half of the value of treasures or shipwrecks found in their jurisdictions. Furthermore, they inherited the property of people who died intestate and without successors, and fines levied by judgments in their courts were paid to their treasuries. The list of honorific rights was quite extensive, but these few examples suggest how important these symbols of power were to lords in a society obsessed with questions of power and status, although no one has claimed that these rights were financially profitable or outweighed the expenditures of justice.[43]

It is in the realm of criminal justice that the line demarcating the competencies of royal and seigneurial courts becomes most visible, because certain crimes were considered royal cases (*cas royaux*), which royal tribunals were granted the sole authority to prosecute. The royal cases encompassed a long list of infractions in which "the majesty of the sovereign, the dignity of his officials, or the safety and tranquility of the public are violated or concerned,"[44] including illegal assembly, murder, sedition, popular uprisings, counterfeiting, heresy, arson, rape, usury, adultery, incest, parricide, and monopoly among others. A lord's officials were obligated to investigate royal cases immediately but then turned over the prosecution to the king's

---

43. Historians seem to agree on this aspect of seigneurial justice, that it was not "profitable" if one looked merely at an account of expenditures (prison, pursuit of criminals, etc.) and revenues (such as the collection of fines, the value of fish taken from rivers) stemming directly from the exercise of it. See, for example, J.-J. Clère, *Les paysans de la Haute-Marne et la Révolution française: recherches sur les structures foncières de la communauté villageoise* (Paris, 1988), 106, or Bois, *Paysans de l'Ouest*, chap. 7, "Le régime féodal," 157–82. The true value of justice was more complex than a direct profitability and lay in the maintenance of a system of power, which is the subject of Chapter 3.

44. Mousnier, *The Institutions of France*, 1:505–6.

courts. In other criminal matters, however, high seigneurial jurisdictions maintained full competence and could sentence malefactors to almost the entire litany of corporal punishments: death, mutilation, thrashing, branding, the *carcan,* and the pillory.

Courts of middle justice heard all civil cases involving real, personal, or mixed actions (except separations of property between married couples and deprival of prodigal sons of control over money) and had cognizance of criminal offenses for which the fine did not exceed three livres. The competence of courts of low justice extended to personal civil cases of less than three livres and criminal infractions for which the maximum fine was one-half livre. By the mid-eighteenth century, inflation had rendered low justice meaningless and therefore nearly nonexistent—it appeared in conjunction with a lord's middle justice when it existed at all—while middle jurisdictions were almost completely inactive in criminal matters.

Besides the *cas royaux,* royal tribunals attempted to guarantee that the king retained ultimate control of justice by invoking Articles 7 and 9, Title 1 of the Ordonnance of 1670 concerning the right of *prévention.* When invoked, *prévention* deprived seigneurial courts of the right to hear a case that royal officials thought was proceeding unnecessarily slowly. Along with a network or appeals and the control of judicial nominees, *cas royaux* and *prévention* were the means by which the monarchy constrained the competence of seigneurial courts and sought to minimize the adverse effects of having granted private persons the exercise of public power.[45]

The Activity of Subaltern Courts

The court sessions of seigneurial justice were very diverse in terms of their setting, frequency, and cases. Although compelled to maintain a court building separate from the demesne as a condition for the exercise of justice, lords apparently considered this an onerous expenditure and often tolerated proceedings in private homes (or even in cabarets, as in the example from St. Seurin d'Uzet). Thus, one finds the court of the *seigneurie* of

45. For a history of the relations between royal and seigneurial jurisdictions, see E. Perrot, *Les cas royaux: Origine et développement de la théorie au XIIIe et XIVe siècles* (Paris, 1910) and J. Riollot, *Le droit de prévention des juges royaux sur les juges seigneuriales* (Paris, 1931). For a recent and very illuminating case study of the interaction between royal and seigneurial courts, see Schneider, "The Village and the State," especially part I.

Jaurezac convened in the town of Coze "in the house of the instructor Pierre Dounoux," the audiences of Breuil d'Arces held in the village of La Croix at the house of the merchant Antoine Careil, and the affairs of the *seigneurie* of Roussillon, le Gagnon, Perissac et le Rail expedited in the house of Antoine Lafon, "place of our proceedings of justice."[46] These were small jurisdictions, however, whose courts convened infrequently and handled but a few judicial matters per session, and most larger courts seem to have occupied a legitimate courthouse.

Court registers distinguished between ordinary and extraordinary sessions, the former theoretically treating feudal and contentious civil matters and the latter dealing with criminal and police matters and the affairs of *incapables* such as minors, absent persons, and the mentally ill. In reality, many jurisdictions covered all civil cases—contentious as well as voluntary *justices gracieuses*—during the more regular ordinary sessions and reserved extraordinary ones for criminal procedures and certain *justices gracieuses,* usually regarding the property of minors, calling for immediate attention. Still other courts heard both civil and criminal proceedings in the same sessions, employing different procedures for the different types of cases.

How well a system of justice serves a society depends to a large degree (but not solely) on its accessibility; that is, on how readily its courts accommodate people's need to protect their goods and persons. Accessibility, in turn, is reflected in the cost of adjudicating and often simply in the frequency of court sessions. For Aunis and Saintonge, Table 2(A) exhibits the diverse frequencies in which various subaltern justices heard cases. The spectrum runs from courts such as St. Antoine du Bois that convened but once or twice annually to those such as the *sirerie* of Pons that operated on a weekly schedule. The overall impression left by a thorough combing of the judicial archives is that the majority of seigneurial justices resembled the *seigneuries* of Ré and the *baronnie* of Chatellaillon in that they held court approximately every month.

Infrequent sessions probably resulted from a combination of the low demand for legal services in small jurisdictions and the absenteeism of judges caused by the multiplicity of offices, although the precise weight of each factor is difficult to determine. For example, during an uninterrupted period of six years in the registers of St. Antoine du Bois, the *sénéchal* appeared only twelve times. Yet in those twelve sessions he dealt with only

---

46. ADCM B 2457, Jaurezac; B 2510, Breuil d'Arces; B 2591, Roussillon, le Gagnon, Perissac et le Rail.

TABLE 2A   The Frequency of Court Sessions

Name of Jurisdiction	Number of Sessions	Number of Years	Average Length of Time Between Sessions
St. Antoine du Bois	12	6 (1779–85)	6 months
St. Seurin d'Uzet	13	2 (1786–85)	7–8 weeks
Huré Lagord	73	9 (1781–90)	Approx. 6 weeks
Chatellaillon	13	1 (1768)	Approx. 1 month
Ré	13	1 (1775)	Approx. 1 month
Marans	49	2 (1769–70)	Approx. 15 days
Pons	48	1 (1777)	Approx. 1 week

TABLE 2B   The Caseload of Court Sessions

Name of Jurisdiction	Number of Sessions	Number of Items Heard	Average Number of Items per Session
St. Antoine du Bois	12	18	1.5
Ré	13	135	10.4
Marans	23	121	5.3
Pons	36	969	26.9

SOURCE: Plumitifs des audiences, ADCM B 4766, St. Antoine du Bois; B 2112, Chatellénie d'Huré Lagord et al.; B 2436, St. Seurin d'Uzet; B 2481, Baronnie de Chatellaillon; B 2149, Seigneuries de Ré; B 3233, Comté de Marans; B 2065, Sirerie de Pons.

eighteen legal matters, including seven initiated by the *procureur fiscal,* signifying that the inhabitants weren't exactly lined up at the courthouse doors only to find them slammed shut for months at a time. On the other hand, contemplate the lot of Jean Seguin, who sued Joseph Dupuy for an unspecified cause on 4 April 1779.[47] Dupuy failed to appear at the hearing, so the judge ordered the parties to return at the next session, rather inconveniently held on 28 April 1780! One can easily imagine Seguin's despair over his inability to obtain justice. Did such dilatory courts cause rural dwellers to seek out extralegal arbitrators, or did tempers simmer until, like the peasants in the mountains of Puy-de-Dome, someone took justice into his or

47. ADCM B 4766, St. Antoine du Bois, 15 April 1779.

her own hands? "It is the custom in these mountains for peasants to render justice themselves [*se fassent justice eux-mêmes*]. They carry their rights with their clubs and with their knives."[48] Other jurisdictions simply fell into desuetude, forcing their inhabitants to supplicate neighboring justices to hear their cases, as did Jeanne Frand when she sought to register an act of acquisition at the comté de Benon. Although a *justiciable* of the chatellénie de Beaumond, the judge of Benon registered her act "in light of the lack of officers for a very long time in the jurisdiction of Beaumond."[49]

In comparison to the sleepy tribunal of St. Antoine du Bois or the phantom tribunal at Beaumond stood the bustling court at Pons, on which at least thirty-five other seigneurial courts depended. The judge at Pons handled an enormous amount of material per session, which is indicative of a high demand for legal services.[50] If the court at Pons proved inaccessible, it was not because of a lack of sessions. A court whose accessibility was more questionable is that of the seigneuries de Ré, where the elevated need for judicial services suggested by Table 2(B) might not have been satisfied by monthly sessions.

What sort of judicial activity went on during these court sessions?—a simple enough question but one not well understood by historians. Although this issue will be explored in greater depth in the following three chapters, Table 3 briefly elaborates on the legal matters covered in several large subaltern jurisdictions. One striking fact from the data is that voluntary civil affairs constituted the majority of issues with which subaltern courts dealt. This is in keeping with the paternal nature of these courts, since a lord, as the community's paternal figure, was expected to perform various benevolent services, especially the protection of property on behalf of minors or absent persons. Hence, it is commonplace in the judicial archives in Aunis and Saintonge to find the *procureur fiscal* acting quickly after the death of a father to gather the children's relatives in order to nominate a guardian. In a three-year period from the registers of its extraordinary sessions, the Comté de Marans appointed 183 guardians and emancipated fifty-eight minors, pointing to the importance of the judiciary

48. In O. Hufton, "Le paysan et la loi en France au XVIIIe siècle," *Annales: Economies, sociétés, civilisations* 38 (1983): 679–701.

49. ADCM B 2790, Comté de Benon.

50. In Table 3, an "item" signifies a hearing and not a sentence rendered. Thus, one case might appear as a procedural item over many sessions before being judged definitively. Because of the procedure in French courts, the number of sentences was a small fraction of the total hearings (items).

for the administration of the property of minors.[51] Table 4 provides evidence that women also often entreated the courts to protect them from the profligacy or maladministration of their husbands.

A second interesting point stemming from Table 3 concerns the low number of decisions per year compared to the total number of procedural hearings. Table 2(B) shows that in thirty-six sessions in 1777 (out of a total of forty-eight sessions for the entire year) the court at Pons heard 969 items. In an entire year, then, the court covered well more than one thousand procedural items but rendered little more than one hundred decisions or judicial acts. A ten to one ratio of procedural matters to decisions hints at dilatory and costly justice, especially when court costs are determined per procedure as was the case in Old Regime seigneurial courts.

Finally, concentrating on Table 4, one notices the scant activity of the *procureur fiscal* outside the realm of *justices gracieuses*. At Pons in 1777 the lord's agent and public party pursued only three parties for the payment of seigneurial dues and one for a criminal infraction and issued a single police ordinance. At first glance, such a picture varies greatly from one in which historians, trained to expect signs of a "feudal reaction" in eighteenth-century France, envision a sycophantic and overzealous *procureur fiscal* out

TABLE 3   The Judicial Activity of Subaltern Courts (In Number of Decisions or Acts)

	Civil		Criminal
	Contentious	Volunary	Plaintes[a] / Police
Taillebourg (1780)	17 (38%)	20 (44%)	8 (18%)
Marennes (1770)	11 (19%)	36 (61%)	12 (20%)
Pons (1768)	26 (27%)	51 (53%)	19 (20%)
Pons (1777)	43 (36%)	56 (47%)	21 (17%)
Pons (1779)	23 (20%)	61 (54%)	30 (26%)
Pons (1787)[b]	19 (16%)	76 (66%)	20 (18%)

Sources: ADCM B 5508, Comté de Taillebourg; B 3329, Chatellénie de Marennes; B 2080, Sirerie de Pons.

[a]A *plainte et information* was a judicial act containing the testimony of witnesses on the facts in a criminal matter. They were used by parties (sometimes the public party but usually by a private party) for pursuing cases in court or, more likely, for encouraging the payment of damages out of court.

[b]In addition to these cases, the judicial register of Pons for 1787 contains 50 acts of homage performed by vassals at the request of the *procureur fiscal*.

51. ADCM B 3232 (registre extraordinaire), Comté de Marans, 1754–1756.

TABLE 4   A Breakdown of the Judicial Acts of a Major Court

I. Sirerie de Pons (1777)
    A. Civil
        1. Contentious
            a. Sentences between individuals   23
            b. Advice of experts   7
            c. Sentences over seigneurial dues   3
            d. Judicial inquiries   10
                                                                     ——
                                                                     43

        2. Voluntary
            a. Protection of minors
                    rendering of guardians' accounts   4
                    lease of property   10
                    emancipations   3
                    opinions of kin (*avis des parens*)   1
            b. Protection of women
                    renunciation of community   6
                    separations of property   6
            c. Repudiation of succession   6
            d. Reports—cadavers, etc.   7
            e. Administration—reception of officials   4
            f. Affixing, lifting judicial seals   1
            g. Matters concerning testaments   1
            h. Other   7
                                                                     ——
                                                                     56

    B. Criminal
        1. *Plainte et information,* private party   18
        2. *Plainte et information, procureur fiscal*   1
        3. Criminal sentences   1
        4. Police ordinances   1
                                                                     ——
                                                                     21

SOURCE: ADCM B 3842, Sirerie de Pons, 1777.

to please his lord by harassing peasants for payment of every sou in seigneurial dues and performance of every manifestation of subordination. Yet
one must not rush too hastily to the conclusion that the fiscal procurator
had evolved into more the public party than the lord's administrator by the
eve of the Revolution, for years such as 1787, in which the *procureur fiscal*
demanded that fifty vassals render homage to the seigneur of Pons, rectify

the imbalance of judicial activity in 1777 and show the close alliance between the courts and the affairs of their lords.

Is there any evidence that the activity of the courts diminished over time, that at the deathbed of the Old Regime the institution of seigneurial justice was experiencing its own demise? I have already suggested in this chapter how inflation conspired to render middle justice in criminal matters, and low justice in all affairs, insignificant—merely an honorific brooch for the lapel of a lord if he or she accepted the burden of the expenses associated with the right of justice—and it is chiefly these courts whose activity and thus numbers diminished over the course of the eighteenth century.[52] However, most jurisdictions of high justice remained vibrant throughout the century even if their activity declined somewhat over time, exemplified by the activity of the court of Pons, which rendered an average of fifty-seven civil sentences per year from 1731 to 1735, thirty-one sentences per year from 1741 to 1745, and a yearly average of twenty-six civil sentences from 1761 to 1765.[53] Finally, Table 5 suggests that there was a steady but minor decrease in the number of functioning seigneurial courts in eighteenth-century Aunis and Saintonge but that the vast majority operated until their abolition by the National Constituent Assembly in the aftermath of the Night of August 4.[54] Although disputants could (as in all times and places) settle their arguments through private arbitration or (in some cases) in royal courts, seigneurial courts were still the most important tribunal of first instance in rural France.

52. Had they been applied, the Lamoignon Edicts of 1788 would have legislated most seigneurial courts out of existence by making the exercise of justice (for example, the upkeep of a prison) prohibitively expensive. See M. Marion, *La garde des sceaux Lamoignon et la réforme judiciaire de 1788* (Paris, 1905).

53. ADCM B 2076. The slow but hardly momentous decline in caseloads in Pons mirrors the pattern in the baronial court studied by J. Dewald in *Pont St. Pierre, 1398–1789: Lordship, Community, and Capitalism in Early Modern France* (Berkeley, 1987), 253–57.

54. Table 5 lists the dates of last entry for the 274 subaltern justices whose records survive in the Archives départementales de Charente-Maritime. A court whose documents exist until only 1750 did not necessarily cease activity in that year, because records are often lost. Therefore, the date of last entry is only a *rough* indication of the cessation of activity. Not surprisingly, seigneurial courts were most successfully circumscribed by royal courts around Paris, although their significance seems to have waned in Provence as well. Z. Schneider paints a picture of royal courts integrating seigneurial courts rather than circumscribing them. The vitality of lords' courts in Aunis and Saintonge reflects that of Brittany, Alsace, Languedoc, Franche-Comté, and parts of Normandy, Burgundy, and the Seine valley. See Lemercier, *Les justices seigneuriales de la région parisienne*; Schneider, "The Village and the State"; and especially J. Markoff's attempt at a national survey in *The Abolition of Feudalism: Peasants, Lords, and Legislators in the French Revolution* (University Park, Pa., 1996), 116 n. 131.

TABLE 5   The Cessation of Records of Subaltern Justices

Time Period	Number of Courts Whose Records Cease
1600–1650	4
1651–1700	30
1701–1725	17
1726–1750	11
1751–1760	6
1761–1770	6
1771–1780	19
	93 (of 274 total courts with records in the archives)

SOURCE: *Inventaire sommaire des Archives départementales de Charente-Inférieure*, Série B: *Justice.*

CONCLUSION

What strikes the historian most about the institution of seigneurial justice is its diversity, which renders conclusions difficult within a small region, let alone across large provinces or all of France. The diverse subaltern justices in Aunis and Saintonge covered a spectrum of sizes, competencies, frequency of sessions, personnel, and hence quality. But one wonders if, for this institution, diversity was not concomitant with confusion. From its obscure origins to the unconvincing theory that "fief and justice have nothing in common," from the crown's inability to ascertain the number of jurisdictions to the interminable and recondite laws governing competencies, from the varied activity of its courts to the wide-ranging quality of its personnel, the institution of seigneurial justice was mired in confusion for contemporaries as well as historians.[55]

The institution of seigneurial justice is intriguing because of its potential to have satisfied the conditions identified by Nicole Castan as necessary for quality local justice: proximity, accessibility, and competence and integrity of personnel.[56] That these courts ought to have been close and therefore accessible is self-evident, and royal courts ought to have functioned as sentinels carefully guarding the nominations and activities of subaltern magistrates. Unfortunately for the justiciables of Aunis and Saintonge, the

55. P. Villard argues that time tended to simplify the institution, especially because of the diminution in the number of jurisdictions. *Les justices seigneuriales dans la Marche*, 129.

56. N. Castan, *Justice et répression en Languedoc*, 214. In this excellent work on Old Regime criminal justice, Castan raises issues that constitute the focus of Chapter 4.

proliferation of jurisdictions constituted the wrench tossed into the gears of justice; there were simply too many courts. A plethora of subaltern justices increased the multiple layers of judicial jurisdiction in France and required a veritable army of personnel whose competence and education eighteenth-century French society could not guarantee and whose integrity was often compromised by the insufficient remuneration offered by their positions. Too often the activity of subaltern courts in eighteenth-century Aunis and Saintonge escaped the watchful eyes of the sentinels of the royal bureaucracy. The inhabitants of the city of Pons offered testimony to the adverse effects of these problems on the administration of justice in their region:

> By way of remonstration the inhabitants expose that the administration of justice in the territory covered by the seat at Pons is most neglected and even almost abandoned in certain areas. The majority of seigneurial justices that depend on the Sirerie of Pons are useless, some because they lack judges or *procureurs postulants* on location, others because the sessions are so rare that it is ordinary for a trial by written procedure [*procès par écrit*] to last five or seven years before being decided [*dans l'instruction*].[57]

In truth, local justice was just one of many victims of the fundamental problems that plagued Old Regime France and finally destroyed it. French kings, neither able to finance the extension of the royal judicial administration into rural France nor willing to attack privileges systematically,[58] actions that would have deprived lords of their rights of justice and would have forced nobles to pay for the extension of royal courts, tolerated the exercise of justice by private persons—by people more concerned for private fiscal matters than control of a public function, by people more inclined to ponder over their account books than law books.

---

57. ADCM C 26obis, cahier de la ville de Pons. Pons was an important court of high justice that served as the court of appeals for numerous other seigneurial tribunals.

58. But see M. Kwass's interesting research on the state's attempt to undermine tax privileges in "A Kingdom of Taxpayers: State Formation, Privilege, and Political Culture in Eighteenth-Century France," *Journal of Modern History* 70 (June 1998): 295–339.

CHAPTER 2

"A Bad Arrangement Is Better Than a Good Trial"

Civil Justice in Seigneurial Courts

A Second Empire legal scholar, M. O. Bourbeau, described the idealized version of seigneurial justice in his massive work on civil jurisprudence: "France had for a long time its village judges. Nothing was lacking to the apparent simplicity of this justice: the rustic nature of the litigants, the familiarity of the judge sitting under the hamlet's elm tree—everything seemed, in this humble creation of feudalism, to contribute to the attractive conception of patriarchal justice."[1] Bourbeau implicitly recognized what was concluded in the previous chapter; namely, that seigneurial justice, because of the frequency of its tribunals and proximity to rural inhabitants, ought to have served well those very inhabitants. However, Bourbeau cited numerous problems, ranging from the incompetence of judges to procedural formalities bordering on parody, that combined to corrupt the system of justice. The end result was that seigneurial courts, rather than constituting the neutral forum in which people settled their differences in a manner that they perceived as fair, enforced a type of class justice in which the superiority of the lord or of the rich was upheld. Bourbeau wrote: "Is it surprising to find that, in these distressing times, the judge of the seigneur was in the eyes of the oppressed the personification of the abuses and vexations that imposed on them a social system against which they dared not protest?"[2]

If, in theory, the state exists primarily to provide for the collective security of its members, then the nonviolent resolution of disputes stands as the state's second most important raison d'être. In this view, law (civil or penal) exists as an integrative mechanism in society, for it embodies

---

1. M. O. Bourbeau, *Théorie de la procédure civile*, vol. 7, *De la justice de paix* (Paris, 1863), 1.
2. Bourbeau, *Théorie de la procédure civile*, 7:3.

collective sentiments, prescribes the obligations of individuals, and assigns
sanctions for acts that deviate from accepted social norms.[3] Civil justice,
then, constitutes the returning of things by an impartial magistracy to their
rightful relationship (i.e., as required by the collective sentiments embodied
in law). Ensuring access to justice and a fair application of the law is necessary to a society's cohesion and a state's legitimacy, for without access to
justice and the law's fair application, people take the law into their own
hands, and conflicts degenerate into violent and lingering vendettas, with
the strongest often imposing their wills on weaker members of society.[4] So
just as inhabitants of a state look to the justice system to provide a forum
for the resolution of disputes in a perceptibly "fair" manner, so too does
the state look to justice as a basis for its legitimacy and as a link to its
inhabitants. Without the willingness of inhabitants to bring their disputes
to official courts of justice, the state's link to, and control of, its subjects or
citizens remains tenuous.

My goal in this chapter is to examine civil justice in the seigneurial
jurisdictions of rural Aunis and Saintonge. I will first comment briefly on
the types of cases brought before the lords' tribunals in order to determine
who used the courts and for what reasons as well as to give a sense of the
conflicts and concerns of people in the French countryside. After discussing
the generation of civil cases, I will examine how the seigneurial courts resolved them. By focusing on the speed of adjudication, the social status of
litigants, and the expense of trials, I will illuminate the inadequacies of
seigneurial justice in the resolution of disputes: it was slow, costly, and
often inaccessible to the poorer members of society. The failure of the
French state to provide a crucial service demanded by rural dwellers must

---

3. This is essentially Durkheim's view of law. See E. Durkheim, "Types of Law in Relation to
Types of Social Solidarity," in V. Aubert, ed., *Sociology of Law* (Baltimore, 1969). For Marxists,
law reinforces social divisions and is therefore instrumental in the maintenance of a society's power
structure.

4. It is important to distinguish between a bias in the law and a bias in the application of the
law. Every society's laws embody certain "biases" that are more or less accepted; just as our laws are
"biased" toward those with property, Old Regime laws had biases towards a social and economic
elite. For example, nobles suspected of crimes were tried in special courts. But a bias in the application
of the law is far more harmful to a state's legitimacy because people no longer view the justice system
as just and stop submitting their conflicts to official courts. As E. P. Thompson lucidly states, "The
essential precondition for the effectiveness of law, in its function as an ideology, is that it shall display
an independence from gross manipulation and shall seem to be just. It cannot seem to be so without
upholding its own logic and criteria of equity; indeed, on occasion, by actually *being* just." See *Whigs
and Hunters: The Origin of the Black Act* (New York, 1975), 263.

have certainly contributed in part to their acceptance of the Revolution in Aunis and Saintonge.

The Cases Before Seigneurial Tribunals

Civil justice neither offered lords financial advantages nor burdened them with many duties; litigants paid for the costs of justice, and if anyone profited from the exercise of justice it was the officials of the court. Because civil justice impinged but slightly on seigneurs (the paramount impact was on the lord's honor, since being the proprietor of a court was highly flattering in its symbolism), its exercise most clearly resembled the fulfillment of a public power. Having little personal business at stake in the functioning of civil justice or in the outcome of trials, lords granted a great deal of autonomy to the operation of civil courts.

The jurisdiction of seigneurial courts in civil cases was extensive, covering all voluntary matters (*juridiction gracieuse*) and almost all adversarial litigation (*juridiction contentieuse*). Voluntary matters included emancipations, the naming of guardians, separations, permission to alienate the property of a minor, the division of property, the affixing of seals and the compilation of inventories, the opening of closed wills, and so on. Although revolutionary justices of the peace would later provide the same services for a fraction of the cost, rural dwellers probably appreciated the proximity of the seigneurial courts that handled this crucial business. Nearly everyone, from well-to-do bourgeois to illiterate peasants, required some of these court services in their lives; hence, as noted in Chapter 1, voluntary civil cases dominate the archives of seigneurial justices. In contentious litigation, seigneurial courts judged almost all of the following cases: contracts, marriages and successions, sales and purchases of land, loans, and financial settlements.[5] The few categories of cases for which lords' courts were incompetent to offer decisions included litigation over the king's patrimony, *bénéfices,* and the recognition of the royal seal. With their having such sweeping powers of jurisdiction over civil cases, it is impossible to regard such courts as insignificant.[6]

Tables 6(A) and 6(B) list a sample of several hundred civil cases from

5. On the civil jurisdiction of seigneurial courts, see Mousnier, *The Institutions of France,* 509. See also Bataillon, *Les justices seigneuriales du bailliage de Pontoise,* 119.

6. Hufton, "Le paysan et la loi," 681–82.

the lower courts of Jonzac, Brizambourg, Taillebourg, Ré, Fouras, Cônac, St. Seurin d'Uzet, and Pons. Together, the cases depict a tableau of quotidian life in eighteenth-century rural France: conflicts between proprietors (often city dwelling) and peasants over land, trials among family members over successions, quarrels over commercial deals gone bad, arguments over a real or perceived threat to someone's honor. Despite the tendency for these conflicts to turn violent and the ubiquitous role of alcohol in precipitating quarrels, most cases did not originate in the irrational, passionate natures of Old Regime peasants. Rather, most disputes stemmed from rational and specific economic interests,[7] with violence serving the primary response of people accustomed to asserting their own rights instead of submitting them to legal proceedings.

It comes as no surprise that cases involving the defense of one's property dominated the dockets of seigneurial civil courts. Whether a case originated in the collection of a debt, a family quarrel over an inheritance, a complaint about damages from a neighbor's livestock, or a lawsuit over the division of produce stemming from a leasehold, rural denizens zealously protected their property. That this was so is quite understandable given the

TABLE 6A   Civil Cases in Lower Courts

Court	Debts/ Billets	Honor/ Assault	Property Dispute	Lease Dispute	Family/ Inheritance	?	Total
Taillebourg	3	—	4	4	3	3	17
Jonzac	14	3	4	10	15	6	52
Brizambourg	8	1	8	10	8	3	38
Fouras	26	2	7	13	16	11	75
St.Seurin	36	6	8	11	6	11	75
Ile de Ré	31	3	3	14	19	12	92
Pons	7	6	10	9	8	1	41
Cônac	17	5	5	13	4	2	46
Total	142	26	49	84	79	47	427

NOTE: Each category includes the following cases:
  Debts: Simple debt, render account of commercial deal, payment for work done, etc.
  Honor/assault: Reparations d'honneur, injures verbales, violences, etc.
  Property disputes: Jouissance, defense de passer/pacager, damages, boundaries, etc.
  Lease disputes: Loyer, bail, saisie de fruits, prix de ferme, rente, etc.
  Family/inheritance: Compte de tutelle, partage, titres, debts from an inheritance, etc.

7. A point well made by J. Dewald in *Pont St. Pierre*, 129.

TABLE 6B   The Social/Legal Status of Frequent Litigants

Status/Occupation	Plaintiffs	Defendants
Agriculture		
Fermier	23	3
Laboureur à boeufs	35	26
Laboureur	34	102
Saunier	9	23
Laboureur à bras	3	12
Journalier	4	16
Women		
Veuve	65	32
Femme/fille	18	14
Military/marine		
Soldat	1	12
Marinier	7	14
Artisans/merchants/shopkeepers		
Négociant	10	1
Marchand	82	45
Farinier/boulanger	19	15
Meunier	17	25
Charpentier	15	9
Aubergiste	3	7
Bourgeois/professionals		
Procureur/avocat	5	3
Bourgeois	5	6
Notaire	17	2
Huissier/sergeant-royal	7	1
Chirurgien	11	4
Curé	6	4

SOURCES: ADCM 5508, Taillebourg, 1780; B 3070, B 3084, B 3087, B 3088, Jonzac (1765, 1771, 1785, 1786, 1788); B 2811, Brizambourg, 1786–87; B 2474, B 2476, B 2477, Fouras (March 1775–July 1775, March 1780–August 1782, August 1788–July 1789); B 2436, St. Seurin d'Uzet (January 1786–July 1788); B 2149, Ré (September 1775–December 1776); B 3842, B 3845, Pons (1777, 1782); B 2282, Cônac (January 1774–April 1780).

precarious nature of life in eighteenth-century France, when the drift from poverty to indigence required no more impetus than the death of a mule, a harsh winter, or the incapacitation of a parent. Perhaps more in need of explanation is the number of cases involving the defense of one's honor, especially considering the risky nature and potentially disastrous expense of civil litigation. But the defense of one's honor carried economic significance in the face-to-face economy of Old Regime rural areas, where community disapproval could lead to the withholding of business. Furthermore, for people with few material goods, one's sense of honor, reinforced by the approbation of society, was often the most cherished possession and merited vigilant defense.[8]

The civil cases in the records of seigneurial courts highlight several aspects of Old Regime social structure. First, they point to the existence of a dynamic, usually city dwelling, minority that purchased, enclosed, and concentrated property and then served as creditors to the inhabitants of the countryside. Although merchants and *fermiers* stood near the narrow apex of the social pyramid of Aunis and Saintonge and combined to form only a minor proportion of the rural population—R. Jousmet's study of notarial records found that merchants accounted for only 1.7 percent of all marriage contracts in Aunis in 1780[9]—they were responsible for a large proportion of the litigation in seigneurial courts. To offer a corollary to the dynamism of a well-to-do minority, one can posit the chronic poverty and indebtedness of the rural majority, who were constantly constrained to pay bills, to repay loans, or to hand over produce as part of leaseholds or sharecropping agreements. The frequency of cases in which merchants or *laboureurs à boeufs* required unpropertied and often destitute *journaliers* or *laboureurs à bras* to repay loaned bread demonstrates just how precarious were the lives of the poorest members of rural society. Second, these civil cases show the fragmented nature of property in rural areas, which gave rise to innumerable conflicts. Not only did landowners sue with regularity to keep others off their property, but also neighbors forced to live at too close quarters complained (and fought) constantly about usurpations of property.

Disputes among neighbors, although commonly exacerbated by clashes of personality, most neatly expose the economic nature of much social agitation in eighteenth-century rural France. In a case from Taillebourg in

---

8. There exists a large body of scholarship on the role of honor in Old Regime sociability. See, for example, A. Farge, *La vie fragile: Pouvoirs et solidarités à Paris au XVIIIe siècle* (Paris, 1986); D. Garrioch, *Neighborhood and Community in Eighteenth-Century Paris* (New York, 1986); Y. Castan, *Honnêteté et rélations sociales en Languedoc (1715–1780)* (Paris, 1974); Reinhardt, *Justice in the Sarladais*; and J. Ruff, *Crime, Justice, and Public Order*. M. Greenshield introduces the concept of "psychic property," which includes one's honor, dignity, space, possessions, and physical person, in *An Economy of Violence*, 2.

9. R. Jousmet, *Fermiers et métayers d'Aunis, 1750–1789* (thèse de doctorat, Université de Rennes II, 1989), 300. On the dynamism and power of *fermiers* in rural France, see J. Jessenne, "Le pouvoir des fermiers dans les villages d'Artois (1770–1848)," *Annales: Economies, sociétés, civilisations* 38 (1983).

1768, Jean and Marie Roulin sued their neighbor, Sebastien Guilloteau, for calling them thieves in a public place.[10] Two days after the Roulins' complaint, Guilloteau entreated the seigneurial judge to investigate the conduct of Jean Roulin. Guilloteau contended that, in the midst of an argument with Marie Roulin over the alleged theft, Jean attacked him, called him names, and threatened to kill him, demonstrating how easily seemingly minor issues of theft were anything but minor to the parties involved and could escalate rapidly into violent disruptions of local order. In another case from Taillebourg, the merchant Jacques Dautriche complained that he "had the misfortune of having as a sole neighbor Pierre Mazière," who sought daily to shoot him, ravage his possessions, kill his domestic workers, destroy his livestock, and set his property on fire.[11] The case's proceedings established that there had been a long-standing feud between Dautriche and Mazière's father over a shared oven around which Dautriche had constructed a wall. After the death of her husband, Mazière's mother had complained continually about the wall, which made Dautriche so irate that he finally grabbed her throat and ordered her, not too politely, to shut up. Later, Mazière received a court injunction preventing Dautriche from cutting wood that belonged to him through the succession of his father. Angrily, Dautriche then filed his lawsuit against his neighbor. Finally, at Brizambourg in 1784, the *laboureur à boeufs*, Louis Jacques, complained of the following "cabal and league" against him by neighbors to whom he had once been "sacredly linked by occupation:"

> Ambition, hatred, and jealousy, these three infernal sisters who afflict the human race at all times with tumultuous divisions, have reunited and taken sanctuary in the hearts of Marguerite David, Marie Saubier, and Marie Roy. . . . Jealous and alarmed to find the supplicant living in tolerable comfort and from time to time augmenting his small fortune with minor acquisitions that his economies allow him, [they] have formed a bond to destroy him by causing the loss of his property or by [verbal attacks and violence].[12]

The struggle to remain solvent in the face of scarce economic resources was so intense that it rent families asunder: at Marennes, a son sued his father for a share of a house left from the death of the mother; at Jonzac,

10. ADCM B 5523, Comté de Taillebourg, 2 November 1768.
11. ADCM B 5523, Comté de Taillebourg, June–August 1757.
12. ADCM B 2810, Seigneurie de Brizambourg, 26 November 1784.

brothers engaged in a long, bitter lawsuit over a minor inheritance. In particular, being named someone's guardian was either a bonanza that offered the opportunity for profligacy with someone else's property, or it was a thankless task for which minors showed little gratitude, depending on whether the mountains of lawsuits accusing guardians of mismanagement were justified. In Mortagne, Paul La Sagelle supplicated the judge from Marennes for one hundred livres from his guardian, Sieur Durozé, in order to support himself during an apprenticeship.[13] The magistrate granted the request even though the guardian had already paid 150 livres for provisions and despite his claim that La Sagelle was notoriously wasteful.

Of course, inheritances opened the floodgates of family enmity, as economic concerns frequently overshadowed the desire to maintain harmony with one's relatives. But even when the death of a relation failed to cause tumult within a family, inheritances inevitably invited litigation from the deceased's creditors. When the curé of St. Etienne, Louis Chevreuse, died in 1762, several merchant creditors sued the inheritors of Chevreuse's estate.[14] They succeeded in having the former priest's possessions sealed and then sold by the *procureur fiscal.* But the judicial sale only set off another round of clamor for payment, this time from Chevreuse's servant, his cook, and his surgeon. Even the bishop of Saintes staked his claim to a piece of the pie by exercising the right of *meilleur meuble* (best piece of furniture): "He has the right to require from all his clergy, whether regular or secular, at the time of their death a piece of furniture . . . commonly called *meilleur meuble;* this right is incontestably paid at the time of death of all curés who die in office." With the likelihood of litigation accompanying an inheritance and with the distinct possibility that one might inherit more in debts than in assets, is it any wonder that many people wanted nothing whatsoever to do with their patrimony? In the year 1777 alone at Pons there were seven repudiated inheritances.[15]

When neighbors or family members were not quarreling over economic issues, it was often parties to even the most basic commercial conventions whose defense of their economic rights and interests ended in court or violence (or both). At St. Seurin d'Uzet, Louis Gouin sued Pierre Neau for violence and verbal insults; he claimed that Neau had called him a *jean foutre* and had assaulted his wife so violently that she would have

<hr>

13. ADCM B 3342, Chatellénie de Marennes, 14 April 1788.
14. ADCM B 3718, principauté de Mortagne, n.d. (1762–63?).
15. ADCM B 3842, Sirerie de Pons, 1777.

died without his intervention.[16] The violence ensued after Neau demanded the return of eleven empty barrels that Gouin had transported from Bordeaux. Gouin refused to do so until Neau reimbursed him for the taxes paid on the barrels during transportation. At Jonzac, the *fermiers* of the *fours banaux*, Jean Frémon and his wife, Marie Giraud, were subject to contumely by people reluctant to recognize their lord's rights:

> At the oven, while collecting the loaves that inhabitants bring here to bake as is the right due to the lord of this court, the named Chasselas, wife of Chouteau . . . in a deliberate slander and with an unparalleled malice, injured [Marie Giraud] in the most flagrant and outrageous manner by calling her a fat cow, a bitch, and a *drolesse*, and by saying that she is poorly regarded and that her lechery had rendered her so fertile that if she continued to make babies in the same manner as heretofore, she would soon have as many children as there are hairs on a steer.[17]

Chasselas then shoved Giraud and threw her fee of one loaf of bread on the ground. Such activity was not only an attack on Giraud's honor, the plaintiffs contended, but also detrimental to the lord's rights. After all, they asked rhetorically, who would be willing to take the lease of the ovens in the face of such insolence?

Although the preceding examples demonstrate the centrality of economic disputes in the social agitation of rural France during the Old Regime, even litigation ostensibly over the defense of honor revealed material concerns. This assertion is most evident when merchants sued for slander or libel. At Tonnay-Boutonne, the merchant Augustin Cadon filed suit against Jean Jean, a cabaret owner, for allegedly exclaiming to cabaret patrons that Cadon, besides deserving the standard litany of eighteenth-century insults (*coquin, gueux,* etc.), handled his business poorly and would soon be bankrupt. Cadon explained why the insults obliged him to sue: "It is certain that this speech will ruin his credit and his fortune, both of which have already suffered, since there is nothing more precious, especially to a merchant, than his probity and his credit, without which it is impossible to

16. ADCM B 2438, Baronnie de St. Seurin d'Uzet, 13 October 1784.

17. ADCM B 3087, Comté de Jonzac, 13 December 1786. A *four banal* was the lord's oven, where subjects were required not only to bake their bread, but also to pay the lord a number of loaves for the use of his or her oven. The *fermier* leased the right to oversee the oven and to collect the lord's dues. It is clear why peasants resented both the lord's monopoly and the *fermiers* who exercised the lord's privilege.

succeed in business."[18] Similarly, a merchant from Varaize, while suing for slander after having been called a *foutu coquin* and a *foutu gueux*, underscored the importance of defending his honor in the interests of his business: "The supplicant is a public merchant who has until now merited general confidence, and if he doesn't stop the indecent and dishonest slander of Bressiaud and his wife [the defendants] he would soon see himself ruined."[19] In small, relatively homogeneous communities where anonymous market economic relationships had not yet supplanted face-to-face commercial transactions, one's financial well-being required recognition by peers of one's upstanding character. Suspected of being dishonest or engaged in activities of which society disapproved—an illicit sexual relationship, for example—a businessperson soon experienced a diminution of customers. A public acknowledgment of probity that accompanied a successful lawsuit could bring a reparation of the plaintiff's reputation as well as his or her business. A good reputation was among the most important capital of anyone engaged in commerce in rural France.

Of course, not all cases involving the defense of one's honor in Aunis and Saintonge reflected economic concerns. In a society keenly aware of gradations of status and the trappings of honor, the slightest offense to someone's sense of self-worth provoked a violent quarrel or a lawsuit. In a case that might be titled "Dandy Roughed Up at the Perruquier," the lawyer Jean Cloquemain sued Baptiste Ponvert, bourgeois, for insults and battery. Cloquemain was visiting Sieur Mesnard, his ordinary *perruquier,* to have his hair powdered. The two men fell into a dispute over a game of *pallet,* at which point Ponvert claimed that Mesnard had won. Cloquemain told Ponvert to mind his own business, and Ponvert responded by calling Cloquemain a *drolle* and by slapping him on the face, causing his hat to fall on the ground. Cloquemain sued for damages, not only because the insult occurred in a public place, but because the slap was to the face, "the most noble part of a man's exterior."[20] In general, notables were quick to sue over slights to their eminence, especially if the insults came from social inferiors. In particular, priests were intolerant of any words or actions that cast the slightest disgrace upon their holy offices, since they considered themselves

---

18. ADCM B 5552, Baronnie de Tonnay-Boutonne, 27 June 1777.

19. ADCM B 5562, Seigneurie de Varaize, n.d.

20. ADCM B 5523, Comté de Taillebourg, March 1766. It is interesting to note that Cloquemain sued Ponvert rather than challenging him to a duel or some other form of violent confrontation such as a fistfight. No doubt his status as a lawyer informed his course of action.

pillars of local communities and worthy or respect. One curé, Jacques Messin of Jonzac, sued for slander three times in 1780.[21] Finally, women of all social backgrounds litigated frequently in defense of their honor. As Anne Deschamps contended in her lawsuit against Jean Genau for verbal insults, "A woman's dearest possession, that which she cannot allow to be taken away without degrading and demeaning herself, is her reputation and her honor."[22]

The preceding comment introduces a concluding point regarding women in this general overview of the nature of cases before seigneurial tribunals. Prevented from practicing most trades, lacking (as did most men in this region) education, discriminated against by inheritance laws and cultural practices favoring sons, particularly in areas under written, Roman law (such as the Saintonge), and penalized in the form of a bad reputation by neighbors for actions that upset the domestic and familial order that rested on a woman's virtue,[23] the lives of women in rural France were exceedingly precarious. With almost all avenues to an independent existence closed for those without a sizeable inheritance, a woman's very survival often necessitated her marriage.[24]

The centrality of marriage to a woman's strategy for defending against economic misfortune explains the frequency of cases of broken promises of marriage and of *rapt et séduction* in the judicial records of seigneurial courts. Although in such cases it is impossible to ascertain whether marriage had actually been proposed, it is clear that women (or girls) and their fathers, who usually accompanied them to the proceedings, placed great importance on potential marriage as a means of preventing future indigence. Furthermore, in many cases the women were pregnant or had recently given birth, and the prospects for an unmarried woman with children were dire indeed. With or without child, the chances of an advantageous marriage decreased for a woman suspected of having had sexual relations with

21. ADCM B 3084. Messin will reappear in Chapter 4 when he and the *procureur fiscal* press criminal charges against Messin's enemies. There appears to have been much enmity between Messin and his parishioners, and Messin was a habitual litigant.

22. ADCM B 5562, Seigneurie de Varaize, 22 May 1787. Deschamps claimed she overhead Genau speaking badly about her husband. When she "pointed out with softness and moderation that he shouldn't speak poorly of an absent person," Genau responded with vulgar epitaphs. Several days later Genau sued Deschamps for slander and claimed that she had called him a *vieux sot* and a *vieux coquin* and other things "one wouldn't expect of an *honnête femme*."

23. N. Castan, *Justice et répression en Languedoc*, 294.

24. For a detailed examination of this point, see O. Hufton, *The Prospect Before Her: A History of Women in Western Europe, 1500–1800* (New York, 1996).

her "fiancé," heightening the significance of the original promise of affi-
ance. When no hope of marriage existed, such cases at least afforded families the opportunity to restore the honor of their daughters.

A few, brief examples will suffice to demonstrate the preceding points.
On 14 April 1777, Jeanne Blanchard and her father, Jean, sued Jean Bernard,
a twenty-year-old *laboureur*, for *rapt et séduction*.[25] According to the plaintiff's complaint, Bernard repeatedly tried to seduce Blanchard with promises of marriage while she was employed watching sheep for Bernard's
family. Upon their finding themselves alone one day, Bernard combined
oaths of marriage with "his brutality," which resulted in Blanchard's pregnancy. Incessant entreaties to fulfill his promises of marriage, to repair her
honor, and "to prevent a weakness of which he was the cause from becoming a source of ruin and humiliation for her" fell upon Bernard's deaf ears,
leaving the Blanchards no course but to implore the law to come to her aid
and to restore the family's honor. Similarly, in the seigneurie du Grand
Breuil et du Petit Breuil en Marennes on 8 April 1779, Marie Joyeux, a
twenty-two-year-old servant, and her father sued Pierre Pasquet, a twenty-
eight-year-old *saunier*, for breaking his promise of marriage. Their complaint recounted the events leading to her pregnancy and the subsequent
lawsuit:

> Since a year ago Pierre Pasquet . . . has sought to marry her [Joyeux]
> with the strongest assertions of his devotion. But since he professed
> the *Religion Prétendue Réformée* [Protestantism], and the fact that the
> difference of his religion from hers—the supplicant professing the
> Catholic faith—was an invincible obstacle to their marriage, Pasquet,
> in order to prove his love, was instructed . . . in the Catholic religion
> and renounced Calvin's heresy last Christmas.
>
> This change proved to the supplicant the sincerity of Pasquet's
> sentiments for her. . . . She had the misfortune to let herself be seduced
> by his promises that he would marry her, and he knew her carnally.[26]

For Blanchard and Joyeux, pregnant and unmarried, the future would have
been bleak. Family support might have softened the harsh edge of poverty,

25. ADCM B 3842, Sirerie de Pons. The case does not include Bernard's interrogation or a
sentence.
26. ADCM B 3347.

but a lack of it might have rendered the expected children orphans or have sent the women down the familiar path of prostitution.

Once betrothed, women often did not find the protection, material or physical, that they had sought in getting married. Jeanne Lorand, the wife of Jacques Goisland, attested to the common profligacy of many husbands in rural France: "[Goisland] is in a daily state of drunkenness from morning to night; liquor has weakened his mind to the point where he has fallen into the most dangerous imbecility. . . . The damage done to his family by his alienation of their property in order to consume wine and brandy . . . forces [me] to break silence."[27] Lorand sought, and won, a judicial decision rendering her husband incapable of all civil acts, including entering commercial contracts or disposing of his property. When a husband's maladministration became unbearable, women resorted to suing for separation. In seeking a separation from her husband, Marie Cartron testified to how the economic motives for her marriage were subverted by her spouse's disastrous lack of business acumen: "By contract of marriage before a notary . . . [Cartron] entered a *société usagère aux meubles et acquêts* [sharing of property] with François Gabion. . . . Cartron has learned that her husband has so poorly managed his business that he has not only dissipated all his property but hers as well through the alienations he has made and the debts he has contracted, so that creditors menace her with rigorous constraints."[28] Often, requests for legal separation followed habitual violence, as was the case when Marianne Poupelin asked for a separation from her husband, the bourgeois Jean-Pierre Georgon. From the beginning of their marriage, Georgon subjected Poupelin to repeated beatings and humiliations, including public spankings. "In addition, her husband has the misfortune of giving himself over to wine . . . and he is not even exempt from other vices, especially the love of women. When he married the supplicant he had venereal disease, which he communicated to her."[29] Worse still, Georgon had the audacity to blame Poupelin for his malady. Alcohol, domestic violence, and the maladministration of property accompanied many marriages in Old Regime rural France. When the husbands on whom they had depended to minimize the precariousness of their lives proved to be the great-

---

27. ADCM B 3087, Comté de Jonzac, 30 June 1786.

28. ADCM B 3842, Sirerie de Pons, 21 June 1777. Cartron won her request for a separation.

29. ADCM B 2438, Seigneurie de St. Seurin d'Uzet, 4 September 1780. The court granted Poupelin's *renoncement à communauté et séparation de biens*.

est threats to their persons and their properties, women depended on the courts for protection. Fathers, husbands, and courts: a woman's guardian often changed; the state of dependency rarely did.[30]

THE COST AND LENGTH OF SEIGNEURIAL CIVIL JUSTICE

Pursuing a grievance in a civil court in Old Regime France was often a very, and sometimes exorbitantly and prohibitively, expensive proposition for two reasons. First, the procedure employed in civil tribunals was conducive to mounting costs, since litigation required numerous complicated proceedings. Although the elaborate nature of proceedings had its origins in the noble ideal of ensuring that the law functioned according to fixed norms, thereby assuring litigants that the application of the law was unbiased, civil procedure in practice invited chicanery and pettifoggery from parties of bad faith. As M. O. Bourbeau commented, civil procedure had degenerated into a "sad parody of judicial formalities, which were created to protect the rights of litigants but had become the instrument of the iniquities of judges and the rapacity of lawyers."[31] In addition, most courts relied on written procedure, which required extra work by attorneys and barristers and resulted in escalating expenses.

The second reason for the high cost of Old Regime civil justice is that court personnel were for the most part unsalaried, meaning that bailiff, attorney, barrister, and judge alike had to earn their living from the expenses generated from civil suits. One needs minimal perspicacity to grasp that this second reason for high costs existed in symbiosis with the first, for complicated procedures invited more work from court personnel, and more work brought more income. Rather than taking a percentage of the value of the object of litigation (which would at least have been an incentive to speed up a trial, since one's wages would have been the same whether a trial lasted one year or two), court personnel received payment based on the amount and nature of the services they contributed to a case. Such a system was a fertile breeding ground for the virus of chicanery about which inhabitants of rural France complained vociferously and that was evident throughout the archives of seigneurial courts in the form of outrageous

---

30. See, for example, the helpful survey by M. Wiesner, *Women and Gender in Early Modern Europe* (Cambridge, 1993).

31. M. O. Bourbeau, *Théorie de la procédure civile*, 7:3.

claims and never ending trials. When the entrepreneur Louis-Augustin Girardeau sued someone for simple libel after that person had questioned his solvency, Girardeau's barrister and attorney saw fit to submit a bombastic sixteen-page history of libels to the judge of Pons.[32]

The same problems of the high cost of justice afflicted royal courts just as surely as they did seigneurial tribunals. After all, they employed the same procedure, and royal judicial personnel earned a living in the same way as did officials of lords' courts, rendering justice prohibitively expensive for most French people.[33] But these problems were exacerbated in seigneurial jurisdictions because of the superfluity of judicial personnel, their relative poverty compared to royal judicial personnel, and the opportunity for fraud afforded by operating outside the professional oversight of the royal bureaucracy. Royal courts commonly discovered anomalies and outright malversation in the charging of expenses in seigneurial courts. For example, a letter from the *procureur général* of the Parlement of Bordeaux in 1768 chastised the judge of Archaic for failing to pay attention to the expenses of cases. "It is absurd and unjust that he [the clerk] expects half the value of your fee for the deposition you prepared. . . . The pretension of the *procureur fiscal* is equally unjust; in fact, it is the height of injustice for him to charge twice for the cost of communication when there is only one party being communicated to."[34] A recent study of a Norman village court shows in detail how and why local tribunals were rife with bribery, corruption, and influence peddling.[35]

How much did civil justice cost in the seigneurial tribunals of Old Regime Aunis and Saintonge? Of course, the cost depended on the nature of the litigation and the value of the object in question. But an examination of the least complex cases of *juridiction gracieuse* illuminates the expensive nature of the costs of civil justice. At Taillebourg, the simple and common act of naming a guardian routinely cost around thirteen livres, including "taxes of four livres fifteen sols for us [the judge], three-quarters that

32. ADCM J 2600, "Mémoire à Monsieur le juge sénéchal civil et criminel des ville et sirerie de Pons" (Saintes, n.d., 1770s?). With grandiose language and an exaggerated sense of victimization, the brief began and continued in the same tone: "Toujours attentifs à reprimer des desodres aussi funestes à la société, les tribunaux, dans tous les temps, se sont-ils montrés les vengeurs inflexibles de la vertu diffamée."

33. On the cost of royal justice (especially for a barrister), see Berlanstein, *The Barristers of Toulouse*, 25–28.

34. ADCM B 2526, Marquisat d'Archaic, 25 November 1768.

35. Z. Schneider, "The Village and the State," especially chap. 6, "Les Chicanneurs."

amount for the *procureur fiscal,* one-half for the clerk and as much for the attorney."[36] Given the fact that, in 1789, a day's labor was valued at one livre, the sum for such a relatively uncomplicated judicial act was not insubstantial; the very same act would routinely cost less than three livres after the revolutionary reforms of local justice. In any case, was a gathering of four officials necessary to legitimate the registration of a guardian, or were these officials merely maneuvering for a piece of the pie? Importantly, nearly everyone required these judicial acts at some point in their lives. A peasant may decide not to pursue a grievance (no matter how convinced of the justice of the cause) because an adversarial act was too expensive, but the same peasant had little choice when requiring the court's service for a voluntary act. At Pons in 1777, the execution of a repudiated inheritance cost more than 409 livres, including 109 livres for the verification and lifting of judicial seals, 20 livres for the assistance of the *procureur fiscal* at the judicial sale, and 48 livres for the judge's *épices.*[37] One wonders how much was left after the sale to pay the creditors.

Even the most basic cases of adversarial litigation took a sizeable chunk out of the purse of an average rural cultivator. At Montendre, cases of *lods et ventes* cost defaulting defendants six livres nine sols, and cases for the payment of *rentes* cost more than eight livres.[38] When lawsuits encountered challenges by the defendant, in other words, when both parties hired lawyers, expenses mounted almost exponentially. Among the most frequent and simple cases in rural France were those in which plaintiffs sued to keep a neighbor or his or her livestock off the plaintiffs' property. Pierre Fevrier filed suit against his brother, Jean Fevrier, for just such a cause on 29 March 1770.[39] The judge sided with Pierre, but the victory afforded little beyond the *Schadenfreude* associated with seeing his rival condemned to pay the hefty court costs of thirty-one livres, since the judge found no grounds for issuing damage payments. The significance of the thirty-one-livre figure will come into full view in Chapter 6 when juxtaposed to the expenses for similar cases under the justice of the peace.

36. ADCM B 5508, Comté de Taillebourg, 1780. E. Guillaume found that the naming of a *tutelle,* including an inventory, normally cost around fifty livres in the *seigneurie* of Murat. See his *Justice seigneuriale et vie quotidienne dans la vallée du Mont-Dore au XVIII siècle* (Clermont-Ferrand, 1992), 104.
37. ADCM B 3842, Sirerie de Pons, 24 April 1777.
38. ADCM B 2403, Marquisat de Montendre, December 1780–July 1782. In such cases, the judge simply declared the plaintiff (the *procureur fiscal*) winner by default.
39. ADCM B 5499, Comté de Taillebourg.

The high cost of litigating in seigneurial courts regularly left the expenditures in a case greater than the amount involved in the lawsuit. The source of contention between François Fagot and François Mulheau, controlleur des Aydes, was a paltry forty-eight sols, but the cost of the trial exceeded thirty-five livres.[40] At Jonzac, an entrepreneur's demand that a day laborer desist from passing on his property cost fifty-five livres.[41] At Cônac, Pierre Foucher sued Jean Delaye for payment of forty-three sols, but the expenses amounted to sixteen livres sixteen sols. When the merchant Michel Bouliaud filed suit against Jean Martin for repayment of eleven livres, the court assessed the costs at thirty-one livres.[42] The examples multiply seemingly without end, but the point is that even the least complicated cases over minimal amounts threatened litigants with enormous costs. Under such circumstances, could the poor risk going to court? Significantly, the plaintiffs in the preceding examples were relatively comfortably situated in the rural social hierarchy. To bring a suit before a seigneurial court, one had to be able to afford a risky trial, to be absolutely convinced of the justice of one's cause, or to burn with the desire to see one's adversary lose in a court of law and pay the expenses.

At times, the high cost of justice appeared to border on a form of social control, in which powerful and wealthy members of society sued their social inferiors and burdened them with court costs as ways to keep them in line or to punish supposedly insolent behavior. Tired of people cutting his crops and foraging in his woods, the squire and partial seigneur of Jarlac, Daniel de Lisleferme, sued the day laborer François Heard before the tribunal of Pons.[43] The sentence ordered Heard to refrain from cutting de Lisleferme's hay in the future and constrained him to pay the plaintiff 20 sols for the value of the hay—indicating how little produce Heard actually took. Incredibly, the judge also ordered Heard to pay the court costs of more than 218 livres, including 26 livres for the involvement of witnesses, 35 livres for the conclusions of the *procureur fiscal,* 10 livres for paper, and 16 écus for the judge's *épices.* In an age where the 140 livres necessary for a family's yearly supply of bread was nearly beyond the means of a *journalier,* the court costs almost certainly signaled a foreclosure on Heard's (limited)

---

40. ADCM B 3070, Comté de Jonzac, 1 June 1765.
41. ADCM B 3088, 7 September 1788. The cost of the case, which began in June of 1786, must have been devastating to a *journalier.*
42. ADCM B 2282, Comté de Cônac, January 1776 and 5 September 1774, respectively.
43. ADCM B 3845, Sirerie de Pons, 15 April 1780.

property. In Old Regime France, a notable's threat of a lawsuit sufficed to have his or her will obeyed by social inferiors—a claim supported by many *cahiers*.[44]

Table 7 contains a list of the expenses in twenty-four civil decisions rendered by the seigneurial tribunal of Tonnay-Boutonne, while Table 8 shows the average and median expenses of cases from several additional subaltern courts. To be sure, the figures are high, but in part they reflect the broad jurisdiction of seigneurial courts that made them responsible for complicated cases whose expenses one expects to be high. The most telling evidence of the exorbitant cost of seigneurial civil justice surrounds the expenses of relatively simple cases—those centering on points of fact and not complex issues of law—that would later be adjudicated at minimal cost under justices of the peace. Among the examples in Table 8, a case over the use of a small plot (*jouissance de terre*) cost seventy livres, a case over a twelve-livre salary cost forty-two livres, a case over straying livestock cost forty-five livres, and so on. Such a judicial system practically guaranteed a wealthy clientele, though of course litigants from all social stations used this tribunal of first instance. Would it give justiciables a sense that justice was just?

The myriad judicial formalities stipulated by French civil procedure in the Old Regime, along with the "pay per procedure" system by which court personnel received remuneration for their services, were conducive to lengthy litigation. In fact, there existed almost no incentives for any court employees to hasten the resolution of disputes.[45] Exacerbating these already colossal impediments to quick trials was a problem specific to seigneurial justice—the multiplicity of offices among judges and the ambulatory nature of seigneurial magistrates—which left judges absent from their jurisdictions for long periods of time. In addition, as one historian writes, "the slowness of procedure, universally denounced, was aggravated by the systematic practice of appeals."[46]

---

44. See the analysis of the *cahiers* in Chapter 5. As the parishioners of Sainte-Marie and Le Bois contended, "The rich drag the poor from court to court."

45. Such an incentive came from the parties themselves. The desire to end disputes out of court probably accounts for the numerous proceedings for which no sentence survives in the judicial records. The cases just fall off the books, probably signaling an out-of-court settlement. Pessimistically, some quarrels might have led to an escalating cycle of violence and retribution, in which case civil disputes were transformed into criminal inquiries.

46. G. Aubin, "La seigneurie en bordelais d'après la pratique notariale (1715–1789)" (thèse de doctorat, Université de Rouen, 1981), 177.

TABLE 7   The Length and Cost of Civil Justice at Tonnay-Boutonne,
1788–1790

Case	Date Begun	Date of Decision	Cost in Livres
1	7/83	3/88	257
2	12/87	5/88	47
3	7/83	3/88	285
4	?	?	6
5	5/89	8/89	9
6	4/89	6/89	12
7	7/89	6/90	17
8	12/79	3/89	605
9	12/79	3/89	?
10	8/82	6/88	397
11	1/81	3/89	63
12	8/87	8/89	118
13	8/88	12/88	86
14	8/86	1/88	41
15	7/89	6/90	18
16	6/86	1/89	180
17	?	?	81
18	?	?	90
19	?	?	23
20	11/88	11/88	8
21	9/87	1/89	40
22	4/88	9/88	14
23	8/88	1/89	119
24	?	?	12

SOURCE: ADCM B 5553, Baronnie de Tonnay-Boutonne, 1788–1789.
? = Data not available.

Tables 7 and 8, indicating the average length of trials in seigneurial courts, speak for themselves. Again, the length of certain cases stems from the nature of the suit in question and is understandable, if not laudable. One lawsuit from Tonnay-Boutonne that required a full decade before receiving a sentence involved four different parties suing and countersuing over an inheritance. But those simple cases hinging on points of fact that ought to have been conducive to celerity still lingered in the courts for time periods ranging from several months (minimally) to several years. One case involving a shoemaker's request for nine livres for a pair of boots was so uncomplicated that the "proof" consisted of the plaintiff's oath that he had

TABLE 8   The Length and Cost of Justice in Several Jurisdictions

Court	Number of Cases	Average Cost	Median Cost	Number of Cases	Average Length	Median Length
Brizambourg, 1786–87	9	32 l.	27 l.	—	—	—
Brizambourg, 1788–89	11	21 l.	13 l.	11	6 months	6 months
Pons 1777	18	40 l.	27 l.	—	—	—
Pons 1782	12	60 l.	34 l.	—	—	—
Cônac	28	41 l.	24 l.	44	13 months	8 months
Jonzac	32	46 l.	37 l.	41	11 months	10 months
Tonnay-Boutonne	24	106 l.	39 l.	18	32 months	16 months

SOURCES: ADCM B 2811, B 2812, Brizambourg (1786–89); B 3842, B 3845, Pons (1777, 1782); B 2282, Cônac (1774–80); B 5553, Tonnay-Boutonne (1788–89); B 3070, B 3076, B 3081, B 3087, B 3088, Jonzac (1765, 1771, 1780, 1785–86, 1787–88).

indeed sold the boots to the defendant.[47] Nevertheless, the lawsuit took ten months of his time. The judge of Cônac deemed the quarrel between two cultivators so frivolous that he threw the case out of court (a rare occurrence when every lawsuit offered the opportunity to make money), but not before the accumulation of eight months of expenses.[48] Of the ubiquitous boundary quarrels between neighbors and proprietors that JPs would later adjudicate in a matter of days by going directly to the site of contention, two such cases took three years and twenty months, respectively, at Cônac.[49] At St. Seurin d'Uzet, the merchant Jacques Guyon sued Jean-Pierre Georgeon, bourgeois, for *inhibition de passage* on 14 January 1779; on 23 May 1782, the judge finally accepted Georgeon's proof that he had been in possession of the right to pass with his wagon and oxen on Guyon's property for thirty years.[50] Louise Vassal's lawsuit against Joseph Guibert for *dézistat* (a request for Guibert to vacate a property), commenced on 13 August 1781, was still being pleaded before the judge of St. Antoine du Bois when the Revolution closed that judicial register forever![51]

This rather bleak portrait of seigneurial civil justice is a general statement about the institution in the region and not a law applicable to every case. Certainly there existed large courts with frequent sessions and competent and conscientious personnel where people, usually of the same social

47. ADCM B 3076, Comté de Jonzac, 2 March 1771.
48. ADCM B 2282, August 1776. The parties shared the expenses.
49. ADCM B 2282, January 1774 and January 1775.
50. ADCM B 2438.
51. ADCM B 4766. The register's last entry was in August 1789.

status, witnessed the satisfactory resolution of their disputes.[52] Yet given the plethora of seigneurial courts, the problems associated with personnel, the ability of litigants (or chicaners) to manipulate the judicial process, and the automatic advantages enjoyed by the well-to-do, serious obstacles stood in the path of even the most well-meaning disputant. Even Pierre Villard's very sympathetic study of seigneurial civil justice contradicts his evidence that the vast majority of *cahiers* in the Marche complained about the length and cost of justice.[53]

But was seigneurial justice the only game in town? In other words, did rural dwellers wary of submitting disputes to lords' courts enjoy other forums where they might witness the satisfactory resolution of their disputes? One such potential avenue for solving quarrels was private mediation, arbitration, or violence, which Steven Reinhardt combines as the concept of "popular justice."[54] That private settlement frequently occurred in Old Regime Aunis and Saintonge is undeniable and can sometimes be documented with notarial records. Given the necessity of finding alternatives to seigneurial courts as well as the fact that people settle disputes informally in all times and places, such a finding is hardly surprising. But quite apart from the difficulty of assessing whether private settlements proved satisfactory and therefore terminated the actual dispute, several problems arise that raise doubts about "popular justice" as an adequate complement to seigneurial tribunals. First, private settlements require a willingness of both parties to negotiate. But for the innumerable cases in which litigants burn with hatred for their adversaries, what can bring them to the negotiating table? Second, social superiors had little incentive to mediate or arbitrate with inferiors given their advantageous position in a formal lawsuit. Third, why should someone owed one hundred livres from a legitimate contract resort to private settlement for payment when a quick and *official* recogni-

---

52. S. Reinhardt argues reasonably that seigneurial jurisdictions "constituted a truly viable alternative to royal justice for . . . commoners involved in petty disputes that did not challenge the status quo." See *Justice in the Sarladais*, 261. Yet litigants who wanted to punish or annoy their adversaries would certainly find in seigneurial courts a conducive environment.

53. Villard, *Les Justices seigneuriales dans la Marche*, especially 208. Villard's study is indispensible for understanding seigneurial courts, especially their origins and evolution over time. However, his conclusions about civil justice for the eighteenth century are based on a limited sample from three jurisdictions, with most cases costing less than fifteen livres. But his figures do not include *épices* and seem to contradict the *cahiers*. Seigneurial justice may indeed have been inexpensive and convenient relative to royal justice.

54. Although a study of criminal justice, parts of Reinhardt's *Justice in the Sarladais*, and especially the notion of "popular justice," are applicable to civil justice as well.

tion of the debt would better restore social tranquility? Finally, private settlements not notarized as contracts have no enforcement mechanism, and
the records of criminal justice demonstrate that even successful private settlements often led to subsequent criminal complaints as minor civil disputes turned into violent vendettas.[55] Under such circumstances, both
"successful" and "settlement" seem inappropriate.

Nor were royal courts the draft that would slake rural dwellers' thirst
for justice, in part because defendants and lords' officials oftentimes insisted—and the law was on their side—that cases be tried in the defendant's seigneurial jurisdiction. In addition, litigating in a distant royal court
might not appeal to villagers, especially when they knew that the same
civil procedure could render a lawsuit there more expensive than one in a
seigneurial tribunal. The proximity of seigneurial tribunals, the fact that
they provided useful services in *juridiction gracieuse,* and their potential to
be less expensive than royal courts probably explain why many *cahiers* in
1789 demanded their improvement but not outright abolition (though
plenty demanded the latter).

CONCLUSION

The considerable length and cost of justice before seigneurial tribunals in
Old Regime Aunis and Saintonge left rural inhabitants, especially the poor,
wary of submitting their disputes to official channels of justice.[56] Although
the plethora of defaults by defendants certainly reflected to some degree the
legitimacy of the plaintiffs' grievances—why hire a lawyer to fight a valid
debt to your creditor?—it also reflected the fear that adversarial litigation

---

55. Of the 477 criminal cases in Sarlat studied by S. Reinhardt, 9 percent refer to successful or
attempted extralegal adjudication. Such evidence confirms the existence of a network of extralegal
settlement but also raises questions about its effectiveness. To be sure, Reinhardt's view of "popular
justice" is nuanced, and he recognizes that "informal modes of dispute settlement were effective in
the Sarladais only among equals." See *Justice in the Sarladais,* 270.

56. If people were wary of official courts, how did the French of the Old Regime earn a reputation for extreme litigiousness? For one, the litigiousness may have been reserved for certain classes.
Second, litigiousness may reflect the fact that cases became bogged down in procedural minutiae
rather than that people were quick to sue. Finally, as J. Dewald argues in *Pont St. Pierre,* a lawsuit
might be only the initial stage of a dispute that reached its final settlement out of court. In this case,
a lawsuit was a warning for the other party to get serious about an agreement. Dewald's argument
helps explain why so many cases in the registers of seigneurial courts simply drop off the books with
no definitive sentence from the judge.

was too risky and expensive to engage in. Eighty-two of 106 cases from the seigneuries de Ré in 1776 witnessed defaults by the defendants, while fifty of seventy-two defendants defaulted at St. Seurin d'Uzet from 1786 to 1788.[57] The contention that defendants defaulted partially from a reluctance to invest the time and money in fighting a lawsuit will receive support in Chapter 6, when the percentage of defaults decreased under the JPs because of the prohibition on lawyers and the inexpensive nature of local justice.

Might one not argue that the "loser pays" system in Old Regime courts allowed the poor the opportunity to bring legitimate claims to seigneurial tribunals? After all, this argument states, the loser would bear responsibility for the expenses generated by the litigation. But this view neglects the extreme risk of litigation regardless of the supposed legitimacy of one's grievance, especially if an adversary increased his or her odds of winning by hiring a capable lawyer or a barrister.[58] Furthermore, the practice of judges accepting *épices* tainted justice with the suspicion of corruption.[59] Whether justified or not, the suspicion of corruption kept many people out of the courts. Finally, a lawsuit usually required significant overhead, since many expenses had to be advanced by the parties; barristers in particular regularly expected the hefty fees of their honoraria at the time they submitted their writings.[60] In an inheritance case from the seigneurie du Grand Breuil et du Petit Breuil the plaintiff advanced 192 livres toward the case's final cost of 413 livres during the six years of litigation.[61] As Robert Forster discovered in his study of the Saulx-Tavanes family, the lord (or any well-off litigant) enjoyed a distinct advantage in any legal battle through the ability to handle the cost overhead.[62]

57. ADCM B 2149 and ADCM B 2436.

58. Although the employment of a barrister was beyond the means of most litigants, almost all parties hired attorneys. According to the 1667 ordinance on civil procedure, certain civil cases (and the majority of those in seigneurial courts), such as contract disputes worth less than two hundred livres, could be classified as *matières sommaires*, which meant that parties could represent themselves in court. But in practice, illiteracy and unfamiliarity with procedural details prompted the overwhelming majority of nondefaulting parties to hire an attorney.

59. J. Carey found that critics of the system of justice in Old Regime France held *épices* responsible for the corruption of justice and blamed venality for the cumbersome size of the judiciary. See his *Judicial Reform in France Before the Revolution of 1789* (Cambridge, Mass., 1981), 26.

60. L. Berlanstein states that a day laborer's simple consultation of a barrister would have cost one week in wages, making the employment of a barrister beyond the means of the vast majority of litigants. See his *The Barristers of Toulouse*, 27.

61. ADCM B 3347, 1784–1790.

62. R. Forster, *The House of Saulx-Tavanes: Versailles and Burgundy, 1700–1830* (Baltimore, 1971), 78.

With a system of civil justice so conducive to expensive and lengthy litigation that conspired to render the courts inaccessible for large segments of the rural populace, it is understandable why the majority of French clung to "the tenacious belief that justice was monopolized and used as an instrument of domination by the rich and the powerful."[63] Such a belief explains the source and persistence of the adage, known not only to the peasants of Aunis and Saintonge, but also to those of Burgundy and Languedoc, "A bad arrangement is better than a good trial."[64] A peasant would do well to accept the wisdom of this adage, since failure to do so could result in financial ruin or worse. Marie Fuger, incensed by a court decision she considered unfair but had been unable to prevent because litigating was too expensive, defended herself from her creditor and the bailiff with a gun and death threats.[65] Her rage gained her nothing but the pursuit of the *procureur fiscal* for *rébellion à justice*. Unable to protect their rights in court, many rural inhabitants defended them with their fists and clubs, with obvious repercussions for rural order as well as the state's desire to penetrate rural areas.

In a sense, seigneurial civil justice constituted the proverbial falling between the stools. For complex cases of civil law that fell within the jurisdiction of seigneurial tribunals, litigants were potentially better served by the more qualified and professional judges of royal courts, which convened regularly and therefore resulted in faster (though still very expensive) adjudication. For the less complex yet very common civil cases that centered on points of fact, civil justice needed a relaxation of its rigid procedural formalities so that judges could decide cases quickly and inexpensively. Faster and less costly decisions would provide access to justice to a segment of the rural populace hitherto excluded from the benefits of a primary service of the state. But such access first awaited a revolution.

---

63. N. Castan, *Justice et répression en Languedoc*, 54.

64. "Un mauvais accord vaut mieux qu'un bon procès." Both Forster's *The House of Saulx-Tavanes* and Hufton's "Le paysan et la loi en France au XVIIIe siècle" cite the existence of this adage in the regions of their research. The adage confirms the practice of extralegal resolution while it simultaneously suggests that "bad arrangements" did not necessarily mean "satisfactory resolutions."

65. ADCM B 3842, Sirerie de Pons, 24 March 1777. The merchant, Antoine Gout, had won a court decision at Pons establishing himself as a legitimate creditor to Fuger and her husband, Ledet. When he arrived with a bailiff to collect, they found Fuger armed and threatening to kill them and screaming about the injustice of a decision that she had been unable to prevent.

CHAPTER 3

Power, Honor, and Profit

Justice in the Defense of Seigneurialism

In October 1790 the inhabitants of the village of Varaize murdered their mayor, Latierce, on the streets of St. Jean d'Angély. The true object of the crowd's wrath, however, was the countess of Amelot, whose properties Latierce oversaw in an apparently ruthless manner. According to the people of Varaize, Mme d'Amelot's Brobdingnagian pride and insatiable greed resulted in the tyrannical administration of her lands: she insisted that dues on leases once paid in cash now be paid in kind (a profitable move in this time of escalating grain prices); other dues once collected in oats were transformed into more valuable payments of wheat; she employed false measures when collecting payments; she prohibited others from using a stream to which she laid claim as the *seigneur justicier*. Despite the "juridically notoriously false" demands of the countess, her tenants saw no alternative to acquiescing in the "open tyranny,"—no alternative, that is, until the Revolution, when they exacted their retributive justice on Latierce. Before 1789, the few who dared to resist her had "seen their fortunes devoured in the jaws of a never ending trial that always terminates [*sic*] to the advantage of our oppressor."[1]

Although the peasants of Varaize had long-standing complaints against the countess and her stewards, it seems that a barrister named Laplanche was instrumental in vociferating their grievances. Laplanche himself was engaged in a trial over the payment of a seigneurial due, *lods et ventes*, during which he had witnessed the judicial seizure of his livestock. Thus, Laplanche possessed his own motives for hostility toward the lord,

---

1. ADCM L 739 (letter of inhabitants of Varaize to Departmental Directory, 3 October 1790). The antiseigneurial events at Varaize are covered in this carton as well as L 147. See also J.-N. Luc, "Les révoltes paysannes de Varaize et des villages voisins en 1790," *Receuil de la société d'archéologie et d'histoire de la Charente-Maritime* 25 (1973–74): 245–57.

and it was he who drafted a bitter letter on behalf of the people of Varaize questioning various seigneurial exactions and condemning the practices of the countess and Latierce. Threatened and scandalized by the insolence of the letter's tone, Latierce denounced Laplanche to the district authorities, who succeeded in having him arrested and incarcerated in St. Jean d'Angély only after four people died trying to prevent it. In return, the inhabitants of Varaize "arrested" Latierce. On 22 October more than two thousand people invaded the unfortified town of St. Jean d'Angély demanding the immediate release of Laplanche. Ultimately and unhappily, they agreed to an exchange of prisoners, but after Laplanche's freedom they once again converged threateningly upon Latierce. The barrister attempted to placate the crowd, and he went so far as to protect his enemy Latierce with his embraces. But it was to no avail; a number of people stabbed Latierce to death while Laplanche held him in his arms.

The case of Varaize illustrates the dynamics of economic exploitation by lords and increasing peasant resentment in the eighteenth century, which led to the antiseigneurial conflagration that scorched the environs of St. Jean d'Angély during the French Revolution. More important for this study, it suggests the crucial role played by seigneurial justice in enabling lords to exploit their tenants and hence in augmenting the hatred of tenants toward seigneurs. If the villagers of Varaize denounced as the violent aspect of Amelot's strategy of repression Latierce's willingness to shoot his rifle at the violators of the countess's rights, they identified "the menaces . . . the subpoenas and the decisions" of her agents as the complementary path by which she employed her legal authority in order to harass them.[2]

This close alliance between socioeconomic power and the rights of justice found an enthusiastic supporter in a barrister at the Parlement of Paris, Pierre Jacquet. Besides constituting an exhaustive historical and jurisprudential treatise, Jacquet's *Traité des justices de seigneur* celebrated the right of justice as the basis of a lord's power. "Monsieur, justice is the most noble part of the fief. It is justice that serves as the foundation of the rights, honors, prerogatives, and preeminence belonging to the *seigneur justicier*."[3] In dedicating the treatise to the duke of Orléans, Jacquet encouraged him to benefit from the power, honor, and profit that emanated from "the property of justice." A lord derived power from naming the officers of justice

2. ADCM L 739.
3. P. Jacquet, *Traité des justices de seigneur, et des droits en dépendant conformément à la Jurisprudence actuelle des différents Tribunaux du Royaume* (Paris, 1764), p. 2.

and those who execute mandates; his honor stemmed from the right to hunt and fish and the preeminent pew reserved for the *seigneur justicier* in the parish church; and his profits were guaranteed by the right to exact fines, to confiscate property, and to claim vacant inheritances.[4] For Jacquet, justice was as much a symbol to buttress the social status and a tool to enhance the economic status of its proprietor as it was a service to be rendered for the sake of the *justiciables*.

In juxtaposition to Jacquet's treatise and the example of Varaize stand the works of several historians who question the significance of the lord's right of justice in the defense of the rural socioecomonic order—of seigneurialism. Indeed, Paul Bois in *Paysans de l'Ouest* goes so far as argue that seigneurialism itself was moribund in the eighteenth-century Sarthe.[5] With light dues only occasionally enforced and whose accumulated value was but a small proportion of a lord's total revenue, Bois doubts that lords mobilized their agents and courts in defense of a moribund seigneurial regime. Thus, he justifies ignoring seigneurial justice altogether in his study.

Pierre Villard and Henri Bataillon, while not altogether denying the continued existence and possibly burdensome nature of seigneurialism in ancien régime France, reject the picture that subaltern justices were nothing but forums for the administration of the private business of their lords. Bataillon discovers that in the Pontoise feudal cases occupied a minor place in the registers of justice, and Villard concludes that in the Marche such cases constituted only about 1 to 2 percent of all affairs handled by the seigneurial courts.[6] For Villard, if there was a "feudal reaction" in the Marche in the latter half of the eighteenth century, seigneurial justice was not the vessel through which lords brought it about.[7]

The implication of the findings of Villard and Bataillon is that perhaps seigneurial justice constituted more of a service rendered—the means by which country dwellers experienced the efficacious and expeditious resolution of their disputes under the auspices of lords familiar with local conditions—than an institution of exploitation. My goal in this chapter is to explore the latter role fulfilled by the lords' courts in ancien régime Aunis

4. Jacquet, *Traité des justices de seigneur*, 4.
5. Bois, *Paysans de l'Ouest*, 178.
6. Bataillon, *Les justices seigneuriales du bailliage de Pontoise*, 120 and Villard, *Les justices seigneuriales dans la Marche*, 215. Bataillon's work is much more concerned with legal than with social questions, so his study of the cases of these justices is more cursory than that of Villard's.
7. Villard, *Les justices seigneuriales dans la Marche*, p. 203.

and Saintonge and therefore to identify how these jurisdictions influenced
lord-tenant relations. Did inhabitants of the countryside of southwest
France experience seigneurial justice primarily as a service (as seen in the
previous chapters) or as a tool of exploitation? Are the roles incompatible?

SEIGNEURIALISM IN AUNIS AND SAINTONGE

Seigneurialism was essentially a system of land tenure and a mode of surplus extraction.[8] An ancient institution, the *seigneurie* originally defined the
relations between a number of peasants and a large proprietor: in exchange
for the latter's protection and grants of agricultural plots to exploit, the
peasants owed their lord certain payments in money, kind, or labor; they
agreed to obey and respect him or her; and they submitted to his or her
justice. In addition to determining land tenures, seigneurialism, by supporting a "jurisdiction of rights" claimed by lords, was a crucial component
of the French social system that made manifest the stratifications between
groups of people and thus reinforced the social hierarchy. Finally, as is
by now clear, the *seigneurie* functioned as a part of the France's judicial
administration.

By the eighteenth century in France, the peasants' need for their lord's
protection had obviously greatly diminished. In any case, had help been
required of the lord, there was a good chance that he or she resided in
a city or at the court in Versailles. Hence, the original justification for
seigneurialism vanished, rendering the institution a poorly disguised means
of economic exploitation. Lords extracted the surplus of their tenants' produce in several ways, the most obvious being the payment of quitrent (*cens*).
Also, tenants in many regions of France were obliged to pay the seigneur a
percentage of the produce harvested each year from their leases. Such payments were called *champarts, terrages,* or *agriers,* depending on the region
and the crop. Furthermore, any purchase or sale of property among tenants
was subject to a substantial tax payable to the lord's treasury (*lods et ventes*).

---

8. My definition of seigneurialism borrows heavily from P. Jones, *The Peasantry in the French
Revolution* (Cambridge, 1988), 44. For an explanation (and qualified rejection) of the difference between feudalism and seigneurialism, see P. Goubert, "Le paysan et la terre: Seigneurie, tenure, exploitation," in F. Braudel and C. Labrousse, eds., *Histoire économique et sociale de la France,* vol. 2, *Des
derniers temps de l'âge seigneurial aux préludes de l'âge industriel (1660–1789),* 120–22.

Finally, lords reserved the right to bring tenants before their tribunals and exact fines for nonpayment of the above dues and other obligations.

Obviously, before attempting to verify the importance of seigneurial justice to the maintenance of the seigneurial system in Aunis and Saintonge, one must first ascertain the strength of seigneurialism itself. Although no study has yet been conducted on the place of the *seigneurie* in the countryside of Aunis and Saintonge, the existing evidence leaves the impression that it was significant. First of all, unlike in provinces such as Languedoc where the maxim "no lord without title" ensured vast alodial lands free of seigneurial exactions, the customs of both Aunis and Saintonge followed the maxim "no land without lord," hinting that few landholders or tenants avoided the burdens of, and interaction with, a *seigneurie*.[9] The proprietors of Aunis corroborated this suspicion in a petition to the National Assembly when they stated that all tenants in the region held their lands from ninety-nine-year leases (*baillettes*) offered by lords in return for the payment of dues.[10]

In addition to scarce alodial lands, extremely heavy harvest dues on the regions' crops attest to the vitality and prominence of seigneurialism in Aunis and Saintonge. At Aigrefeuille in Aunis the *terrage* claimed 12.5 percent of the harvest on more than one-third of the vineyards, while almost all land was subject to an expropriation of at least 10 percent of the wine crop (Tables 9[A] and 9[B]). Harvest dues in Saintonge ranged from approximately 11 percent to 14 percent of the crop.[11] On the Ile d'Oléron, 16.7 percent of cereal production went to the seigneurs, who also enforced the due (*agrier*) on vine production at an exorbitant rate of 25 percent! Coupled with the rapacious demands of royal tax agents, the tithe, and the need to set aside seed for the next planting, harvest dues took a sizeable bite out of rural tenants' production and must certainly have been handed over begrudgingly to lords.

Another means of determining the importance of seigneurialism is to quantify the proportion of a lord's total revenue that came from seigneurial exactions. If the income from tenant dues paled in comparison to that generated from other economic activities (such as mining or draining

9. "Nul seigneur sans titre," in Languedoc, versus the maxim "nulle terre sans seigneur" in Aunis and Saintonge.

10. Archives nationales, D XIV 2 (Mémoire, March 1790).

11. For a comparison of the harvest dues listed in Table 9(A) and (B) with those of other regions, see P. Jones, *The Peasantry in the French Revolution*, 46.

TABLE 9A   Harvest Dues, *Terrage* on Wine at Aigrefeuille

9 journaux at	1/6 of harvest
636 journaux at	1/8 of harvest
861 journaux at	1/10 of harvest
135 journaux at	1/16 of harvest
137 journaux at	no terrage

1778 journaux in 306 tenures (1 journal = 0.8 acres)

SOURCE: C. Laveau, "Le monde rochelais de l'ancien régime au Consulat," 323.

marshes but especially the direct exploitation of the demesne, including valuable forests) it is probable that lords focused on managing these latter activities more than on using their rights of justice to enforce the payment of seigneurial dues. Reconstituting eighteenth-century incomes is a difficult endeavor, and the data must be approached cautiously; indeed, for the same region of Toulouse Robert Forster calculated that feudal rights accounted for 8 percent of the total seigneurial revenue (i.e., income from land, excluding such items as annuities) of twenty of the wealthiest families, whereas Jean Bastier fixed 18.8 percent as the mean revenue stemming from those dues on forty-eight *seigneuries*.[12] Without generalizing, then, the

TABLE 9B   Harvest Dues — Various Territories

Territory	Due	Crop	Rate
Ile d'Oléron	champart	grains	1/6
	agrier	vines	1/4
Saintonge	agrier	vines	1/7 to 1/9
	champart	grains	1/7 to 1/9
Seig. of Fouras	agrier	—	1/6
Seig. of Landrais	agrier	vines	1/8
		grains	1/7
Seig. of Paille	agrier	—	1/6
Seig. of Benon	agrier	—	1/6
Seig. of Gemozac	agrier	—	1/10

SOURCES: AN D XIV 2 (Ile d'Oléron, Saintonge); ADCM C 267 (cahiers of Fouras, Paille, Benon, Gemozac, Landrais).

12. R. Forster, *The Nobility of Toulouse in the Eighteenth Century: A Social and Economic Study* (Baltimore, 1960), 185–87; Bastier, *La féodalité aux siècles des lumières*, (75–77). Perhaps the discrepancy in figures can be explained by the fact that Forster studied rich *families* who likely possessed extensive

figures concerning seigneurial revenues established for Aunis and Sain-tonge by J.-N. Luc suggest that feudal exactions were extremely important to at least some lords, who must have viewed the rigorous collection of them as a paramount desideratum (Table 10).[13] Hovering around 50 percent of seigneurial revenue, feudal dues escalated to an astounding 87 percent of all seigneurial revenue in Beauvais-sur-Matha because of a diminutive demesne and a heavy impropriated tithe.

Finally, the sheer number of subaltern jurisdictions demonstrates the vitality of the *seigneurie* in Old Regime Aunis and Saintonge. As the tribu-nal of first instance encountered by country dwellers in many of the most important transactions of their lives—civil disputes, the nomination of guardians, the registration of acquisitions, and so on—the ubiquity of sei-gneurial justices, along with scarce freeholds, significant harvest dues, and a high percentage of revenue from seigneurial exactions, reminded peasants of the central place held by the institution of the *seigneurie* in this region.

Justice and the Administration of the *Terrier*

Table 11 shows for various territories the percentage of those contentious civil cases concerning the interests of a lord and inaugurated by his or her agents, either a *procureur fiscal* or a *fermier*.[14] The data dispel any lingering notion that seigneurial courts did nothing but hear litigation stemming from the exploitation of the *seigneurie*.[15] However, it would be equally erro-neous to contend that a small ratio of feudal cases to total cases relegates the former to the status of insignificance in a study of seigneurial justice. A small percentage is not necessarily tantamount to insignificance, and a few court sessions every year or several years sufficed to administer properly a

---

demesnes and forests, thereby decreasing the proportionate value of seigneurial dues, while Bastier examined *seigneuries*, which, if devoid of vast demesnes, relied more on tenant dues.

13. Luc, *Paysans et droits féodaux*, 63–67. Luc's admirable study is indispensable for understand-ing the French Revolution in Aunis and Saintonge.

14. Normally a fiscal procurator initiated such cases, but if the collection of seigneurial rights was leased (the *seigneuries* of the Ile de Ré in 1787, for example), the *fermier* often sued for their payment.

15. D. Sutherland rightly criticizes A. Giffard's famous study of local justice in Brittany for the latter's view that lords' courts did little but manage the lords' business. However, just because the majority of cases did not pertain to the lord does not mean that justice was solely a benign service that had no role in the maintenance of seigneurialism. See D. Sutherland, *The Chouans: Social Origins of Popular Counter-Revolution in Upper Brittany, 1770–1796* (Oxford, 1982), especially 182–84.

TABLE 10   Seigneurial Exactions as a Percentage of Total Revenue

Seigneurie de Beauvais-sur-Matha		
Demesne	1,220 livres	(13%)
Seigneurial dues	8,180 l.	(87%)
—terrage	2,080 l.	
—rentes (cens)	500 l.	
—banalités, péages	1,300 l.	
—lods et ventes	200 l.	
—dime inféodée	4,100 l.	
Seigneurie de Charron		
Demesne	3,002 l.	(54.5%)
Seigneurial dues (terrage)	2,498 l.	(45.5%)
Seigneurie de Cressé		
Demesne	3,098 l.	(47%)
Seigneurial dues	3,326 l.	(53%)
—agrier	2,655 l.	
—rentes (cens)	81 l.	
—rentes (moulin)	550 l.	
—lods et ventes	100 l.	
Comté de Cosnac		
Demesne	17,226 l.	(45.5%)
Seigneurial dues	20,485 l.	(54.5%)
—agrier	12,609 l.	
—rentes (cens)	3,925 l.	
—droits de greffe	100 l.	
—lods et ventes	3,851 l.	
Seigneurie de Migré		
Demesne	1,724 l.	(28.5%)
Seigneurial dues	4,296 l.	(72.5%)
—terrage	2,760 l.	
—dime inféodée	230 l.	
—rentes (cens)	640 l.	
—corvées/banalité	506 l.	
—lods et ventes	160 l.	

SOURCE: J.-N. Luc, *Paysans et droits féodaux*, 65–66.

lord's affairs. For example, the *procureur fiscal* of the seigneurie des Grois appeared at forty-nine hearings concerning seigneurial rights on 27 August 1766 and at sixty hearings on 2 November but then did not pursue another such case until July 1770, suggesting that the management of the lord's interests occurred cyclically.[16] In other *seigneuries*, among them the

16. ADCM B 2103, Seigneuries des Grois et al.

marquisat d'Archaic and the marquisat de Montendre, the fiscal procurator appeared only in the registers of extraordinary or voluntary cases. Does this imply that some lords almost never used their rights of justice to pursue their economic interests? The survival of separate registers in Archaic and Montendre for cases introduced solely by the *procureur fiscal* casts doubt upon this view. These mammoth registers of hundreds of pages paint pictures of zealous agents and reinforce one's wariness about equating a low percentage of feudal cases or even the extended absence of a *procureur fiscal* in the archives of civil justice with a lord's economic inactivity.

Frequently there exists very direct evidence that the *procureur fiscal* worked closely with his lord to guard the latter's interests. In a letter from the lord of Aigrefeuille, Depont, to his fiscal procurator, Faurie, Depont complained that a tenant whose contract had expired refused to vacate a property. To facilitate the tenant's removal, Depont wrote, "I am sending you the attached contract of said [tenant] Boneau so that you can act against him." In another item of correspondence between Depont and Faurie, the lord demonstrated the instrumental role of his judiciary in pro-

TABLE II Percentage of Civil Cases Concerning Lords' Rights

Seigneurie	Cases About Lords' Rights	Total Judgments	Percentage	Types of Seig. Cases
Cônac 1786–88	6	50	12	4 rentes 2 lods et ventes
St. Seurin 1786–88	7	34	20.5	6 rentes 1 lods et ventes
Fouras 1775	23	57	40	8 show title 6 unknown 6 rentes 2 lods et ventes 1 seizure
Fouras 1780–82	4	35	11	3 rentes 1 declare prop.
Fouras 1788–89	12	34	35	9 lots et ventes 2 rentes 1 grazing
Taillebourg 1780	2	19	10.5	1 lods et ventes 1 unknown
Ré 1775–76	3	106	3	1 lods et ventes 1 dues on salt 1 show title

SOURCES: ADCM B 2282, Cônac; B 2436, St. Seurin d'Uzet; B 2474, B 2476, B 2477, Fouras; B 3842, Pons; B 5505 Taillebourg; B 2149, Ré.

tecting his rights and interests: "Please warn the widow of Louis Guignet, barrel maker, and others that if, within one week, they do not come to pay the three years of arrears on the dues of fifty livres which was due last 1 January that they shouldn't be surprised to find themselves constrained to do so by the path of justice."[17] It was through the path of justice and the efforts of the *procureur fiscal* that the lord asserted and received legitimation of his or her interests.

The significance of seigneurial justice to a lord's interests lay in the supervision of the *mouvance*, all of a *seigneurie's* property that was not part of the demesne, and in the upkeep of the *terrier*. A *terrier* was for all intents and purposes the "constitution" of a *seigneurie;* it enumerated the rights of a lord and identified each piece of property and its owner as well as the dues and conditions for enjoyment falling on that property. Historians have long considered the renewal of letters of *terrier* to be synonymous with a feudal reaction in which lords, fueled by the necessity to augment their revenues in the eighteenth century, rediscovered ancient rights and dues, in turn fueling the antiseigneurial discontent of the rural masses. Although the issue of a feudal reaction is beyond the scope of this study, one can state with certainty that the renewal of the *terrier* was a lord's call to arms, a sign of renewed vigor in the administration of the *seigneurie,* and a message unwelcome to the inhabitants of rural France. The inhabitants of Aigre-feuille were so incensed by the message of the renewal of their lord's *terrier* that they armed themselves with pitchforks and chased away the *feudiste* Sarralbe.[18]

While awaiting the *présidial* of Saintes's authorization of the renewal of his *terrier*, the marquis d'Archaic wrote a letter instructing his fiscal

---

17. For both quotations, ADCM E 487 (10 July 1772 and 25 April 1770, registres de correspondence), fonds famille De Pont des Granges.

18. Cited in R. Forster, *Merchants, Landlords, and Magistrates: The Depont Family in Eighteenth-Century France* (Baltimore, 1980), 91. For a contemporary work on the renewal of the *terrier,* see Poix de Fréminville, *La pratique universelle pour la rénovation des terriers et des droits seigneuriaux,* 5 vols. (Paris, 1752–57). For the classic statements on the feudal reaction, see G. Lefebvre, *Les Paysans du Nord pendant la Révolution française* (Lille, 1924) and M. Bloch, *French Rural History: An Essay on Its Basic Characteristics,* trans. J. Sondheimer (Berkeley, 1966). For a current criticism of this idea, see F. Furet, "Feudal System," in F. Furet and M. Ozouf, eds., *A Critical Dictionary of the French Revolution,* trans. A. Goldhammer (Cambridge, 1989). As Lefebvre notes, the surest way to ascertain a "reaction" is to study two different *terriers* from the same *seigneurie,* which is difficult because of a lack of documents. The chronology for this study is too short to examine the issue of a reaction. In any case, letters of *terrier* can signal increasing or more efficient extraction without constituting a reaction (i.e., reasserting old rights). In *Paysans et droits féodaux,* J.-N. Luc states that the *présidial* of Saintes granted thirty-six renewals of *terriers* from 1754 to 1789.

procurator on how to proceed in administering his lands.[19] This correspondence clarifies brilliantly both the economic importance of a new *terrier* and the role to be played by seigneurial justice in the renewal. The marquis empowered the *procureur fiscal*, Léonard, to do everything "that he judges necessary for the profit and advantage of the lord and the improvement of his revenues." The marquis being unhappy with his present judicial officials, presumably for their actions prejudicial to his revenues, the first item he insisted on was that Léonard fire them and hire replacements. Then, he ordered the return to his jurisdictions of all trials "unduly carried before the presidial courts [of Saintes and Angoulême] . . . by individual inhabitants and *justiciables*." Evidently, both *justiciables* and the lord—the former by avoiding seigneurial courts and the latter by insisting on bringing trials back to them—implied that these tribunals benefited the seigneur's interests.

To maximize revenues, it was essential for Léonard to know who possessed property in the *seigneurie* and to determine what dues were associated with those properties. Hence, the marquis instructed Léonard to constrain all vassals to render *aveu et dénombrement*—detailed accounts of noble fiefs, including the territorial dimensions and dues to be paid on them—and *déclarations en censive*, which were the same accounts but for nonnoble lands. Anticipating resistance of the part of the inhabitants because these declarations and the communication of titles usually exposed the neglect of certain dues, the lord admonished Léonard to proceed "by the path of feudal seizure." Once Léonard attained a clear picture of the status of the property in the *seigneurie*, he was encouraged to purchase properties amicably or by *retrait féodal* in order to augment the demesne. Finally, the marquis requested his fiscal agent to mobilize the judicial apparatus for his profit—"to litigate, to oppose . . . and generally to do all that you deem good for my interests."

Similarly, the renewal of the *terrier* in Montendre demonstrates the paramount significance that lords attached to this document.[20] Identifying the *seigneurie* foremost as a jurisdiction of rights, the marquis of Montendre claimed the right of high, middle, and low justice as the basis for all his other privileges (Table 12), which he intended to pursue with zeal. In order to know the *rentes* due to him, he requested all proprietors to give declarations of property or *aveu et dénombrement* before the *sénéchal* of his court.

19. ADCM B 2522, Marquisat d'Archaic, 9 December 1751.
20. ADCM B 2403, Marquisat de Montendre, 23 January 1782.

Predictably, recalcitrant inhabitants were to be constrained to appear at the court of Montendre "in order to see them condemned to pay and to recognize the rights and dues to which their properties are subject." The entire process of renewing the *terrier* was necessary, according to the marquis, because after repeated mutations of property, "he believed that the best means of recognizing these [new] *censitaires* and vassals as well as the payments that they owe was to proceed with a new *terrier*."

Only by keeping abreast of the dimensions, dues, and owners of property could lords exploit their tenants. As a fitting result, the records of seigneurial jurisdictions abound with litigation over *aveux et dénombrements*, declarations of property and communications of titles (rural denizens especially hated the latter; seigneurial agents frequently questioned the validity of titles). Table 13 corroborates this assertion; indeed, for a six-year period in Archaic, declarations of property, *aveux et dénombrements*, and

TABLE 12   Rights Claimed in *Lettre de Terrier*, Marquisat de Montendre

Justice	Right of high, middle, and low justice listed first as the foundation of all other rights.
Chasse/pêche	Sole right to hunt and fish; material benefits but also symbolizes lord's social preeminence.
Cens	Quitrents on all non-alodial properties in the *seigneurie*.
Agriers ou champarts	Right to collect harvest dues on arable land.
Lods et ventes	A tax on all sales or exchanges of property, levied at ⅙ or ⅛ of the value of the transaction. Justified because lord was ostensible owner of property (*seigneurie directe*) who granted its use to lessee (*seigneurie utile*). Tax was for "alienation" of lord's property without permission.
Retrait féodal/prélation	The lord's right to reunite a piece of property with the demesne by reimbursing the purchaser for the price paid to acquire the property. Same justification as lods et ventes.
Marché/foire	Sole right to hold markets and fairs and tax goods sold there.
Mesurage d'huile	Sole right to measure oils and levy a tax for doing so.
Banalité de four	A lucrative monopoly requiring all inhabitants to bake their bread in the lord's oven.
Péage	Seigneurial tolls. Justified because lords theoretically responsible for the upkeep of roads, bridges, etc.
Guet et garde	A right forcing tenants to contribute to the maintenance of the chateau.
Bians et corvées	A right constraining tenants to work on their lord's demesne.

SOURCE: ADCM B 2403 (lettre de terrier), Marquisat de Montendre.

the communication of titles accounted for 180 of 295 hearings concerning the lord's rights. Similarly, a 123-page judicial register from Chatellaillon contained only the declarations of property made in the barony from 1753 to 1770.[21] When, as they usually did, tenants dragged their feet in fulfilling their duties, lords flexed their muscles and tightened the judicial screws. A Monsieur Briard, bourgeois, knew this all too well when the court of Montendre required him to declare his possessions in the territory, to show his titles, and to pay arrears if any were discovered, upon "the failure of which we [the judge] will order that the said properties will be and will remain reunited with the demesne."[22]

Since at least thirty-nine *seigneuries* in Aunis and Saintonge renewed their *terriers* in the period 1750–89, the lively seigneurial jurisdictions in Archaic and Montendre were not exceptional. Moreover, a renewal of the *terrier* was not the only means by which a lord ensured the supervision of the *mouvance* within his jurisdiction. The majority of lords kept abreast of property mutations by maintaining separate registers of acquisitions, in which tenants notified seigneurial agents of purchases of land or wood and received the necessary judicial act legitimating the transaction. Certain registers in the comté de Marans and the seigneurie de St. Hilaire, for example, contained nothing but notifications of acquisitions; the register from St. Hilaire granted 232 judicial acts of acquisition for the period 1770–81.[23]

Not only did registers of acquisitions maintained by seigneurial courts contribute to a lord's management of the *terrier* without a need to resort to a lengthy and vexatious renewal, but they also allowed lords the immediate exercise of their rights. One such right was that of *retrait féodal* or *prélation*. According to the complex laws governing seigneurial property relations, the lord was theoretically the "proprietor" in possession of all nonalodial land in the territory who "leased" property to usufructuaries, often in perpetuity. Thus, in theory all property transactions between tenants alienated the lord's property without his or her permission. *Retrait féodal*, then, recognized the lord's status as proprietor by authorizing him or her to recover all sold property and to reunite it with the demesne by indemnifying the purchaser for the price of the sale. Although *retrait féodal* offered lords the

21. ADCM B 2481, Baronnie de Chatellaillon.
22. ADCM B 2403, Marquisat de Montendre, 4 July 1782.
23. ADCM B 4298 (registre d'acquisitions), Seigneuries de St. Hilaire et al.; ADCM B 3248, Comté de Marans.

means to increase their demesnes, it was not a particularly inexpensive one because the land was simply repurchased at its market price. Therefore, the judicial archives portray *retrait féodal* as a right more often claimed than exercised. However, when tenants acquired property at bargain prices, lords sometimes invoked *retrait féodal* to reap the spoils, as did the Depont family in Aigrefeuille five times from 1730 to 1778, often despite the contestation of those tenants whose business acumen had first identified the bargains.[24]

Another right stemming from acquisitions was that of *lods et ventes*. This right proved more profitable than *retrait féodal* because it required no expenditure on the lord's part; hence, one encounters it frequently in the records of seigneurial justice. A tax of one-sixth or one-eighth of the acquisition's value, the *lods et ventes* could be a substantial windfall for lords, as was the case when the judge of Tonnay-Boutonne in 1786 ordered Gabriel de St. Laurent, an administrator for the navy at Rochefort, to pay fifteen hundred livres in *lods et ventes* as a proportion of the principal of a recent purchase.[25] In order to escape these 17 percent taxes on transactions, tenants apparently often avoided registering them. In May 1787 the *sénéchal* of St. Seurin d'Uzet sentenced Pierre Bernard to reimburse the lord thirty-one livres for *lods et ventes* from a purchase made nine years earlier, in 1778. Again in the same jurisdiction, the *procureur fiscal* won his case demanding that Jean Binaud, merchant, pay twenty-four livres *lods et ventes* for one-sixth of the value of wood he purchased from a verbal contract with a Monsieur Guillon.[26] How did a fiscal procurator learn of verbal sales of wood or of acquisitions made almost a decade earlier? Most likely the efficacious management of a lord's interests necessitated a combination of administrative zeal on the part of the fiscal procurator (for example, in tapping networks to discover who has purchased wood or land) *and* the weight of the seigneurial judicial system in constraining tenants to register acquisitions, to exhibit contracts, to communicate titles, and to declare property.

JUSTICE IN DEFENSE OF THE LORD'S MATERIAL INTERESTS

The most direct manner in which lords employed the judicial apparatus for their benefit was by enforcing payment of the fundamental dues (*rentes*)

---

24. Cited in Forster, *Merchants, Landlords, Magistrates,* 88.
25. ADCM B 2551, Baronnie de Tonnay-Boutonne, 8 June 1786.
26. ADCM B 2436, Baronnie de St. Seurin d'Uzet, 3 May 1787 and 1 June 1786.

required of all socage tenants, the first of which was the *cens*. Hence, on 16 January 1762 the fiscal procurator of the marquisat of Mirambeau, Duburg, constrained twenty-two tenants to appear before the court for failure to pay their *rente*,[27] while 52 of the 295 hearings relating to "affaires particuliers au Marquisat" d'Archaic from 1759 to 1765 treated the nonpayment of *cens* (Table 13). As anyone familiar with a *terrier* knows, the assessment of the *cens* varied enormously and without discernable principles from plot to plot, from garden to garden, and from house to house, often ranging from a few sols to several chickens to a quantity of grain or a combination thereof. Although the *cens* were generally light burdens on tenants, their minimal value (when taken individually) did not deter lords from insisting on their collection. Of the six *rente* cases initiated by the fiscal procurator of St. Seurin d'Uzet in 1786 and 1787, one was for three chickens, a second was for six quarts of grain, two chickens, and fifty-two sols, and yet another concerned two years of *cens* worth six quarts of grain.[28] Still, *rentes* were often more substantial, as seen when the mason Pierre Brissard was sued by the *procureur fiscal* of Cosnac for the failure to pay the *cens* evaluated at nine livres, four bushels of grain, and seven chickens.[29]

Lords also enforced in their courts the payment of the other fundamental *rente*, the harvest dues. Thus, in 1788 the *sénéchal* of Sablonceaux, "at the request of the *procureur fiscal* . . . condemns Demoiselle Pain to pay 120 l. for the value of the agrier at one-sixth of the produce . . . unless she prefers the value to be regulated by an estimation of experts. He also condemns her to pay a fine of 7 s. 6 d. as the custom warrants."[30] Courts records often did not specify whether "*rente seigneuriale*" referred to the *cens* or harvest dues, but lords and tenants evidently litigated less frequency over the latter because they were usually collected on the spot (*quérable*) by seigneurial agents, minimizing the opportunity not to pay them.[31] For example, on 25 September 1787 the *procureur fiscal* of Marennes obtained a court order proclaiming the opening of the harvest.[32] He announced the various fiefs subject to harvesting, each on a different day from the first

---

27. ADCM B 2248 (registre des audiences), Marquisat de Mirambeau.
28. ADCM B 2436 (registre des jugements), Baronnie de St. Seurin d'Uzet, 1786–88.
29. ADCM B 2275, Comté de Cosnac, 13 May 1765.
30. ADCM B 4235, Sablonceaux, 12 June 1788.
31. Opposed to *quérable* dues stood *portable* ones, or those that tenants brought to the lord's château. Already disliking dues as economic burdens, tenants resented their *portable* status as an additional mark of subservience. A case of 1 September 1787 (ADCM B 3341; Marennes) is a good example of a dispute over whether the *champart* and impropriated tithe were *quérable* or *portable*.
32. ADCM B 3341.

TABLE 13   Hearings Concerning Seigneurial Rights, Marquisat
            d'Archaic, 1759–1765

Management of terrier		
Declaration of property	160	(54%)
Communication of titles	4	(1%)
Return of titles	4	(1%)
Render aveu et dénombrement	12	(4%)
Reprise d'instance	4	(1%)
Reinforce social order		
Declaration of faith and homage/fidelity	4	(1%)
Control dues on property		
Payment of dues (cens and harvest dues)	52	(18%)
Exhibition of contracts	10	(3%)
Payment of lods et ventes (property sales)	8	(3%)
Payment of lods et ventes (wood sales)	3	(1%)
Render accounts of harvest	5	(2%)
Determine boundaries between cens/agrier	2	(1%)
Droits casuels (occasional dues)		
Payment—rights of banalité	12	(4%)
Render bians et corvée	15	(5%)
TOTAL	295	

SOURCE: ADCM B 2524 (registre des affairs particulier au marquisat, 1759–65), Marquisat d'Archaic.
Note: These figures reflect the number of hearings and do not represent the number of decisions concerning each item.

through the twelfth of October, and prohibited all tenants and proprietors from gathering crops except on the specified day for that land. The court injunction allowed for the control of seigneurial dues (because the lord's agents assessed the value of each tenant's harvest and evaluated the due) while it simultaneously guaranteed their immediate payment. Such was the close interaction between the lord's fiscal management and the judiciary.

The pursuit of some of the lighter *rentes* seems ridiculous for its pettiness, but it is important to remember that the accumulated revenue from them often contributed substantially to a lord's income. Furthermore, the collection of *rentes* fulfilled more than an economic function; it served as a reminder that the lord was master. As a *portable* due incumbent upon every house owner and every proprietor of a garden—in other words, even those inhabitants too poor to possess plots subject to harvest dues—the payment of the *cens* was a ritual that clearly delineated the social hierarchy and ensured that the *seigneurie* impinged upon the lives of everyone within it.[33] Those who "forgot" their subordinate status and neglected to pay their *rentes* in St. Seurin d'Uzet quickly received notification of it with an order from the lord's court to pay the *cens* and litigation costs, with a fine of 7 sols 6 deniers (perhaps one-third of a day's wages for a laborer) for good measure.[34]

Rentes acquired far greater value and fiscal significance when lords sued for the payment of arrears. The dizzying complexity of a *terrier* guaranteed that even the most conscientious *procureur fiscal* let slip the payments of certain tenants, and a careless seigneurial agent or an indifferent or absentee lord offered tenants ample opportunity to neglect their responsibilities. In addition, unproductive years and chronic indebtedness often caused rural dwellers to miss payments and required lords to seek reimbursement for arrears. If the *cens* of a half bushel of grain easily fell within the budget of a widow cited before the tribunal of Fouras, then the decision that she also pay for twenty-nine years of arrears might have been unrealistic, this sum being beyond her means.[35] Were arrears the avenue of increasing peasant indebtedness?

A case in 1782 between the fiscal procurator of the marquisat de Montendre and M. Pelluchon, royal notary, highlights the significance of arrears payments to the incomes of lords and explains why seigneurial courts were employed in their rigorous enforcement.[36] Pelluchon paid dues of nine bushels two *picotins* of wheat and four bushels four *picotins* of oats on his property; that is, in theory his property was assessed at that rate, but he (and maybe those from whom he inherited) had not paid the *rente* since 1743! In 1773 the *procureur fiscal* had sued Pelluchon for, and won, twenty-nine years of arrears, and again in 1777 he sued for (and won) that year's *rente* and three years' arrears. Thus, Pelluchon faced the unenviable task of paying thirty-three years of dues, which, according to the *forleaux* of the *marquisat*, added up to the considerable sum of 1,242 livres.[37]

33. Paul Bois argues for the weakness of seigneurialism by stating that dues, because they fell on property, affected only the relatively few peasant proprietors and not the large mass of landless subtenants. My view is that because Aunis and Saintonge were regions of micro-ownership and because dues were levied on houses and gardens as well, the *seigneurie* touched nearly everyone.

34. ADCM B 2436 (registre des audiences, 1786–88). The customs of Saintonge allowed for a fine of 7 s. 6 d. for nonpayment of the *cens;* those of Aunis did not.

35. ADCM B 2477 (registre des audiences), Fouras, 1788–89.

36. ADCM B 2403 (registre des affaires particulier au marquisat), marquisat de Montendre, 1780–82.

37. *Forleaux* were detailed tables of the prices of commodities in an area maintained so that dues and other debts in kind could later be converted to cash sums. For example, the value of Pelluchon's wheat payment would have been 15 l. 3 s. 3 d. in 1744 but was worth 38 l. 6 s. in 1777.

Decisions requiring the payment of twenty-nine years' arrears abound in the annals of seigneurial justice, twenty-nine being crucial because that was the maximum number of years the customs of Aunis and Saintonge afforded a lord to demand back payments of dues. Why had so many lords allowed dues to go unpaid for such extended periods of time? Was this a sign of lax seigneurial administration or of a veritable rebellion on the part of inhabitants who incessantly defied lords by withholding dues? The latter view is unlikely because lords possessed the authority and ability to carry out foreclosures. And rather than pointing to administrative neglect, litigation over arrears payments of twenty-nine years actually seems to have been a harbinger of a lord's increasing interest in rendering the *seigneurie* more profitable. Indeed, where requests for arrears of twenty-nine years occurred most frequently—Fouras, Archaic, Montendre, Aigrefeuille—they coincided with the renewal of the *terrier,* which gave lords the chance to identify those mutations of property that had resulted in the inability to determine who owed what. Table 13 shows that among the forty-five decisions by the *sénéchal* of Montendre in 1781–82 ordering the payment of dues, ten of them stipulated that the defendant also pay twenty-nine years' arrears.

Another view of arrears, and one casting aspersions on the actions of lords, would suggest that lords deliberately neglected the collection of *rentes* for certain periods of time only to sue tenants for hefty arrears payments at a later date, thereby increasing the likelihood of foreclosure. Although the notary Pelluchon's finances might have allowed him to pay his twelve hundred livres in arrears, most defendants could ill afford back payments of twenty-nine years; that failure could lead to deepening debt and finally a loss of property. Such a view corresponds neatly to the putative hunger of lords for expanding their territories—Marc Bloch's famous "reconstitution of the demesne"—but remains only speculative in the absence of direct evidence of the motives of lords regarding arrears.[38]

The power of the seigneurial judiciary in policing the lord's material interests extended beyond the ability merely to demand the payment of dues or the recognition of other rights; a *procureur fiscal* threatened to seek feudal seizure (*saisie féodale*) in the case of especially recalcitrant tenants. In

38. On the reconstitution of the demesne, see Bloch, *French Rural History,* 135 ff. Bloch suggests that lords anxious to enlarge their demesnes consciously failed to collect dues for long periods of time. Lulled into a false sense of security, tenants could not pay their arrears, became insolvent, and were forced to sell their property or saw it confiscated.

a lawsuit of 4 March 1768 against Jean Citeau, "onetime cabaret owner and presently day laborer"—a manifestation of the familiar drift into economic hardship—the judge of Marans permitted the fiscal procurator "to have seized the land and other real property that [Citeau] possesses in the *censive* of this *seigneurie* according to the customs"[39] for Citeau's failure to exhibit valid titles for his property. Although the laws governing feudal seizure were complicated, they authorized a lord to seize a tenant's property and produce if the latter failed to pay dues, to cultivate a leasehold, or to render homage or a requested *aveu et dénombrement*. At times seizure was only a temporary safeguard—the judge of Tonnay-Boutonne ordered the return of Madame Lorancie's property on the condition that she fulfill her duties within a week and pay nearly one hundred livres for the cost of the feudal seizure[40]—but for serious infractions and very hostile tenants the act of seizure became a sanction, granting seigneurs the right to keep the produce of a property. The ultimate sanction authorized a lord to reunite seized property with the demesne; the customs of Saintonge and St. Jean d'Angély granted such reunions when tenants neglected to cultivate lands subject to the *agrier* for three consecutive years. The repeated failure to pay dues apparently could also lead to a permanent seizure as seen in Semoussac: "On May 23, 1786 the judge of the chatellenie of Semoussac grants the fiscal procurator the right to reunite with the demesne all the buildings and cultivable land from the *baillette* of M. Quesson. This tenant has not paid for many years his dues of ten *quartiers* two *boisseaux* of wheat, two chickens, and two ducks. On 27 June 1786 the judge places the fiscal procurator in '*possession réelle et corporelle*' of the property concerned."[41] Although actual feudal seizures occurred relatively rarely in the judicial archives of the region, the *threats* of seizure were commonplace, lending some judicial bite to the barks of seigneurial agents urging people to recognize the lord's rights. Even those tenants who exasperated the seigneur by filibustering in the payment of dues and who were wealthy enough to endure heavy court costs by doing so probably shuddered at the prospect of a *saisie féodale*.

The process of collecting *rentes* itself presented dishonest and avaricious agents with another means of exploiting tenants, as the people of Varaize well knew. Abuses in dues collection in the Saintonge reached the point where the Parlement of Bordeaux could no longer ignore "the public

39. ADCM B 3246 (assizes), Comté de Marans, 4 March 1768.
40. ADCM B 2551, Baronnie de Tonnay-Boutonne.
41. ADCM B 5314; cited in Luc, *Paysans et droits féodaux*, 59.

clamor" and threatened lords with stiff fines and damage payments if their courts failed to remedy the malfeasance. Among the abuses cited by the parlement, the most notorious were the following: "In the jurisdiction of the *Sénéchaussée* [Saintes] there are several unequal measurements; oftentimes the cupidity of *fermiers* or stewards causes them to substitute arbitrarily one for the other while receiving dues. . . . [Furthermore], when tenants or debtors carry their dues in kind to them, they almost never find it to be of good enough quality, and under this pretext they make tenants and debtors pay in money above the fair value."[42]

That both the *présidial* of Saintes and the Parlement of Bordeaux found it necessary to act is evidence of the probable widespread nature of the abuses committed by lords' agents in the collection of dues. Was it realistic for the higher courts to expect subaltern justices, frequently peopled by the same agents responsible for the abuses, to police their own *seigneuries* in this matter? Whether this was realistic or an exercise in willful self-delusion, the parlement demanded that seigneurial jurisdictions standardize measurements, maintain *forleaux* for the equitable resolution of arrears disputes, and accept payments in kind if the produce was in good condition.

Finally, along with obliging tenants to pay the basic seigneurial dues falling on land, the seigneurial judicial apparatus protected the economic interests of lords by constraining justiciables to recognize other dues claimed by lords. The main occasional right (*droit casuel*) was the right of *banalité* forcing inhabitants to use the lord's oven or winepress, which in effect gave the seigneur a monopoly over these highly remunerative activities. Despite the near universal denunciation by jurists and rural dwellers of this right, which they saw as nothing but a vestige of the violent usurpation of feudal lords, Réné-Josué Valin, a commentator on the customs of Aunis, identified *banalité* as one of the two occasional rights most often exercised in the region.[43] From 1759 to 1765 the court of Archaic held twelve hearings concerning cases of *banalité* (see Table 13), and J.-N. Luc discovered twenty such cases for 135 *seigneuries* in the year 1788.[44]

Perhaps even more heinous than the *banalité* in the eyes of rural inhab-

---

42. ADCM B 3073 (Arrest de la cour de Parlement portant homologation du règlement fait par le siège présidial de Saintes pour la préception des rentes, 24 September 1768); Jonzac, 24 September 1768.

43. Valin, *Nouveau commentaire*, 1:20.

44. Luc, *Paysans et droits féodaux*, 55.

itants was the seigneurial *corvée,* which required them to perform several days (usually three) of labor per year on the lord's behalf. Valin vilified the *corvée* and questioned its validity under any circumstances. "One cannot guard too cautiously against a right so onerous that, despite the longest possession of it and the titles ordinarily shown in defense of it, must be regarded as an illicit exaction."[45] Many historians have thought that seigneurial *corvées* had fallen into desuetude by the eighteenth century, but their frequent enforcement continued unabated until the Revolution, especially in certain territories such as Archaic and Pons. On 28 November 1788 the *sénéchal* of Pons condemned Pierre Laurent, vine cultivator, "to serve or have served in his stead . . . the *bians et corvées* in question as well as those to be ordered in the future, and for having disobeyed to pay 7 s. 6 d. in fines toward the Sirerie," and to pay the court costs.[46] The question of whether or not the *corvée* constituted an economic burden to peasants is perhaps secondary to the symbolism contained in the right, for rural inhabitants hated dues in manual labor as a mark of ancient servitude.

Is it possible that seigneurial courts—tribunals that sanctioned such questionable rights, that employed the language of obedience, that fined tenants and burdened them with bloated court costs as well—were regarded by country dwellers as anything but the lords' allies? Witness the alliance between a lord's court and the economic exploitation of peasants implicit in the *cahier* of St. Crespin:

> Seigneurial *corvées,* a right still more odious, have only been tolerated until now because they were supposedly attached to the sword or accorded to lords as indemnification for various concessions, such as the right to graze animals or to forage in forests, that they had granted to tenants. The inhabitants of this parish enjoy no such concessions and always serve the *corvées* in order to avoid an ever dangerous trial vis-à-vis a lord, but they dare to hope that the Estates General will charge to their defense and avenge their oppression.[47]

Clearly, the people of rural Aunis and Saintonge often perceived seigneurial justice not as an independent forum for the *resolution* of disputes over the lord's rights—for example, to determine the validity of the *corvée*—but rather as one party's forum for the *enforcement* of those rights.

45. Valin, *Nouveau commentaires,* 1:38.
46. ADCM B 2065, Sirerie de Pons, 28 November 1778.
47. ADCM C 263bis.

JUSTICE IN DEFENSE OF THE SOCIAL ORDER

In 1770 the judge of the sirerie de Pons finally rendered a decision in a long and bitter case pitting the curé and his (unspecified) abbey against the house of Pons. At issue was who enjoyed the right to display a coat of arms at the entrance of the church, the Pons family alone or the religious house as well. In a thinly veiled attack on the honor of the lord, the priest reminded the judge of Madame de Pons's shameful conversion to the *religion prétendue réformée* (Protestantism) in the seventeenth century. Nevertheless, the *sénéchal* concurred with the conclusions of the fiscal procurator and forbade the brethren, at the risk of a one-thousand-livre fine and criminal prosecution, from displaying their arms on the cathedral.[48]

This case exhibiting a seigneur's jealousy over the trappings of his social preeminence, and of the justice system's defense of it, is but one of the many contained in the judicial archives of Aunis and Saintonge. Besides protecting the material interests crucial to a lord's economic status, seigneurial courts closely guarded the rights conferring honor and prestige upon their proprietors. Cloaked in these honors and wearing badges of prestige, lords were able to reinforce their social superiority over their *justiciables,* which in turn helped justify the economic exploitation of them. Hence, one discovers the marquis of Archaic demanding that holders of fiefs render him faith and homage, even though the ritual was anachronistic in a period when vassals no longer followed their lords to war.[49] In a society so fixated with questions of status, the marquis must have relished the decision ordering the powerful Marquis de Pons to render him faith and homage for the fief of Brie.

Perhaps the issue of hunting constituted the greatest battlefield in the eighteenth-century rural war for social status.[50] In addition, the social questions pertaining to the hunt overlapped with material issues, for often illicit hunting supplemented the meager incomes and diets of country dwellers, while other times it destroyed cultivators' crops. Michel Alnet, the *fermier* of the seigneurial revenues of Marignac, expressed this dual significance of the hunt in a complaint before the tribunal of Pons:

48. ADCM B 3329, Sirerie de Pons, 4 January 1770.
49. ADCM B 2524, Marquisat d'Archaic, 11 February 1762.
50. For an overview of hunting in France, see A. Chastel, ed., *Le château, la chasse, et le forêt* (Bordeaux, 1990), while J. Markoff, in *The Abolition of Feudalism,* 118–24, examines the views of the *cahiers* on hunting. For a comparison with hunting in eighteenth-century England, see E. P. Thompson, *Whigs and Hunters.*

The precautions taken by sovereigns from time immemorial to prevent actions prejudicial to harvests or production of the land, and thereby to encourage cultivators, have become almost useless. The hunt, an exercise previously reserved for people with status [*personnes de condition*] and possessing fiefs, today seems permitted to everyone. The penalties pronounced in articles 28 and 29 of the 1669 ordinance for those in contravention of them, contain nothing frightening for the inhabitants of the countryside. Those whose slight fortunes seem to have placed them above the masses, they believe everything is permitted to them and they hunt in broad daylight.[51]

When the judge of Tonnay-Boutonne decried the frequent discoveries of dead game in the barony, and when the *procureur fiscal* of Marennes spoke of the epidemic of destroyed pigeons belonging to the lord, they implied that inhabitants hunted for economic reasons—because they considered these creatures a nuisance to their property.[52] Yet the frequent prosecutions of "bourgeois" for hunting and for insolence toward seigneurial agents signifies that carrying firearms and the act of hunting were most likely also symbolic challenges to the lord's social status. In another case heard by the court of Pons, Charles du Sablon, seigneur of les Brives, complained that his *garde-chasse* (ranger) discovered one Girard jeune's dog holding a rabbit. When the ranger confiscated this illegal possession, Girard actually had the nerve to threaten him with a criminal investigation. "An enterprise of this nature," lamented Sablon, "demonstrates the audacity and insolence of this individual and at the same time leads to nothing less than the annihilation of the rights of lords."[53]

Whether those in contravention of hunting laws were more an economic or a social affront to lords, seigneurial agents mercilessly pursued them. Jean L'houmeau, a miller in the *seigneurie* of Archaic, was convicted of hunting and received the huge but standard fine of one hundred livres, payable to the lord; worse, the court costs of 112 livres exceeded the fine itself and rendered his transgression very painful indeed.[54]

---

51. ADCM B 3845, Sirerie de Pons, 25 August 1780.

52. ADCM B 5552, Tonnay-Boutonne; B 3329, Marennes. See S. Reinhardt's work on peasant reactions in the Périgord in 1790 to honorific privileges, "The Revolution in the Countryside," in S. Reinhardt and E. Cawthon, eds., *Essays on the French Revolution: Paris and the Provinces* (College Station, Tex., 1992).

53. ADCM B 3845, Sirerie de Pons, 19 December 1781.

54. ADCM B 2695, Marquisat d'Archaic, 2 January 1767.

Still, the steady incidence of illegal hunting in Aunis and Saintonge, the repeated audacity of offenders in threatening or even firing upon *gardes-chasse,* the increasing exasperation of lords in the face of their tenants' disobedience, and finally the reliance on draconian measures bordering on the ludicrous all manifest the lords' unsuccessful prosecution of the war against hunters. Nowhere was this more evident than at Pons; there, the fiscal procurator, "in light of the great number of abuses . . . in the hunt and the sale of game, [could] no longer permit himself to maintain his silence without betraying his mission" and therefore obtained the following decree from the judge:[55] (1) It was illegal to purchase any game (confiscation, twenty-livre fine). (2) It was illegal to purchase, make, or sell traps (stocks and thirty-livre fine; whipping, branding, five-year banishment for second offense). (3) Taking, selling, and buying eggs of game birds was forbidden (one-hundred-livre fine). (4) Hunting without possessing a fief was prohibited under pain of a one-hundred-livre fine (the *carcan* and a three-year banishment for the second offense). (5) Hunting with setters or mastiffs invited an additional one-hundred-livre fine. (6) All dogs had to be on leashes except shepherds' dogs when working. A *garde-chasse* could kill any unleashed dog (stocks if dogs unleashed). (7) Everyone, including fief owners, was forbidden to hunt on seeded lands until after the harvest (five-hundred-livre fine, possible loss of fief ["greater penalty for those without fiefs"]). There is little sign in the registers of seigneurial justice at Pons that inhabitants heeded the warnings of the lord's agents and ceased their vexatious hunting. In fact, such strict judicial measures might have represented an admission of the seigneurs' impotence in the face of inhabitants' incessant resistance.

The People and the Judicial Authority

In the marquisat de Mirambeau on 16 May 1772, the *procureur fiscal* introduced eleven cases for the payment of seigneurial dues.[56] No defendants appeared at the hearings. The judge postponed his decisions until the following session on 30 May, but when all eleven defendants defaulted again, he ordered them to pay their *rentes* and the court costs. This habit of defaulting among defendants when the plaintiff was the lord's agent was not

---

55. ADCM B 3861, Sirerie de Pons, 7 April 1759.
56. ADCM B 2251, Marquisat de Mirambeau.

an aberration confined to Mirambeau, for one of the most obvious yet striking facts stemming from Montendre is that inhabitants almost literally never showed up at such cases. In 178 hearings relating to ninety-two non-criminal cases pursued by the fiscal procurator, the defendant appeared in only three of them.

How might one interpret this epidemic of defaults among rural inhabitants? Was it a sign of docility, an unwillingness even to deign to challenge a lord's claim by confronting his or her agents in a court? Was it tantamount to a collective sigh and shrugging of the shoulders as if to say "what can we do?" just as the people of Varaize acquiesced in the tyranny of the countess of Amelot and her bailiffs? Perhaps the near absence of cases in which individuals sued their lords or seigneurial agents gives weight to the view that the redoubtable judicial apparatus cowed tenants into submissive relations with their lords. Similarly, when the *cahiers* of Chérac and Saint-Medard requested that seigneurial justices be restricted to the cognizance of cases involving the rights of lords, their inability to imagine the abolition of these rights implied that rural inhabitants ascribed to seigneurial power a permanence about which they could do little.[57]

On the other hand, despite the marked power that the judiciary offered its proprietors, perhaps the act of defaulting constituted a form of resistance to the lord through the symbolic repudiation of the legitimacy of his court. Why show up for a case you cannot win? Such a strategy, of course, would not ease the burden of seigneurial exactions, but at least it would point out that inhabitants considered seigneurial justice a contributor to their exploitation and not an unbiased institution that decided between the competing claims of equal parties. It is very likely that through defaults, tardiness in payments of dues, and the repeated ignoring of judicial decisions, rural denizens used passive resistance and "the force of inertia"[58] to combat seigneurial power, which exasperated lords by draining the time and energy of their agents. For example, in a case begun 7 April 1775, the fiscal procurator of Fouras demanded that Pierre André Fiénat declare his property in the *seigneurie*. Four months later, in August, the *sénéchal* not surprisingly decided in favor of the lord of Fouras's agent and ordered the defendant to furnish his declaration within a week under penalty of feudal seizure. By 6 September, Fiénat still had not complied, and the judge this time granted

---

57. ADCM C 267, Saint-Medard; C 260bis, Chérac.
58. S. Dontenwill, *Une seigneurie sous l'ancien régime: "L'étoile" en Brionnais du XVIe au XVIIIe siècle (1575–1778)* (Raonne, 1973), 107.

him three days in which to obey. Only in late March 1776, nearly a year after the initial lawsuit, did Fiénat make his declaration after fearing that the threat of seizure would become a reality. The court expenses of Fiénat's stubbornness might have cost him dearly, but what alternatives existed for him to protest the seigneur's authority?

As noted, it was over the issue of hunting that the populace proved most contentious, and their passive resistance often drifted into active opposition to the lord and his employees. The position of *garde-chasse* in particular earned an individual the acerbic hatred of the rural masses and was frequently the target of their violence. In Pons, both Pierre Marchegay, *garde-chasse* in 1777, and Sir Vuiliaume (illegible), inspector of the hunt in 1780, killed dogs caught holding game and promptly became the recipients of the owners' verbal abuse and vicious baton blows.[59] The countess of Amelot exacerbated the hatred of the people of Varaize by confiscating their rifles in an attempt to limit hunting on her territory, and that hatred ultimately led to the murder of the countess's steward.

In truth, determining whether tenants were docile or were passively or actively hostile toward their lords requires an understanding of the strength of the *communauté d'habitants* in a region, for this institution, when strong, offered an entire community the means by which to contest a lord's claims,[60] whereas seigneurial courts pitted mere individuals against lords. In Languedoc, strong communities effaced the power of lords, while vibrant communities confronted the even greater power of lords in a struggle for dominance in Burgundy.[61] Since no study exists on the status of the peasant community in eighteenth-century Aunis and Saintonge, it is difficult to determine who had the upper hand in lord-tenant relations. But one can say without equivocation that within those relations the institution of seigneurial justice was a powerful ally of the lord; and the rural populace knew it. The inhabitants of Le Thou, when informed that the National Assembly had abolished certain feudal rights including the right of justice, responded with relief: "God be praised, we will no longer be pursued by *les procureurs fiscaux.*"[62]

59. ADCM B 3842 and B 3845, Sirerie de Pons.
60. See H. Root's study of strong Burgundian communities that, encouraged by royal intendants, often challenged the power of lords in royal courts; *Peasants and King in Burgundy: Agrarian Foundations of French Absolutism* (Berkeley, 1987).
61. See both P. de Saint Jacob, *Les paysans de Bourgogne au dernier siècle de l'ancien régime* (Paris, 1960) and Root, *Peasants and King in Burgundy.*
62. AN D XIV 2, 5 March 1790.

Conclusion

In a very influential work on the origins of the French Revolution, William Doyle argues that "privilege was universal" in the ancien régime, that few people did not enjoy some unique right, fiscal exemption, or other special treatment. By doing so, of course, he dilutes the importance of seigneurial-ism and the amount of resistance to it before the Revolution by rendering it just one of the myriad privileges that were familiar and frequently bene-ficial to inhabitants of France. Hence, Doyle minimizes, if not altogether discounts, rural social issues in his explanation of the origins of the French Revolution.[63]

On the other hand, Peter Jones, while not denying the universality of privilege in the eighteenth century, questions whether an assertion of the widespread nature of privilege justifies jettisoning seigneurial rights in an explanation of the social climate in France on the eve of the Revolution. For the school of thought that denies the significance of seigneurialism, Jones writes that "what is lacking is the groundwork; nobody seems to have bothered to find out how 'privilege' impinged on the population in practice; how far seigneurial authority still permeated daily life in the eighteenth century."[64] My goal in this chapter has been to explore seigneurial justice as a privilege enjoyed by lords as well as its role in protecting the lords' other social and economic privileges. As such, I hope it has clarified how rural inhabitants experienced the reality of privilege. Simply because privi-leges were common did not make them benign, and seigneurial justice was an important component in the lords' exploitation of their tenants.

Justice carried a dual function within the *seigneurie:* it first allowed lords to supervise the *mouvance* in their territories and then allowed lords to collect the exactions falling upon the usufructuaries and other inhabi-tants. If the *terrier* was the constitution of a *seigneurie* that defined every-one's rights and duties, then seigneurial justice was, paradoxically, the executive branch[65] that guaranteed those rights, usually belonging to the lord, and enforced the fulfillment of duties. Armed with the right of justice, the wish of a seigneur resembled a command. As early as 1694 the inten-dant of La Rochelle, Begon, criticized seigneurial *corvées* as "an exaction

---

63. W. Doyle, *Origins of the French Revolution* (Oxford, 1980), 117. Any future attempt to ignore rural social issues must now confront Markoff's impressive *The Abolition of Feudalism.*

64. Jones, *The Peasantry in the French Revolution,* 43.

65. Luc, *Paysans et droits féodaux,* 65.

contrary to the customs and laws," but he failed to eliminate them because they "are authorized by the possession and by the authority of those who benefit from them."[66] This is a striking example of how lords defended even illicit rights, which would have been impossible without the harassment and authority of their courts. Through seigneurial tribunals, the claim to, or usurped possession of, some privilege attained the status of a right defended by a territory's *usages*.

I have not argued in this chapter that seigneurial justice was the only pillar upholding the exploitation of rural dwellers in Old Regime France. After all, the magistrates of the royal judicial bureaucracy were lords themselves, so the defense of seigneurialism extended beyond the confines of the *seigneurie*. But royal magistrates were members of a professional body whose duty was to oversee and control a public function, the administration of justice, whereas the personnel of seigneurial courts were much less independent of the lords who expected them to act in their private interests.

Furthermore—and this is where seigneurial justice attains its paramount significance—a *seigneurie's* jurisdiction of rights was coterminous with its justice. Thus, any claim to a right or any measure of exploitation received an immediate and forceful sanction in a court of law. Because it was nearly impossible to distinguish between the rights claimed by lords and the proceedings that enforced those claims, it is understandable that the economic exactions and social pretensions of lords acquired a certain reality, a sort of permanence or "imprescriptibility"[67] for the rural inhabitants of Aunis and Saintonge. On this imprescriptibility rested the power of lords.

Any tenant who dared to challenge the imprescriptibility of a lord's rights found him- or herself subject to the legal intimidation of the seigneur's judicial power and the threat of an expensive lawsuit. The rather melodramatic *cahier* of Landraye expressed well the role played by justice in buttressing the power of the seigneur: "Some lords don't want their tenants to have sheep, whose fleece would serve to cover their nakedness; and if one of the tenants decides to have some, well, then, that is a declaration of war between him and his lord, and the bailiffs are continually at his door. Without a doubt, that's wrong on the part of lords, but what can the weak do against the strong? It's the fable of the wolf and the lamb."[68]

66. M. Begon,"Mémoire sur la généralité de La Rochelle," in *Revue de Saintonge et Aunis* 2 (1875): 40.

67. To borrow a term used by P. de Saint-Jacob, in *Les paysans de la Bourgogne du Nord,* 58.

68. ADCM C 267 (37).

CHAPTER 4

The Short Arm of the Law

Seigneurial Justice and the Maintenance of Law and Order

On 11 May 1780 Sieur Pierre du Morisson complained to the public prose-cutor (*procureur fiscal*) of the sirerie de Pons that certain unknown individu-als had scaled the walls surrounding his property and had broken the lock on his home.[1] The malefactors then entered the premises, burned titles and smashed household objects, and finally fled with sixty-two livres in cash and sundry items. The *procureur fiscal* reacted to the report of crime in his jurisdiction with remarkable celerity, for within one week he had obtained the arrest warrants for Antoine Robin and Jacques Gaudin. The wheels of the judicial apparatus continued to move quickly, requiring little more than one month to complete the byzantine criminal procedure that included the taking of depositions from twenty-five witnesses, allowing the judge to decide the case on 12 June. Although the *sénéchal* ordered the continuation of the investigation against Gaudin, he concluded that sufficient evidence existed to convict Robin of breaking and entering. As a reparation for his transgression, Robin was sentenced to death, to be hanged by Pons's execu-tor of high justice, but not before being subject to torture in order to iden-tify his accomplices. After his strangulation, Robin's corpse would be exposed publicly as a macabre monument to his iniquity and as a deterrent to the criminally inclined inhabitants of Pons.

In another case from Pons, the judge sentenced the widow Marguerite Berteau to genuflect before the church of St. Martin in order to demand pardon from God and Justice.[2] Passersby could learn of Berteau's violation of the law and breach of morality by reading the sign hanging from her

---

1. ADCM B 3845, Sirerie de Pons. All sentences of capital or corporal punishment rendered by seigneurial courts were automatically appealed to a parlement. On the process of appeals, see Villard, *Les justices seigneuriales dans la Marche,* 239 ff.

2. ADCM B 2066, Sirerie de Pons, 11 July 1775.

neck: "Convicted of the crime of hiding pregnancy." In addition to ordering the ritual of public humiliation, the magistrate banished Berteau from
the jurisdiction for a period of nine years, which, if she did not have family
outside of Pons to take her in, probably placed her in a precarious economic
condition and might have been the equivalent of issuing her a prostitution
license. Berteau's accomplices—Marie Guillet, Elisabeth Péré, and Marguerite Gaudin—received the only slightly less severe sentence of seven
years' banishment for their complicity in the crime.

Finally, at Tonnay-Boutonne in the autumn of 1767, a well-to-do *laboureur à boeufs*, François Gourit, accused Jeanne Priou of a nocturnal theft
of his grain.[3] Priou asserted her innocence and remonstrated that the grain
in her possession was simply the produce of her own plots. The case produced a mountain of paperwork—the depositions of witnesses, interroga-
tions of Priou, the confrontation of the witnesses and the accused—but the
calculations of the fiscal procurator demonstrating that Priou's land was
insufficient to produce the quantity of grain discovered in her house convinced the judge of her guilt. Unmoved by any sentiment of clemency, the
sénéchal of Tonnay-Boutonne condemned Priou to be taken outside the
courthouse and stripped to the waist so that the executor of high justice
could flagellate her and then brand her with the letter *V* (for Voleuse de
Bled, or grain thief). Besides subjecting Priou to corporal punishment, the
judge banished her for a period of nine years and levied the considerable
fine of four hundred livres, payable to the "seigneur of this court."

That courts controlled by private persons were still imposing sentences
of death and corporal punishment on malefactors almost to the eve of the
French Revolution is eye-opening; in fact, forty-seven such sentences from
the *généralité* of La Rochelle from 1741 to 1765 were meted out by seigneurial courts.[4] But the astonishment this may cause is somewhat mitigated by
the knowledge that these sentences went directly to Parlement on appeal.
Jeanne Pinard, condemned to be hanged by the high justice of Archaic in
1766 for the crime of hiding her pregnancy and the subsequent exposition
and inhumation of the infant, owed her life to the Parlement of Bordeaux,
which altered her sentence on appeal to read:

> We condemn said appellant Pinard to be delivered in the hands of the
> executor of the high justice to be attached by him to the *carcan* of

3. ADCM B 5552, Baronnie de Tonnay-Boutonne, 7 September 1767.

4. ADCM C 177 (crimes dignes de mort, peines afflictives). There was a total of 790 capital
and corporal sentences in the region for those years.

Archaic for three consecutive days, one of which will be market day, from 10 a.m. to noon, having around her head a sign bearing these words: *for hiding pregnancy*. She will also be whipped twenty-four times on her naked shoulders, six times in each of the four cantons of the place. In addition we banish her for the period of three years from the jurisdictions of Guyenne and Saintes.

Since the sign on Pinard's neck made no mention of exposing or inhuming the infant, the magistrates of Bordeaux's sovereign tribunal apparently overturned that conviction from Archaic's seigneurial court.[5]

More important than the recognition that lords' courts still issued sentences of *peines capitales et afflictives* is the impression left by these few examples that seigneurial justice constituted an active and efficient component of a redoubtable Old Regime repressive structure. A high level of activity might be seen in the case against Marguerite Berteau, for it demonstrated that the tentacles of seigneurial criminal justice extended even to matters of morality. Furthermore, the substantial fine of four hundred livres in Tonnay-Boutonne suggests that the protection of the public through the prosecution of crime existed in symbiosis with the lord's desire for profit; that is to say, fines were motives for seigneurial agents to remain active in the pursuit of crimes. And although the mere month it took to convict Robin of the crime of burglary might point to carelessness in prosecution rather than efficient speed, an examination of the prodigious dossier seems to belie this view, for it contained the following procedural items: the original complaint to the fiscal procurator; the depositions of twenty-five witnesses; the interrogation of the suspects; the judge's decision to rule the case *à l'extraordinaire*;[6] a report of Robin's attempted escape from jail; two seigneurial police reports of stolen items located at Robin's domicile; the reading of depositions in front of the witnesses and the accused simultaneously; the confrontation of witnesses and the accused; the confrontation of accused to accuser; the interrogation of the accused *sur la sellette* (on the

---

5. ADCM B 2695; copy of sentence from the Parlement of Bordeaux, 15 December 1766, appealing the sentence from the marquisat d'Archaic, 10 November 1766. Who actually carried out the sentence? The parlement states that Archaic had an "executor" of high justice (and it almost certainly had a *carcan*), but I do not know who actually whipped Pinard.

6. Such a decision kept the trial secret, denied the accused the right to counsel and to hear the charges against him or her, and authorized the use of torture if the evidence pointed toward the party's guilt.

guilty seat); the conclusions of the *procureur fiscal;* the judge's decision and sentence.

My goal in this chapter is to explore the role of seigneurial justice in the repressive structure of ancien régime France. In other words, what part did lords' courts play in the maintenance of law and order? The historiography of eighteenth-century French criminal justice has focused on royal courts and especially the sovereign tribunals of the parlements that served as the final stage of appeals and heard the most important criminal cases. But outside of Nicole Castan's excellent work on justice in Languedoc, very little is known about how seigneurial jurisdictions treated crime, despite their centrality to the daily lives of inhabitants in rural France.[7]

Thus, it is important to ask very basic questions about how the courts of lords dealt with the subject of crime in their territories. Were seigneurial agents really so active, quick, and efficient in their police work and the prosecution of crimes as the few preceding examples suggest? Were they truly so intolerant of crime that thefts of relatively minor sums routinely merited capital punishment and struck fear into potential lawbreakers? Could criminal justice prove profitable so that the security of justiciables offered by criminal prosecutions coincided harmoniously with a judicial agent's need for remuneration and a lord's financial concerns?

After answering these questions about the role of seigneurial justice in the maintenance of rural law and order, one can then speculate on the implications of this role for the rural dwellers of Aunis and Saintonge. Did a conscientious judicial apparatus render inhabitants secure in their persons and property; or did an overzealous and intrusive apparatus cause friction between people and a repressive authority; or, finally, did a weak and inefficient rural repressive force require rural communities to police themselves? The answers to this last series of questions will shed much light on how the inhabitants of Saintonge and Aunis viewed the judicial system both before 1789 and after the French Revolution reformed the perceived abuses in the realm of criminal justice.

---

7. For good studies of royal criminal courts, see Reinhardt, *Justice in the Sarladais;* Ruff, *Crime, Justice, and Public Order;* and especially N. Castan, *Justice et répression en Languedoc.* Castan's study is one of the entire criminal justice system in the region, from seigneurial courts to the Parlement of Toulouse. Hufton's "Le paysan et la loi au XVIIIe siècle"; Reinhardt's *Justice in the Sarladais;* and Dewald's *Pont St. Pierre* also contain recent and helpful sections on seigneurial criminal justice.

The Organization of Old Regime Criminal Justice

Like so many of the institutions of Old Regime France, the administration of criminal justice was clouded by overlapping or ill-defined geographical and jurisdictional boundaries.[8] In a hypothetical case of theft perpetrated in the territory of the comté de Jonzac, for example, the seigneurial agents were normally responsible for the investigation, prosecution, and sentencing involved in bringing the criminal to justice. But if the theft was committed by a *gentilhomme*, the case became the responsibility of the royal *sénéchaussée* of Saintes. For yet another scenario in which the malefactor was a vagrant or if the deed was committed on a royal highway, the royal constables of the *maréchaussée* had jurisdiction over the crime. In other words, when a miscreant transgressed the law, the nature of the crime was the most important but not the only factor in determining which court would pursue the case, for the status of the criminal and the place and circumstances of the act complicated the matter of assigning the duties of prosecution. The French Revolution would later establish concrete lists of criminal acts, divided into categories of felonies and misdemeanors, and clearly specify the authorities responsible for investigating and prosecuting these criminal activities, but prior to 1789 the administration of criminal justice was impeded by a confused organizational scheme.

For the most part in rural France, the responsibility for investigating and prosecuting crimes in the first instance rested with three institutions: the ordinary royal courts (*bailliages et sénéchaussées*), the extraordinary *prévotés des maréchaussées*, and seigneurial tribunals. Ordinary royal tribunals had cognizance not only of crimes committed in the territories for which they were the tribunals of first instance (usually large towns or cities), but, as stated in Chapter 1, also of cases classified as *cas royaux* even if perpetrated on a *seigneurie*. Seigneurial agents in theory investigated *cas royaux* committed in their territories, but they had to relinquish prosecution to royal agents. It seems that royal officials were much more efficient in policing and prosecuting crimes in urban areas than in the countryside, where the judicial bureaucracy's personnel and financial resources were simply ex-

---

8. R. Mousnier's *The Institutions of France Under the Absolute Monarchy* is indispensible for making sense of the organization of Old Regime justice. S. Reinhardt's *Justice in the Sarladais* also has a succinct and useful overview of criminal justice in chap. 2, "Official Justice in the Sarladais." For an excellent study of criminal justice in Paris, see Andrews, *Law, Magistracy and Crime*, vol. 1.

tended beyond efficacy. Hence, law and order in rural areas was largely the concern of other institutions.

One such institution was the *maréchaussée*. Constables of the *maréchaussée* constituted a rural police force, on the one hand, by watching over royal highways, surveying the actions of soldiers, and monitoring the incidence of vagrancy. On the other hand, they combined their police roles with judicial functions by summarily prosecuting the crimes of popular sedition and armed assembly and crimes committed by vagrants.[9] In such cases, the lieutenant of the *maréchaussée*, untrained in law, served as the presiding judge. The numerical weakness of the constables rendered them absent from some rural areas for extended periods of time.[10] When present, the appearance of this armed, mounted, and often undisciplined group of constables could be as fearsome to peasants as the bands of marauding mendicants and soldiers the *maréchaussées* were supposed to control.

The substantial list of felonies and misdemeanors not covered by the categories of *cas royaux* or *cas prévotaux*, including assault and burglary committed by domiciled rural dwellers, fell within the competence of seigneurial courts. Hence, the ubiquitous rural crimes concerning physical and verbal violence stemming from economic and neighborhood disputes were the responsibility of the lords' tribunals. Moreover, *procureurs fiscaux* served as rural police magistrates who investigated transgressions of the law that royal or seigneurial officials later judged. Rather than fulfilling an ancillary or supporting role in criminal justice, then, the lords' tribunals were in principle expected to handle a large proportion of crimes committed in rural France.

In theory, a case received the classification of *grand criminel* or *petit criminel*, which roughly corresponded to *crimes* (felonies) and *délits* (misdemeanors).[11] In many cases, a private party filed a petition of complaint demanding the payment of damages and requesting the public prosecutor to punish the crime. Courts encouraged civil plaintiffs to come forward in all criminal matters, for even in joint actions the civil party covered the expenses; only in very serious cases without a private party would the public party consider initiating criminal proceedings at the expense of the crown

9. For studies of the *maréchaussées*, see R. Schwartz, *Policing the Poor in Eighteenth-Century France* (Chapel Hill, 1988) and especially the thorough work of I. Cameron, *Crime and Repression*.

10. O. Hufton states that only one member of the *maréchaussée* existed for every seven thousand French people. "Le paysan et la loi au XVIIIe siècle," p. 679.

11. This discussion follows closely that of Reinhardt, *Justice in the Sarladais*, 71–84.

or lord. After the initial investigation, the magistrate listened to the advice of the public party and decided whether the transgression disturbed the entire public order, in which case he ordered the public prosecutor to treat it as a crime and to seek punishment for it. If the case remained entirely a private matter, the public party (the *procureur fiscal* in seigneurial courts and the *procureur du roi* in royal ones) avoided involvement and the civil party could demand reparations but not punishment for the misdemeanor. Plaintiffs routinely stated that the gravity of the actions committed against them merited both reparations and punishments, but public prosecutors just as routinely ignored their pleas.[12]

Any transgression not deemed a *crime* by a magistrate could be *civilisée;* that is, subject to less costly civil procedure for the goal of seeking damage payments. However, all felonies required the implementation of costly and elaborate criminal procedure, which seigneurial agents often sought to avoid because any irregularity in the complex procedure found upon appeal to a royal court had to be repeated at the cost of the lord.[13] The first stage in a criminal case was the inquest, in which a public or private party filed a petition of complaint and the magistrate took the depositions of witnesses. Next, the judge interrogated the accused, who lacked counsel and was unaware of the evidence against him or her. Criminal proceedings then continued to the stage of recall and confrontation. Here witnesses restated, and swore oaths to the veracity of, their testimony, after which the suspect could object to the witnesses' testimony and cross-examine them. If the defense of the accused appeared strong, the magistrate might then hear the testimony of defense witnesses, although this procedural act was rare, since few seigneurial or royal prosecutors risked accumulating expenses in a case

12. The criminal complaints at Taillebourg from 1757 to 1769 (ADCM B 5523) are almost formulaic in their descriptions of the events leading to the suits. In cases involving physical violence, for example, the plaintiff cites the following: (1) a loss of much blood; (2) the attack was unprovoked; (3) the plaintiff might have been murdered without the intervention of others; (4) the defendant has had a long-standing but irrational hatred for the plaintiff; (5) the plaintiff expresses surprise over the attack; (6) the defendant blasphemed the holy name of God during the attack. In other words, plaintiffs inflated the severity of attacks and overstated their innocence in order to position themselves for large damage payments or to encourage the public party to file a joint suit. The reports of surgeons usually attested to injuries much less severe than those claimed by plaintiffs, and the depositions of witnesses often showed that violence was rarely sudden, unprovoked, or irrational. Instead, it was often a result of a long-standing feud—usually over an economic issue—between the parties.

13. For the 1670 Criminal Ordinance, see Isambert et al., *Réceuil général des anciennes lois françaises depuis l'an 420 jusqu'à la Révolution de 1789,* vol. 18 (Paris, 1829). For a history of French criminal procedure, see A. Esmein, *Histoire de la procédure criminelle en France et spécialement de la procédure inquisitoire depuis le XIIIe siècle jusqu'à nos jours* (Paris, 1882).

for which the evidence was insufficient.[14] Finally, the judge might employ torture (*la question préparatoire;* abolished in 1780) against a suspect if evidence was significant but insufficient for a conviction. Torture was also used after convictions in order to force the criminal to reveal the identities of accomplices (*la question préalable;* abolished in 1788).

The retribution meted out for criminal convictions by judicial magistrates fell into the categories of capital punishment (*peines capitales,* including the death penalty, life in the galleys, life banishment, life in prison), corporal punishment (*peines afflictives,* including whipping, branding, the *carcan,* the galleys for a limited time), and dishonoring (*peines infamantes,* including temporary banishment, public admission of guilt, begging pardon). Lords of high justice possessed the capability to punish criminals in all of these ways, although only when two law graduates accompanied the judge in his decision. Any sentence of capital or corporal punishment by a seigneurial court was automatically subject to appeal in a parlement.

In summary, not only did seigneurial courts have broad powers of punishment, but they also had significant police powers as well as jurisdiction over a large and important list of crimes, especially the commonplace rural *délits* that could give rise to family feuds, extralegal revenge, and endemic community violence if left unresolved. Furthermore, the inability of royal courts to penetrate the countryside and the frequent absences of the *maréchaussée* assured that the official responsibility for law and order in rural areas rested with the lords' tribunals.[15] How well did this institution fulfill its significant theoretical role in practice?

SEIGNEURIAL CRIMINAL JUSTICE IN PRACTICE

One of the most glaring absences from the archives of eighteenth-century seigneurial justice in Aunis and Saintonge is evidence of a sustained pattern of activity in criminal matters, despite the important role assigned to these courts. For the large comté de Taillebourg, seigneurial agents investigated only ninety-three criminal cases for the period 1757–69 (Table 14), or fewer

14. Reinhardt, *Justice in the Sarladais,* 78. See also Ruff, *Crime, Justice, and Public Order,* chap. 2, "Old Regime Justice in Practice."

15. J. P. Gutton found that only twenty-eight officers of the *maréchaussée* policed the entire Lyonnais, rendering the institution an obviously weak and ineffective repressive force. *La société et les pauvres: L'exemple de la généralité de Lyon, 1534–1789* (Paris, 1970), 159–211.

than eight complaints per year. More significant, the fiscal procurator, commissioned to safeguard the public interest, appeared as the public party in only three cases: once for a hunting violation; once to prosecute the violence of a passenger from outside the community; and once in conjunction with a peasant for the theft of a mule. Is it possible that only three transgressions of the law involved the public interest and merited punishment in this period of increasing population, prices, and social dislocation? Similarly, only fifteen criminal complaints led to criminal trials in the comté de Jonzac from 1751 to 1762, meaning that the court heard little more than one criminal case per year.[16] The public party participated in only two prosecutions, including one case against an illegal hunter for which there was obviously no civil party (the seigneur was not technically a civil party in these cases); in the other instance, the *procureur fiscal* joined a cabaret owner in prosecuting a case of excessive violence. Both of these cases occurred prior to 1754; in other words, the public party of Jonzac failed to prosecute a crime for at least eight years.

In the rare event that seigneurial agents acted in criminal matters on their own initiative, it was often to protect the interests of their lord. Hence, hunters dominated the ranks of defendants in cases pursued by fiscal procurators. Likewise, the lord of Brizambourg's eight hundred *journaux* of valuable forest ensured that his agents remained busy, because of the "crimes committed there almost daily."[17] In a case involving disrespect for the seigneur of Jonzac, the fiscal procurator provided a sycophantic eulogy for the lord's wife, whose life the Supreme Being had just terminated. Although "one could neither respect too greatly her memory nor begin to render her the dignities and honors that are due," vandals led by Monnerot fils américain nonetheless desecrated the black flag flown at the courthouse in her honor. In addition, they disturbed the peaceful repose of the mourners in Jonzac by pounding on doors and responding to the question "Qui est là?" with the retort "C'est moi qui ai chié là!"[18] The entire scandalous affair was "an unpardonable malignity," according to the *procureur fiscal*, who demanded an immediate prosecution, because of the lack of respect shown for the memory of the countess as well as the lack of "submission to the lord of

16. ADCM B 3090.

17. ADCM B 2810, Seigneurie de Brizambourg, 18 May 1784.

18. The translation "Who's there?"; "I shit there!" cannot convey the rhyming play on words of the original French.

TABLE 14   Criminal Cases, Comté de Taillebourg, 1757–1769

Crimes

Violences verbales (death threats, etc.)	11
Injures verbales (insults, attacks on reputation)	24
Violence (coups, voies de fait)	34
Theft	11
Property damage	7
Burglary	1
Seduction	1
Hunting	1
	93

Plaintiffs and Defendants

Social or Legal Category	As Plaintiff	As Defendant
Procureur fiscal	3	—
Bourgeois	6	5
Professionals	11	2
Curé	6	—
Merchants	20	3
Artisans	17	31
Fermier	1	1
Laboureur à boeufs	5	10
Laboureur	3	1
Laboureur à bras	10	24
Day laborers	2	6
Servants	3	4
Women*	18	19
	105	106

SOURCE: ADCM B 5523, Comté de Taillebourg.

*Judicial records identified women not by their social status (as the case for men), but rather by their legal status, i.e., as widows, wives, emancipated girls, or minors.

this court."[19] Finally, the fiscal procurator of Croix-Chapeaux felt obligated to put an end to the incidence of illegal nocturnal grape harvesting, for such actions were prejudicial to the rights of the seigneur.[20] Thus, to a large extent, the duties of *procureurs fiscaux* to safeguard the interests of the public were supplanted by their roles in safeguarding the interests of the lord. The rest of the "public" were free to constitute themselves as civil parties in criminal matters and to demand reparations for injuries but almost always did so without the involvement of the public party (Tables 14 and 15).

When the public party did file a joint suit with the civil party in a criminal complaint, it usually occurred in cases that posed serious threats to the established social order. For example, the public prosecutor of Marennes in 1770 filed a suit with the civil party, the butcher Jacques Cailleton, against Cailleton's servant, Jean Basset.[21] Cailleton had discovered an open

TABLE 15   Criminal Complaints Filed by Private and Public Parties in Various Lower Courts

	Total Criminal Complaints	Number Filed by Public Party	Number with Known Suspect	Plaintiff Where No Suspect
Pons 1777	19	1	18	Proc. Fiscal
Marennes 1768	11	1	10	Notaire
Marennes 1783	15	3	13	Proc. Fiscal, Saunier
Marennes 1788	14	4	12	Proc. du Roi, Bourgeois
Jonzac 1751–62[a]	15	2	15	
Jonzac 1768	7	1	7	
Jonzac 1783–84	6	2	5	Proc. Fiscal
Taillebourg 1757–69	93	3	90	2 Fermiers, Bourgeois
Total	180	17 (9%)	170 (94%)	

SOURCES: ADCM B 3842, Pons; B 3327, Marennes, 1768; B 3340, Marennes, 1783; B 3343, Marennes, 1788; B 3090, Jonzac, 1751–62; B 3073, Jonzac, 1768; B 3086, Jonzac, 1783–84; B 5523, Taillebourg.

[a]These figures reflect criminal trials, complaints that actually led to court prosecutions. As such, there was obviously always a known defendant. Other criminal complaints, after investigation, might have led to damage payments outside of court or the dropping of cases altogether, meaning that they never came to trial.

19. ADCM B 3087, Comté de Jonzac, 22 April 1786.
20. ADCM B 2096, Chatellénie de Croix-Chapeaux, 1759.
21. ADCM B 3329, Marennes, 15 September 1770. Basset was found guilty, sentenced to one year in prison in Bordeaux, fined twelve livres, and ordered to pay the court costs of eighty-one livres and the sixty livres it cost to transport him to Bordeaux.

trunk in his house missing fifteen écus and that Basset had fled the environs. According to the fiscal procurator, domestic thefts were shocking examples of insolence and betrayal that ruptured the entire social hierarchy. In Jonzac, the fiscal procurator often rushed to the defense of that other pillar of the community, the priest Jacques Messin. In one case judged *à l'extraordinaire,* the public party worked diligently to secure the prosecution of the servant Jean Lesne for referring to the priest's two female employees as "the servants of the whoremonger."[22] It is unknown whether Messin actually scandalized the community with his sexual improprieties. Perhaps another case involving Messin from 1780 sheds light on why he provoked the wrath and disrespect of the villagers of Jonzac. In this case, Messin and the fiscal procurator pursued two day laborers, Rousseau and Girard, for "the insolent manner in which they pay the tithe."[23] Inhabitants of Jonzac apparently resented the heavy nature of the tithe and Messin's rigorous enforcement of it, resulting in tensions between the priest and his flock. Regardless of the source of this conflict, however, it is important to note how few infractions that did not affect the interests of the lord or pose serious threats to the social order provoked seigneurial agents from their slumber in criminal affairs.

The pronounced inactivity of seigneurial agents in criminal matters stemmed from one fundamental problem: the high cost of criminal justice. The lords' efforts to avoid expenses and their never ending concern with the financial repercussions of their undertakings—whether the private administration of their demesnes or the public administration of their courts—rendered rural law and order yet another victim of the confusion of public and private interests in the institution of seigneurial justice.

The paramount cause for the excessive, even prohibitive, cost of criminal justice was that the procedure stipulated by the crown's criminal ordinance of 1670 proved elaborate and time-consuming. The ordinance's original goal was guided by two overriding desires: that irrefutable proof exist for conviction and that, once convicted, the guilty received swift and severe punishment. But it made criminal procedure cumbersome and costly in practice (not to mention barbaric, in its use of torture and the prohibi-

22. ADCM B 3084, Comté de Jonzac, 1780. The judge ordered Lesne to publicly avow the upstanding life of Messin, to pay thirty livres in fines toward church repairs, and to pay the court costs of 116 livres. Such costs were almost assuredly beyond the means of a *domestique,* leaving the priest and the lord responsible for reimbursing the judicial agents and the witnesses.

23. ADCM B 3084, Comté de Jonzac, 1 September 1780.

tion of counsel for the defense, as Enlightenment critics such as Beccaria pointed out). The expenses involved in a criminal trial almost invariably reached at least one hundred livres (see the example in Appendix 1). Not only did the costs of paper escalate with every required procedural act, but also witnesses proved especially expensive, since the judge and the clerk both received a fixed payment per witness for each deposition, recall, and confrontation, and witnesses received a per diem sum for their involvement in a case. Furthermore, the expenses generated from guarding suspects in jail—for food, straw, the jailer's wages—and transporting them between prisons were often staggering; it cost sixty livres alone to transfer a convict from the prison in Marennes to that of Bordeaux.[24] Such costs intimidated both private and public plaintiffs from pursuing cases for which there was little hope of recovering the expenditures.

Many cases avoided hefty criminal expenses, since courts often subjected misdemeanors to civil procedure, but all serious crimes followed the procedure specified in the ordinance of 1670. In the latter case, the existence of a civil plaintiff or of a defendant wealthy enough to cover court costs relieved the seigneur of the burden of investigating or prosecuting crimes at his own expense. But when no aggrieved civil party came forward— whether out of fear of reprisal, because of despair over recuperating expenses from an impoverished defendant, or in the absence of a specific malefactor from whom one could demand damages—and when defendants were too poor to reimburse the lord for the costs of adjudication, the lord theoretically bore the financial loss as a duty incumbent upon him or her for possessing the prerogative of justice.

In ninety of the ninety-three criminal complaints at Tonnay-Boutonne from 1757 to 1769, the plaintiff's petition identified a specific defendant; that is to say, plaintiffs constituted themselves as civil parties in criminal cases, thereby undertaking responsibility for court costs, when they perceived the opportunity to exact damage payments from known defendants. In the three cases without suspects (and all serious enough to be classified as felonies), the plaintiffs—two *fermiers* and a *sieur bourgeois*—came from the top of the rural social hierarchy and were thus able to incur the expenses of a criminal investigation even without the possibility of being reimbursed by damage payments. Hence, misdemeanors pursued by civil parties and capable of being *civilisée* dominate the archives of seigneurial criminal jus-

24. ADCM B 3329; Marennes.

tice in Aunis and Saintonge, and this blurring of criminal and civil justice allowed rural society to enjoy some semblance of protection from its miscreants.[25]

Besides the unwillingness of seigneurial agents to prosecute crimes, the condition of the prisons in the region is another manifestation of the reluctance of lords to finance their duties regarding criminal justice. The maintenance of a functional prison was not only a symbol of the power of a lord of high justice, but also one of the most costly conditions demanded by the crown for the exercise of the right of *haute justice*. Yet a report by the intendant of La Rochelle titled "The State of the Prisons" exposed that "the poor condition of the courthouses and prisons merit the greatest attention," signifying that lords neglected their responsibilities to safeguard the populace with secure prisons and guarantee the majesty of justice with dignified courthouses.[26] The house of detention on the Ile de Ré was so dilapidated that "it needs to be rebuilt rather than repaired." At Tonnay-Boutonne, the prisoner Joseph Albert entreated the judge to release him, claiming that horrible prison conditions threatened his life: "The supplicant was captured by virtue of this arrest warrant and detained in the prison of Tonnay-Boutonne, that is to say in one of the most horrific holes where the least light of day has never penetrated and where the prisoner is continually suffocated by pestilent odors."[27] Not only was the prison unhealthy, but its state of disrepair was so advanced that the jailor Pierre Caillaud petitioned the judge to be excused from responsibility in case of the escape of Albert or any subsequent prisoner: "The prisons of this court are not secure enough to prevent the evasion of the accused; besides, the jailor's

25. Of course, this could also suggest a very low incidence of crime. Although one need not expect rates of delinquency comparable to those of the present day, the pronounced absence of crimes from the dockets of seigneurial courts (despite their jurisdiction over them) is far too striking to attribute to the orderliness of eighteenth-century rural society, especially since socioeconomic conditions left contemporaries increasingly insecure about the threats of rising criminality. In any case, the evidence cited in the rest of this chapter explains why I attribute the paucity of criminal cases to problems with the justice system and not solely to the low incidence of crime in the region.

26. ADCM C 180, n.d. (1769?). In truth, the state of royal courts and prisons seemed little better than those of lords.

27. ADCM B 5552, Tonnay-Boutonne, 15 December 1777. Albert had claimed that Sebastien Niguet owed him money. When he demanded payment from Niguet's wife, she called him "canaille," to which he responded that she was a "garce, putain, et coquine." Later he boasted to Niguet in public that he knew the latter's wife carnally and that Niguet's child was a bastard. Niguet pressed charges, resulting in Albert's imprisonment for interrogation and trial even though he was obviously not a dangerous criminal.

chamber is presently outside the state of being occupied."[28] Simply put, the jailer could not even guard the prisoners. Throughout the region, dilapidated prisons exhibited that the burdens of the expenses associated with criminal justice hindered the fulfillment of lords' duties in this realm.

Another source of evidence demonstrating the desire of seigneurs to avoid the costs of criminal justice, already cited in Chapter 1, stems from the attempts of the royal treasurer to charge subaltern tribunals for proceedings undertaken at royal expense but that were theoretically the responsibility of lords. From March 1739 to June 1747, lords in Aunis and Saintonge objected to ninety-nine demands for reimbursement in criminal cases for which they were ostensibly responsible, but that the crown claimed to have investigated or prosecuted at its expense—a substantial sign of the neglect of lords or of the dishonesty of the royal treasury; in either case, it hinted at problems in the administration of criminal justice.[29] In Table 16 I enumerate as examples the sums and reasons for which the crown requested reimbursement in the year 1745; these sums and reasons range from thirteen livres for the bread and straw of a prisoner detained at royal expense to a whopping 554 livres for the cost of an entire case of theft that the agents of the comté de Rassé failed to prosecute.

For nearly every entry in the intendant's records of a sum sought by the royal treasurer there existed a parallel response from a lord stating why a criminal case, and hence its costs, fell within someone else's jurisdiction.

TABLE 16   Royal Demands for Reimbursal by Seigneurs for the Costs of Criminal Procedures, Généralité of La Rochelle, 1745

Sum	Cause	Seigneurie
13 l. 10 s.	Bread and straw—case of theft	Lonzac
130 l. 17 s.	Criminal procedures, bread, straw	Nieul le Verouil
32 l. 11 s.	Case of theft of nets	Charente
141 l.	Cost of witnesses, bread, straw	Soubise
93 l.	Wages of sergeants	Aubterre
80 l. 10 s.	Bread, straw—case of theft	Mirambeau
18 l.	Bread, straw—case of assault	Dolus d'Oléron
554 l. 14 s.	Criminal trial—case of theft	Rassé

SOURCE: ADCM C 179.

28. ADCM B 5552. The judge responded tersely to place irons on Albert's feet.
29. ADCM C 179.

Thus, the duke de St. Simon, as the seigneur of Rassé, protested the 554 livre charge by denying that this *seigneurie* carried with it the right of high justice. "[He] maintains that he possesses only low justice in the County of Rassé and that, although the King elevated this fief into a County, it was without granting the right of high justice."[30] Monsieur de Sallignac, the *seigneur haut justicier* of Mons, claimed that the homicide purportedly committed by Thomas La Fon took place on a *grand chemin* (highway) and not a village road, removing the burden of prosecution from the lord. Similarly, the royal minister Trudaine requested the intendant of La Rochelle to investigate the following claim:

> The lord of high justice of Angliers has opposed article 13 of the Roll of Recovery of the Costs of Justice in the Généralité of La Rochelle of January 1739 in which he is included for the reimbursement of the costs of the case pursued by the *lieutenant criminel* of La Rochelle against Foulin fils, Baudry, and others accused of homicide. The defense of this *seigneur haut justicier* is that the homicide in question resulted from the Rebellion of the accused relative to the execution of a judgment rendered by the *juges consuls* of La Rochelle against Foulin père. As a consequence, [it is] a *cas royal* over which the officers of the justice of Angliers do not have jurisdiction.[31]

In a case of assault committed on his territory of Moindreau, Paul François de Pont des Granges asked his son Jean-Samuel, the intendant of Moulins, to use his substantial influence to persuade the *procureur général* to prosecute the transgression at royal expense.[32] In sum, the ledgers for the recovery of expenses show that royal officials and seigneurs waged a battle over the issue of the costs of criminal justice, with ministers endeavoring to prod lords from their inactivity in criminal matters, and lords working strenuously to deny responsibility for criminal cases. In this battle the proliferation of seigneurial tribunals and its resultant confusion over jurisdictions obviously benefited the lords by obstructing the crown's attempts to administer criminal justice.

The inactivity of seigneurial agents in criminal matters, the failure of lords to maintain functional prisons, and the struggle between royal and seigneurial tribunals over the cost of prosecutions all point to the lords'

---

30. ADCM C 179 (letter of the minister Trudaine to the intendant Barentin), 26 June 1747.
31. ADCM C 179, 8 April 1739.
32. ADCM E 487, fonds famille de Pont des Granges, 1 June 1766.

derogation of duty in the criminal justice system of Old Regime France. The result of this derogation, then, is obvious: crime frequently went unpunished in rural areas, at least by seigneurial authorities. R.-J. Valin, a contemporary observer of the rural local justice system in Aunis, offered a bitter indictment of seigneurs for their reluctance to pursue crimes and lamented the accompanying sorry state of law and order in the region. Valin denounced

> the repugnance that they [lords] show toward ensuring the investigation of crimes committed in the confines of their *seigneuries,* because of the considerable expenses charged for these types of procedures, without their being able to reap any profit. . . . They all endeavor to avoid these expenses, and this often favors the evasion of criminals. . . .
>
> It is so easy to place serious crimes in the ranks of *cas royaux, présidiaux, ou prévôtaux* [*maréchaussée*], that they don't believe themselves to have jurisdiction over any of them. But, to reiterate, what guides them is the interest they have in avoiding the expense. Nevertheless, they don't always avoid it, and when the crime is recognized as falling within the competence of a seigneurial justice, they are obliged to furnish the costs for the procedure, unless they wish to renounce the right of high justice. I know of no one who has resolved himself to this sacrifice.[33]

Valin's strictures demonstrate yet again how lords' private financial concerns victimized their justiciables, in this case by failing to provide for the security of persons and property. Unlike civil and seigneurial cases, which proved rewarding to judicial officials and lords, respectively, pursuing crimes simply threatened lords with the burdensome costs of investigations that led nowhere, of meaningless condemnations in absentia, and of prosecutions of destitute criminals who could pay neither court costs nor fines.

Many *cahiers* corroborated Valin's assertion about the lack of law and order in the countryside of Aunis and Saintonge, although not all of them attributed the neglect of crime to the conscious efforts of seigneurs to avoid the costs of investigating criminal affairs. The petition of Forges demanded "that there be taken efficacious measures for the punishment of crimes too neglected in the countryside, that the police that is almost forgotten there

33. Valin, *Nouveau commentaire,* 1:18.

be put in vigor, and that the officers of justice have more force in their
hands than they do now."[34] Likewise, the *cahier* of Beauvais-sur-Mathas
complained that "the exercise of the police is absolutely neglected by their
[lords'] officers," but excused the fiscal procurators for this neglect by
claiming that they were simply overwhelmed by the task, especially in *seigneuries* covering several parishes.[35] The *cahier* of St. Martin d'Aix specified
a unique cause—its location on an island—as the reason for its problems
of justice. According to the inhabitants of St. Martin, the lack of communication with, and the cost of transportation to, the mainland prevented
the frequent appearance of the officers of justice, "which is harmful to law
and order [*ce qui nuit à la bonne police*] and makes contestation eternal."[36]
Importantly, all three of these *cahiers* mentioned the inadequacy of the rural
police force, which probably encouraged malefactors and certainly aided
the evasion of criminals.

Even if seigneurial agents conscientiously attempted to fulfill their
roles in the criminal justice system, they often encountered the lack of
community cooperation as an obstacle. The *procureur fiscal* of Tonnay-Boutonne wrote to the judge on 13 December 1777, complaining that "there
often occur crimes meriting the animadversion of the public but that remain without pursuit and punishment because of a lack of individuals to
file complaints or to denounce the authors and the accomplices of these
crimes."[37] Instead, the public party came to know of crimes only if rumors
(*la voix publique*) reached his office. In this particular case, the fiscal procurator was scandalized to hear that a certain Daniaud was suspected of com-
mitting several burglaries in the jurisdiction without denunciation. It may
be that victims refused to risk paying for the expenses of a criminal complaint. In another scenario, perhaps a fear of reprisal prevented victims
from voicing their complaints through official channels, or maybe the community intended to exact its own justice on Daniaud. But whatever the
reason for the reticence of the inhabitants of Tonnay-Boutonne, they exhibited little confidence in the ability of seigneurial agents to deal ade-
quately with the subject of crime in the territory.

Another example from Tonnay-Boutonne demonstrates the reluctance
of inhabitants to involve seigneurial officials in local affairs. Informed by

34. ADCM C 267 (29).
35. ADCM C 263.
36. ADCM C 262bis.
37. ADCM B 5552, Baronnie de Tonnay-Boutonne.

public rumors that the twelve-year-old son of a *laboureur* had recently died from wounds inflicted by another person and been buried, the fiscal procurator asked the judge to order the exhumation of the corpse. According to the *procureur fiscal*, "the father of said [unnamed] child has not accused the authors of this crime because, as local gossip has it, he has received from them damage and interest payments with which he is satisfied."[38] If the rumors were true, this example points to the existence of an extrajudicial network for the resolution of some criminal cases, in which parties, whether out of a desire to avoid the expenses of official judicial channels or because of community pressure, mediated their own disputes.[39]

To summarize, it is instructive to look at the case of St. Martin de Ré, which illuminates the problems associated with criminal justice, especially its costs, in seigneurial jurisdictions.[40] In three letters from 1701, the *procureur fiscal*, Durand, wrote to his lord, the baron of St. Martin, describing a case of aggravated assault committed against a soldier stationed at the island's garrison. Durand first wrote on 3 January stating in an obsequious tone that "the fiscal procurator [i.e., Durand himself], for the good of his lord, has done everything so that he might spare him the costs of the pursuit of the crime; but one also sees that he fears the garrison." In other words, Durand was caught between his lord's explicit pressure to avoid expenses by quite frankly ignoring crimes, and the soldiers' wrath, which necessitated swift action in punishing their comrade's assailant. Despite the obvious desire of the lord to avoid involvement in the matter, Durand exclaimed that "the crime is so enormous and so public that it isn't possible for me to remain silent especially since the entire garrison demands justice," and so he asked the lord to authorize his steward to furnish sums necessary to pay for the investigation of the case.

38. ADCM B 5552, Tonnay-Boutonne, 27 September 1776.

39. Although beyond the scope of this study, the idea of a realm of popular or community justice is defended by many authors, including N. Castan, in *Justice et répression en Languedoc* and O. Hufton, in "Attitudes Towards Authority in Eighteenth-century Languedoc," *Social History* 3 (1978): 281–302. S. Reinhardt's argument in *Justice in the Sarladais* is that three competing systems of criminal justice—royal, seigneurial, and popular—competed for hegemony in eighteenth-century France, with royal tribunals gaining the upper hand. Furthermore, T. G. A. Le Goff and D. Sutherland argue that the inability of royal and seigneurial authorities to penetrate rural communities left the latter responsible for maintaining their own social equilibrium. These communities resented the interference of the new revolutionary officials, providing the Breton countryside with a counterrevolutionary impetus. "The Revolution and the Rural Community in Eighteenth-Century Brittany," *Past and Present* 62 (1974): 96–119.

40. The three letters from 1701 cited in this example may be found in the Bibliothèque municipale de La Rochelle (BMLR), 663 Folio 46, 663 Folio 43, and 663 Folio 41.

By 24 February, at which time the baron still had failed to authorize funding for the case, Durand found it necessary to scold his lord by reminding him of his duty to provide justice for all inhabitants of his territory. He regretted being harassed in the prosecution of this case by the lord and his steward "even more so since this [a conviction] would do much to reassure the people and since there are other events to fear [without a conviction]." Durand warned that popular retribution and an escalation of violence would ensue upon the authorities' failure to punish the culpable party. In closing, he requested yet more money to finance the food of the person taken suspect and repairs for the prison.

On 30 March 1701 there was still no cooperation from the baron or his steward. Nonetheless, the expenses mounted. This time Durand requested 130 livres for the costs of the assistance of two barristers from La Rochelle who aided the judge of St. Martin in his decision. Furthermore, the appeal to parlement—evidently the judge sentenced the defendant to capital or corporal punishment, making the appeal automatic—would require the prisoner to be transported to Paris. Apologetically, Durand insisted, "I did everything I could to avoid this expense." Nowhere were the contradictions inherent in the institution of seigneurial justice more striking or more evident than in this example from St. Martin de Ré, for the fiscal procurator was caught between his mission to satisfy the public's demand to safeguard its interests and his duty as the fiscal agent of the baron, his employer. It would be interesting to know if Durand's unenviable predicament led to his dismissal.

The problems surrounding criminal justice in St. Martin remained unresolved until 1755, when Charles d'Argental, the baron of the Ile de Ré, became so exasperated by the financial burdens of pursuing malefactors that he relinquished the right of high justice to the king.[41] The crown's executive order documenting this transfer of the right of justice cited the Ile de Ré as an area "where crime is frequent and where punishment is very rare," especially because of the tension between soldiers and the local populace, who preyed on each other and who harbored the criminals that did so. Consequently, the investigations of seigneurial officers, when they led anywhere at all, resulted only in "a vain condemnation" of a suspect long since gone from the island. The crown noted that this near guarantee of impunity "only encourages criminals, multiplies the crimes and burdens

41. BMLR 121 Folio 72 (lettre patente du roi), 15 May 1755.

the seigneur with a multitude of expenses that never procure any utility, [and] that the sole remedy would be for High Justice to be exercised in our name."

This passage highlights the inadequacy of seigneurial justice in the realm of law enforcement, already cited in the *cahiers*. Could a single *procureur fiscal* and perhaps a sergeant or two constitute an adequate police force in a rural area? The inutility of investigations implied in the royal letter suggests that rural law enforcement was too weak to pursue cases and apprehend suspects in a timely fashion, which might have made their efforts in criminal justice worthwhile. As it stood, the crown and lords realized that the pursuit of crimes was often a waste of time and money in the absence of public cooperation or a larger and more efficient police force.

Although d'Argental's relinquishing of high justice constituted a severe blow to his aura of power, he could take refuge in knowing that he preserved all the honorific and seigneurial rights associated with middle and low justice. Furthermore, the crown "discharges said d'Argental from all costs of justice that have been or will be incurred in the said *seigneurie*, even . . . for the criminal trial that is presently taking place against two soldiers of the navy for the crime of theft committed by them *avec effraction*." At last, the lords of St. Martin were rid of the wearying costs of criminal justice.

A Partial Reform of Criminal Justice

Why didn't the solution in St. Martin de Ré, in which the lord gave up the right of high justice, serve as a model for the reform of criminal justice in all of rural France? After all, the terms were favorable for lords, whose lucrative role in civil and seigneurial cases went unscathed. First of all, even had the monarchy possessed the financial resources to do so, it lacked the political will to attack the power of lords in this manner. Secondly, lords clung tenaciously to the power symbolized in the right of high justice, not simply because this right flattered vain social pretensions, but especially because it reinforced the lord's status as master, on which rested the imprescriptibility of the lord's right to exploit the *seigneurie*. As Valin implied, rather than divesting themselves of the prerogative of high justice, seigneurs simply preferred to avoid the inconveniences associated with its costs despite the manifest deleterious effects for the inhabitants of their territories.

Nevertheless, the French crown did address the glaring problems of seigneurial criminal justice throughout the kingdom by passing the edicts of February 1771 and March 1772. Unable to dissimulate any longer that the issue of crime vexed the rural populace, the crown wrote:

> Always occupied with the well-being of our peoples, we have consid-
> ered that the costs involved in the pursuit of crimes committed in the
> boundaries of the seigneurial justices were for lords of high justice a
> very heavy charge and oftentimes a motive for favoring impunity; we
> believe that we have to assure more and more the repose of our sub-
> jects, the maintenance of public order, and the punishment of crimes
> by making *seigneurs hauts justiciers* find that it is to their individual
> advantage to pursue guilty parties and by furnishing them with the
> means to discharge themselves of the expenses of criminal proce-
> dures.[42]

Rather than directly assaulting the lords' right of high justice, the solution offered by the monarchy combined a series of incentives for lords to
pursue crimes and provided punishments in the event of their failure to do
so. Hence, the crown promised to reimburse lords for all expenses involved
in the investigation of cases that seigneurial agents turned over to royal
officials for prosecution. Conversely, when royal officials informed seigneurial agents of crimes committed in the latters' territories, the costs of
the investigation (for all cases) and prosecution (if a case within the jurisdiction of seigneurs) were borne by the lord. Prior to the edicts of 1771 and
1772, lords were in a sense penalized in the form of heavy expenses for their
diligence in pursuing crimes, whereas after 1772 they were penalized for a
lack of diligence. In effect, these edicts were attempts to reform the administration of criminal justice by rendering seigneurial agents judicial police
officers responsible for the investigation of crimes at royal expense while
diminishing their role as magistrates who prosecuted cases and dispensed
justice.

André Giffard declares the reform of 1772 an unenforced failure in Brittany, and John Markoff also raises the important question of how well the
edict was enforced. On the other hand, Steven Reinhardt, citing the royal
court's growing criminal caseload in the Sarladais from 1770 to 1790, argues

---

42. Edit du roi, March 1772. Reprinted in Giffard, *Les justices seigneuriales en Bretagne*, 343–44.

that the reforms of 1771–72 "probably revitalized seigneurial courts in the area of criminal justice." [43] For the region of Aunis and Saintonge, at least one piece of evidence suggests the efficacy of these reforms. From 1780 to 1790, only five lords complained of costs charged to them by the royal treasury for a putative failure to fulfill their obligations in criminal cases.[44] Compared to the ninety-nine complaints for the years 1739–47, the figures hint that these reforms served as the impetus for lords to heighten their denunciation and investigation of criminal acts and point to the smoother, more cooperative administration of criminal justice.

Of course, as Nicole Castan remarks, the threat to charge lords for the neglect of crime was nothing new and proved empty in large royal jurisdictions where royal officials simply could not penetrate into the remote countryside.[45] Similarly, in the absence of an augmentation of the rural police force, the reforms did nothing to prevent the easy escape of suspects or to protect judges, plaintiffs, and witnesses from the frequent revenge of malefactors and their allies, the fear of which also hindered rural criminal prosecutions. Finally, even if the reform of 1772 removed the impediments facing seigneurial courts in the pursuit of malefactors, rural law and order still suffered from the crown's own lack of enthusiasm for prosecuting crimes such as violence and theft that impinged mostly on private subjects rather than on public order or royal majesty.[46]

An example from Marennes in September 1789 sheds light on how the reforms of 1771 and 1772 might have encouraged subaltern courts to pursue crimes that had previously received scant interest. "Informed by public notoriety" that certain unknown individuals entered the house of the demoiselles You, merchants, where they committed several thefts *avec effraction,* the fiscal procurator filed a criminal complaint requesting the judge to investigate, "since it is in the public interest to ascertain the facts in order to inflict upon the guilty persons the punishment that they deserve." The judge then prepared to interview witnesses, and he ordered the commander of the Milice nationale to search the inns and cabarets in the vicinity in the hope of discovering the "unknown outsiders [*quidams étrangers*] or other suspects" in

43. Giffard, *Les justices seigneuriales en Bretagne,* 127, and Markoff, *The Abolition of Feudalism,* 116 n. 129. Markoff writes, "It is likely that these edicts were only spottily enforced." For Reinhardt's argument, see *Justice in the Sarladais,* 239–41.

44. ADCM C 181.

45. N. Castan, *Justice et répression en Languedoc,* 117–21. In Languedoc, for example, the gigantic *sénéchaussée* of Nîmes encompassed five dioceses and served more than 630,000 inhabitants.

46. See especially Ruff, *Crime, Justice, and Public Order,* 44.

possession of the stolen goods. Significantly, even without a private complaint by the You sisters, and with little likelihood of apprehending the
malefactors—the crime occurred on 8 September, eight days before the public party heard rumors about it and filed his complaint, leaving ample time
for the evasion of the criminals (especially if they were not from the area)—
the officials at Marennes nevertheless pursued an investigation and manhunt
for which the expenses promised to be enormous.[47] Prior to 1772 such an
exercise in futility dissuaded even conscientious lords from pursuing crimes,
but after the reforms, the crown (now the nation, in this example from
September 1789) underwrote the costs of the investigation. In effect, lords
guided by their cupidity feared the pursuit of legal transgressions before 1772;
thereafter, it became a motive for activity in criminal matters.

Although Castan considers the reforms of 1771–72 "a very relative pal-
liative,"[48] they constituted an important step forward in the administration
of Old Regime criminal justice for several reasons. First, they proclaimed
the existence of a problem of crime in seigneurial jurisdictions. Next, they
confronted a major practical source of the problem—the cost of justice to
lords. Finally, they began to reconceptualize the role of the officials of local
justice in the criminal justice system by attempting to turn them into judicial police officers, the rural eyes and ears of urban magistrates more financially and professionally competent to prosecute crimes. After 1772, the
inadequacies of Old Regime criminal justice probably stemmed less from
problems specific to seigneurial courts than from more general problems
relating to state finances. Later, the reforms of the French Revolution
would build upon those of 1771–72 by defining the justice of the peace as a
police agent who investigated but did not prosecute serious criminal matters. But the revolutionaries also understood that without attacking an important source of the problem—the exercise of the right of justice by
private persons, which relegated the supervision of the public well-being to
a secondary position after the issue of profitability—the public interest
would remain the interest of a few.

SEIGNEURIAL JUSTICE AND THE POLICING OF RURAL FRANCE

Seigneurial jurisdictions, in addition to constituting a major component of
the Old Regime criminal justice system, had another important repressive

47. ADCM B 3343, Marennes, 16 September 1789.
48. N. Castan, *Justice et répression en Languedoc*, 121.

function in its role in the rural police. The eighteenth-century conception of *la police* was much broader than today's meaning of the maintenance of security and order; rather, it covered the supervision and regulation of the social life of the group for which the police was responsible.[49] Indeed, perhaps the most famous contemporary treatise on the police, Delamare's *Traité de la police*, cited eleven broad categories subject to police activity, including religion, morals, health, the supply of food, public order, commerce, science and liberal arts, and the poor.[50] The right of police, then, theoretically offered lords the broad power of surveillance over the population of the *seigneurie*. Did they in fact exercise this power? Although the subject of the police in urban areas or of their activities in specific realms such as the control of foodstuffs or the poor has received much attention from historians, the role of seigneurial jurisdictions in policing remains largely unexplored territory.[51]

The *sénéchal* and fiscal procurator, as a jurisdiction's police agents, not only enforced the police ordinances of the crown and superior courts, but also issued laws to ensure the good order of their own *seigneurie*. Thus, in the interests of public safety, the judge of Croix-Chapeaux in 1770, following an outbreak of rabies, asked all residents to kill stray dogs and forbade all inhabitants regardless of their social stature from discharging their firearms during funerals or holiday processions.[52] To ensure public order in St. Fort, the judge issued a police ordinance threatening people with a thirty-livre fine and a stint in prison for running in the streets and creating a scandal or for wearing masks.[53] At Pons, proprietors' neglect of the roads adjoining their property disrupted commerce, so the judge issued a decree requiring inhabitants to make repairs. Moreover, he ordered the public

49. Dontenwill, *Une seigneurie sous l'ancien régime*, 77. For an extended explanation of the Old Regime concept of police, see A. Williams, *The Police of Paris, 1718–1789* (Baton Rouge, 1979), 5–16.

50. N. Delamare, *Traité de la police*, 4 vols. (Paris, 1705–38). Poix de Fréminville's *Dictionnaire de police* (Paris, 1756), offers another contemporary description of the role of police in eighteenth-century France.

51. For the police of urban areas, in this case Paris, see Williams, *The Police of Paris*, or Farge, *La vie fragile*. For works on the police in specific realms, see for example, S. Kaplan, "Réflexions sur la police du monde de travail, 1700–1815," *Revue historique* 26 (1979): 17–78, or Schwartz, *Policing the Poor in Eighteenth-Century France*. T. Brennan's article "Police and Private Order in Early Modern France," *Criminal Justice Review* 13 (1988): 1–20 summarizes succinctly the historiography of the subject of *la police*.

52. ADCM B 2096, Chatellénie de Croix-Chapeaux, 1770.

53. ADCM B 2330, Chatellénie de St. Fort, 27 January 1763. This ordinance most likely referred to the incidence of charivari or the activities of bands of youth in the region.

declaration of the ordinance so that no one could claim ignorance in case of subsequent fines.[54]

A combing of the archives of justice in Aunis and Saintonge shows that for the most part, the activity of seigneurial agents in police matters was relatively infrequent and did not extend beyond the issues that affect localities in all times and places—the upkeep of roads, the concern for public health, the maintenance of order, and so on. However, the seigneurial police were exceptionally active in two areas: the defense of religion and the supervision of the local economy. By focusing their activities on these two realms of police responsibility, lords (and the crown) identified the protection of Catholicism and the control of foodstuffs as the pillars upholding order in the countryside of France.

The value of the established church in France came not only from the sense of morality that it instilled in people, but also from the blessing it gave to the entire social order. As a result, the preservation of French society was inextricably linked to the defense of the sanctity of the Catholic Church. In rural Aunis and Saintonge, the defense of the church—so crucial to the positions of both king and lord—led to close police supervision, and often harassment, of the paramount religious and secular threats to the established religion: Protestants and cabarets. On 29 August 1777 the judge of Jonzac, citing both royal and seigneurial ordinances, fined two couples one hundred livres apiece and ordered them under threat of bodily punishment to take their children to the parish church in order to receive a Catholic baptism.[55] In 1773, again at Jonzac, the judge issued a police ordinance forbidding Protestant burials without his permission.[56]

Cabarets, of course, offered rural inhabitants an enticing alternative to a church service on their day of rest. Therefore, it is commonplace to discover judges outlawing cabaret owners from opening shop or serving alcohol while mass was in session, as was the case in Fouras in 1780, Tesson in

54. ADCM B 3861, Sirerie de Pons, 15 September 1758.

55. ADCM B 2368; Comté de Jonzac. The couples, Samuel Arneau and Elisabeth Gobeau and Pierre Mercier and Jeanne Arneau, ignored the judge's decree, which increased their fine to two hundred livres on 26 September.

56. ADCM B 2362, Comté de Jonzac, 31 December 1773. The intent of the decree might not have been to harass Protestants but rather to ensure that the fiscal procurator, the party responsible for the public interest, could ascertain the cause of death and verify that it was natural. As such, it might have been intended to bring Protestants within the administrative fold of the *seigneurie*.

1773, St. Fort in 1763, Pons in 1759, and Jonzac in 1771.[57] Concerned with "the contempt of religion and the forgetting of the divine church" that cabarets encouraged, the *sénéchal* of Tesson included a prohibition on public dancing in cabarets in his ordinance. There are signs that people often resented or simply ignored the attempts of the police to enforce proper respect for the established church. In a criminal case from Taillebourg, the curé complained that he scolded a *jardinier* who had just come out of a cabaret on Sunday, only to be met with such scandalous epithets as "fucking bugger."[58] At Jonzac, the judge Landreau hurried one Sunday to the cabaret of the widow Barré, whom he had learned was in contravention of his police ordinance prohibiting the public consumption of alcohol during mass. Once they arrived, the judge and his clerk found four patrons at a table laden with three bottles of wine. After Landreau explained the police rules, the customer Latorce quipped sarcastically "that [we] will consent to obey them just as soon as [we] will have finished the bottles."[59] Landreau did not appreciate the humor and found it grounds for a criminal complaint. In another manifestation of insubordination, the widow Barré neither signed the police report nor indicated whether she was capable of doing so, for which she received an immediate fine of three livres. As the setting for a large percentage of the physically and verbally violent local conflicts in Aunis and Saintonge, the cabaret attracted a good deal of police attention and stood as the antithesis of that institution of morality and good order—the church.[60]

But by far seigneurial agents channeled most of their police work into controlling the economic life of the *seigneurie*, making *la police* practically synonymous with supervision of the local economy.[61] Not only were seigneurial agents responsible for directing a community's most important annual economic events, planting and harvesting—activities crucial to the lord's economic interests—but they also labored diligently to protect inhabitants from market forces and to ensure the availability of basic commodities at reasonable prices. In this sense, local agents imitated royal officials

57. ADCM B 2476, Fouras; B 2456, Tesson; B 2330, St. Fort; B 3861, Pons; B 3076, Jonzac.

58. ADCM B 5523, Comté de Taillebourg, 8 August 1763.

59. ADCM B 3076, Comté de Jonzac, 10 March 1771.

60. On the role of the cabaret in Old Regime society, see T. Brennan, *Public Drinking and Popular Society in Eighteenth-Century Paris* (Princeton, 1988).

61. See the study by C. Bouton, *The Flour War: Gender, Class, and Community in Late Ancien Régime French Society* (University Park, Pa., 1993).

by making the ready availability of certain foodstuffs, or the enforcement of consumers' demands for a moral economy, the focal point of a strategy for law and order.[62]

Since authorities considered the accessibility of staples to be the surest means of guaranteeing public peace, they frequently set price limits on food, especially meat and bread. Registers for food prices existed in nearly every seigneurial jurisdiction, with mundane entries such as the following from Pons on 10 March 1759. "[The judge] has priced veal at six sols per livre, sheep at five sols and beef at four and a half, and as a consequence prohibits butchers from selling meat above this price."[63] In the same police register, the judge compelled bakers to sell bread at or below the price that he designated, and he required them to consult and sign the price register every Saturday. Any baker not in compliance with the police decree would be fined one hundred livres. At Jonzac in 1780, the judge slapped a fifty-livre fine on a baker for selling bread above the set price.[64] That the baker could do so is evidence that the scarcity of grain and the laws of supply and demand would have enabled bakers to secure a high price for their goods had the seigneurial agents not intervened.

The establishment of a fair price for bread was meaningless without any attempt to ensure an adequate supply of grain in the region, so the seigneurial police labored, through moral suasion, threats of criminal prosecution, and outright requisitioning, to keep granaries and bakeries full. The problem of the grain supply proved particularly acute in Aunis and Saintonge, where the cultivation of vines for eau-de-vie to the neglect of grain cultivation left inhabitants vulnerable to famine during poor harvests. At Pons in 1760, the fiscal procurator lamented the "misery" caused by the lack of grain in the official seigneurial market and demanded an ordinance from the judge forcing merchants to bring their stocks to market for sale and distribution at regulated prices (under penalty of confiscation and a five-hundred-livre fine). Significantly, he regretted not only that "the public experiences the horrors of scarcity," but also that the merchants' failure to sell grain in the market constituted "a considerable loss for the lord of

---

62. For the classic statement on the idea of a moral economy, see E. P. Thompson, "The Moral Economy of the English Crowd in the Eighteenth Century," *Past and Present* 50 (1971): 76–136. Seigneurial agents probably worked in conjunction with subdelegates in promoting a policy aimed at provisioning each region, but the sources that would prove this are insufficient in the departmental archives of Charente-Maritime.

63. ADCM B 3861, Sirerie de Pons.

64. ADCM B 3084, Comté de Jonzac, 1780.

the present *sirerie* concerning his right of *minage*."[65] At Taillebourg, the fiscal procurator's desire "to ameliorate the misery and the calamities of the people" resulting from the absence of grain led him to ask the judge for permission to search the homes of merchants and to requisition grain found on the premises. In addition, he wanted the judge's permission to confiscate any grain that merchants sought to sell outside of the public market.[66] In 1789, the unfortunate inhabitants of Taillebourg once again experienced the hardships of scarcity. The *procureur fiscal* stated: "He receives daily the cries on the part of the public that there is no bread to be found for the money, and on the part of bakers who cannot procure any flour. . . . The rarity of this commodity merits the most serious attention."[67] To remedy the situation he demanded again the authority to requisition grain at a specified price.

The maintenance of a moral economy pitted seigneurial police and consumers against the enemies of a regulated market. As a result, much time and effort of the local police went into surveying the activities of merchants whose economic outlook opposed the moral economy and whose livelihood suffered because of the regulation of the market. The fiscal procurator of St. Fort explained how one of the surest means of fulfilling his mission to guard the public interest was to police the local merchants: "[The *procureur fiscal*] remonstrates that one of the principle duties of his office obliges him to defend the public interest by maintaining good order and the service of the police. . . . He believes that he can give no greater sign of his vigilance in this regard than in searching to eliminate the abuses that merchants, bakers, cabaret owners and others can commit by . . . selling at false weights and measures."[68] From 12 to 18 December 1772 the *sénéchal* of Jonzac fined ten butchers for selling their merchandise at illegal prices, evidence of either widespread collusion among them or that the judge's fair prices were anything but fair for butchers.[69] Later, working on tips by local inhabitants that several merchants routinely committed fraud in their businesses, the judge and fiscal procurator at Jonzac on 11 September 1780 summarily sentenced four merchants to pay fifty livres each in fines: a butcher for using false weights and three bakers for selling bread at higher prices than those set by the judge.[70]

65. ADCM B 3861, Sirerie de Pons, 26 April 1760 & 20 April 1758.
66. ADCM B 5499, Comté de Taillebourg, 24 April 1770.
67. ADCM B 5517, Comté de Taillebourg, 19 May 1789.
68. ADCM B 2330, Chatellénie de St. Fort, 27 January 1763.
69. ADCM B 2368, Comté de Jonzac.
70. ADCM B 3084, Comté de Jonzac.

Police agents reserved their deepest suspicions for people involved in provisioning the local populace with bread, the staple of France's diet. Unable to conceive of the problem of scarcity as a result of overdependence on viticulture, of poor harvests, or of an inadequate system of distribution, the seigneurial police of Aunis and Saintonge attributed the misery of the region to the greed or criminal networks of merchants and therefore identified repression as the solution. Thus, informed by public complaints, the judge of Marennes fined several bakers one hundred livres, and threatened recidivists with a 250-livre fine, for failing to use proper quantities of flour and grain in their bread, despite the protests of bakers that no flour could be purchased at the local market.[71] At Taillebourg, the police attributed the lack of flour and grain in the market to the immorality of merchants and millers who, "insensitive to the unhappiness of their neighbors," refused to sell to bakers, instead dealing their goods at high prices to merchants who exported them from the region.[72] In Pons, the police went further than denouncing the immorality of merchants by exposing "a criminal intelligence among the *marchands greniers* who form grain warehouses in different parishes . . . from which they sell at an excessive price to individuals."[73] As a result, the judge issued an ordinance forbidding this criminal intelligence of entrepôts—in effect, the ordinance forbade the sale of grain and flour anywhere but in the lord's market—under pain of confiscation and a massive five-hundred-livre fine.

By stating that misery occurred "in the middle of abundance"[74] only because of the criminal networks of merchants, the local police legitimated the popular fear and hatred of merchants, who they were convinced plotted to profit at the expense or even lives of the poor. In addition, by displaying such an attitude, the police revealed that their strategy to maintain good order in the countryside was essentially a repressive one that coerced merchants to abide by the laws regulating the local economy. After 1789, this drama in three acts—popular and officials calls for *taxation* (price controls), noncompliance by certain segments of society, and the official response of repression—would be performed again, with drastic implications for the course of the French Revolution.

71. ADCM B 3341, Marennes, 8 August 1785.
72. ADCM B 5499 (4 April 1770), B 5517 (19 May 1789), comté de Taillebourg.
73. ADCM B 3861, Sirerie de Pons, 26 April 1760.
74. ADCM B 3861, Sirerie de Pons, 20 April 1758.

Conclusion

Seigneurial jurisdictions, especially prior to 1772, when they faced the prospect of enduring massive costs for the pursuit of crimes, proved negligent in the fulfillment of their duties; as such, they were a weak part of France's repressive structure. Without a doubt, the greed of some lords informed their inactivity in criminal matters, as the critic Valin suggested. But one need not categorically accuse seigneurs of bad faith, for oftentimes the decision not to investigate a crime was a function of pragmatism, with an understaffed police force, frequently hindered by an uncooperative public that harbored criminals or feared their retribution, deciding that the pursuit of a lawbreaker would be expensive but would not guarantee prosecution and punishment. But whatever the motive—cupidity or common sense—money stood as the supreme concern, and negligence was the undeniable result. That finances were the main concern of lords is underscored by the fact that the activity of seigneurial courts in remunerative feudal and civil cases was as pronounced as the inactivity in burdensome criminal cases. Therefore, the conclusions about seigneurial criminal justice in the Saintonge and Aunis mirror those of Nicole Castan for Languedoc, where "seigneurial jurisdictions simply refused to participate in the repression of crime."[75]

Again, the actions of the crown were not completely immune to the financial concerns that guided lords in criminal matters. In his regional study of royal justice, Julius Ruff finds that a desire to minimize expenses limited public prosecutors to involvement in only one-fourth of criminal cases for which defendants were known.[76] Furthermore, the quarrels between royal officials and lords over the costs of justice exhibit the crown's own efforts to avoid the burdens of criminal cases. But although both the crown and lords experienced fiscal pain in their roles in criminal justice, the degree of pain cannot have been the same, for the crown commanded massive (though still insufficient) public resources in its fight against wrongdoers, whereas just a few criminal cases per year could threaten the solvency of individual lords.

Clearly, then, the crown and lords reacted differently to crime and its cost because of the different financial resources at their disposal. But an-

---

75. N. Castan, *Justice et répression en Languedoc*, 214.
76. Ruff, *Crime, Justice, and Public Order*, 44.

other, and possibly more important, reason for the different attitudes toward crime revolved around the conception of the king as the embodiment of the entire public. A private lord might have considered various crimes (especially hunting or theft from his woods) an affront to his or her authority, but as the case of St. Martin de Ré makes clear, such issues were usually clouded by the private concern of profitablility. For the crown, on the other hand, a crime was an attack on the sovereign himself, because the king was the source of all justice, or the public body par excellence. Hence, as Michel Foucault argues, criminals rebelled against the king's law, rendering retribution a political necessity in order to buttress royal authority.[77] For royal officials, the political significance of pursuing lawbreakers often overshadowed the similarly compelling financial concerns that informed the attitude of private lords toward crime.

The reluctance of seigneurial and royal officials to prosecute crimes left many transgressions unpunished in rural areas, a reality to which many *cahiers* attested. Did this leave inhabitants of the countryside feeling victimized by a perception of increasing criminality in the late eighteenth-century, or did a self-policing mechanism operate in the void left by seigneurial authorities? Whether or not people felt victimized requires a study of popular ideas about what constituted crime for various social groups, which is beyond the scope of this chapter (for example, hunting disturbed cultivators whose crops were damaged by those in pursuit of game, while it hardly constituted a crime for those who hunted to supplement a meager diet). Many of the criminal complaints in the judicial records of Aunis and Saintonge did stem from long-standing disputes, suggesting that revenge—a primitive but inexpensive mode of self-policing—was the first stage of seeking justice and that conflicts only reached official channels when they erupted violently and acrimoniously beyond the control of families, the neighborhood, or the community. A study of the nature and practice of "popular justice" in Aunis and Saintonge would serve as a beneficial complement to a study of seigneurial justice.[78]

77. M. Foucault, *Discipline and Punish: The Birth of the Prison,* trans. A. Sheridan (New York, 1979), 54.

78. For the most thorough studies of "popular justice," see Reinhardt, *Justice in the Sarladais,* and Greenshield, *An Economy of Violence in Early Modern France.* Again, I do not doubt the existence of private settlement in any of its forms (mediation, arbitration, or violence). However, an acknowledgment of occasional private settlement should not lead us to minimize the problems of local justice, as if every problem not handled by the court somehow received efficient treatment in some "tribunal" of popular justice. Violence is particularly problematic. Certainly rural dwellers who beat a tax collec-

The sentences of torture, hanging, public humiliation, flogging, and banishment from Pons and Tonnay-Boutonne that introduced this chapter stand as exceptions to the normative wariness of seigneurial tribunals in criminal matters. Pierre Douilles, ordered in 1753 by the seigneurial judge of Bassac to be broken on the wheel for assault with a rifle, must have cursed his unlucky fate. Surely he knew that for every prosecution and punishment of a case such as his, there were countless of his partners in crime who, eating warm meals at home, savoring their pipes in a cabaret, or lying in the arms of a lover, enjoyed their immunity from the short arm of the law.[79]

tor or thieving vagabond were expressing through violence notions of community standards and did not require or want the involvement of legal officials. However, when a casual insult, boundary dispute, or contested business transaction escalated into a cycle of violence until it reached royal criminal courts, that violence was indicative of a legal system that did not satisfactorily end the dispute in its early stages. In late eighteenth-century France, violence, ripostes, and vendettas say as much about a legal system as they do about an "organic community." In fairness, both Reinhardt and Greenshield point out that growing recourse to official courts demonstrate the increasing number of individuals and social groups who were unwilling to accept expressions of "popular justice."

79. ADCM C 177.

PART II

The Revolutionary Justice of the Peace

CHAPTER 5

From the *Procureur fiscal* to the *Juge de paix*

The Revolutionary Changes in Local Justice

When Boucher d'Argis wrote of "these vampires who suck in the last drop of blood of the cadavers to which they attach themselves," he was not addressing the readers of a gothic thriller.[1] Rather, his audience was the Estates General and his topic the reform of local justice. The vampires of whom he spoke were the judicial personnel—judges, *procureurs fiscaux,* clerks, sergeants, notaries—of seigneurial courts whose cupidity victimized the justiciables (cadavers) of rural France by transforming peoples' attempts to attain justice into interminable charades with the sole purpose of lining the pockets of magistrates and court auxiliaries. Another commentator from 1789 on the French system of local justice argued that if the National Assembly truly desired to restore France's ancient liberties it ought to begin with the destruction of seigneurial justice. Fouqueau de Pussy censured this institution in the harshest terms and especially scorned the person who stood as its quintessence, the *procureur fiscal:* "The fiscal procurators exercise an incredible despotism. . . . [They] are all stewards, confidantes, and protégés of seigneurs. They are tyrants who get the attorneys who oppose their wills fired. Never have justiciables oppressed by lords, their stewards, or their *procureurs fiscaux* found a defender."[2]

In contrast to seigneurial justice, whose personnel invited comparisons with vampires and tyrants, the revolutionary justice of the peace often reaped lavish praise from the observers of the institution of local justice.

1. Boucher d'Argis, *Cahier d'un magistrat du Châtelet sur les justices seigneuriales* (Paris, 1789), 30. Oddly, this treatise did not advocate the abolition of seigneurial justice. It only called for the reduction of the degrees of justice and the control or abolition of court auxiliaries (especially sergeants). Boucher d'Argis's stated goal was "to conciliate the respect due to feudal proprietors and the interests of the people of the countryside" (30–31).

2. Fouqueau de Pussy, *Idées sur l'administration de la justice dans les petites villes et bourgs de France pour déterminer la suppression des juridictions seigneuriales* (Paris, 1789), 42, 45.

The representative Thuriot exclaimed to the National Convention in 1793, "The most beautiful institution for which we are indebted to the Constituent Assembly, that which has been the most useful to society, is the institution of the justice of the peace."[3] Several years and a vastly changed political climate failed to diminish the enthusiasm of legislators for the new local judicial order, as seen in the declaration of Regnier to the Conseil des Cinq-Cents that "the greatest institution of the Revolution is the justice of the peace."[4] Similarly, an unsolicited comment by cantonal administrators of Néré to their departmental colleagues in the Year VII lauded both the institution and its present officeholder. "This establishment, which is one of the greatest benefits of our revolution and whose advantages we recognize daily, is currently conferred to a man who combines probity, impartiality, and speed with a genuine desire to fulfill his functions well."[5] To be sure, much of the support for the institution was self-congratulatory in nature, coming from legislators, administrators, and judicial personnel with a stake in the Revolution's success. Nonetheless, its sincerity is indisputable; revolutionaries truly believed in the beneficial changes wrought by their creation of the justice of the peace.

What had the revolutionaries done to render local justice, once the private domain of lords, their supposedly tyrannical agents, and avaricious practitioners, one of the greatest benefits of the Revolution in their eyes? In this chapter I will explore the principles that guided the creation of the institution of the justice of the peace. Comparing the conception, competence, organization, and personnel of the justice of the peace to those of seigneurial justice illuminates the basis of the revolutionary rhetoric praising the advantages of this institution. Following this description of the Revolution's theoretical basis for and reorganization of local justice, in the subsequent chapters I will examine the institution in practice in order to determine whether the enthusiasm of commentators was justified and to assess its effect upon the people of rural Aunis and Saintonge. Did the

---

3. *Le moniteur universel* 16, 8 June 1793, 591.

4. *Le moniteur universel* 26, 23 frimaire IV, 718.

5. ADCM L 158 (brumaire VII). The comment was part of the canton's response to a departmental inquiry into the political situation in various localities. That it was unsolicited is undeniable, since neither the JP nor local justice was a rubric included in the inquiry (such rubrics were *esprit public, fêtes, instruction,* etc.). Furthermore, this comment about the JP was not simply a matter of the canton sycophantically telling the department what it wanted to hear, since the cantonal response was otherwise harsh in its criticism of local roads, the lack of public education, and the mediocre *esprit publique.*

Revolution actually fulfill its promises of providing swift, fair, and inexpensive justice, of mitigating the litigious passions of French people, and of protecting peasants from the avaricious practices of seigneurs and lawyers?

The Criticism of Seigneurial Justice in 1789

Although the *cahiers de doléance* of 1789 constitute a fascinating and rare portrait of French opinion on the eve of the Revolution, the interpretation of them presents historians with some perplexing problems.[6] Did they accurately reflect the concerns of the rural masses; or did a coterie of village *grands* dominate the primary assemblies, thus skewing the complaints to reflect only the interests of a well-to-do and influential elite; or did royal subdelegates and seigneurial officials effectively repress any spontaneous and autonomous expression of local opinion? In particular, any analysis of the attitude of *cahiers* toward seigneurialism is problematic, since the seigneurial judge often presided over the primary assembly at which people voiced their most basic local concerns. Under such circumstances, the possibility of conscious or unconscious self-censorship by assembly participants looms large, for how many peasants risked angering their lords with cries for relief from seigneurial exactions (or, for that matter, how many judges would allow such criticisms of their employers to be voiced officially in the *cahiers*)? Criticism of seigneurial justice, which attacked not only the integrity and livelihood of the judge who presided over the meeting but also one of the most cherished symbols of a lord's power, might have required a very intrepid assembly indeed.

Perhaps this caveat about self-censorship partially explains the essentially moderate hostility toward seigneurialism exhibited by the *cahiers* of Aunis and Saintonge. According to J.-N. Luc's thorough study of the existing *cahiers* from the Charente-Maritime, only 77 of 202 (38 percent) primary assemblies referred to the *seigneurie,* while a mere 63 (31 percent) were explicitly critical of some aspect of this institution. Those parishes mentioning seigneurial justice represented 15.5 percent (31 of 202) of the

---

6. For interpretations of the *cahiers,* see G. Taylor, "Revolutionary and Nonrevolutionary Content in the *Cahiers* of 1789: An Interim Report," *French Historical Studies* 7 (1972): 479–502; and J. Markoff and G. Shapiro, *Revolutionary Demands: A Content Analysis of the Cahiers de Doléances of 1789* (Stanford, 1998). In chapter 9 of Markoff's and Shapiro's book, the authors argue persuasively for the "authenticity" of the *cahiers,* thereby minimizing some of the concerns expressed in the following discussion.

total.[7] Although this figure implies that seigneurial justice constituted only a mildly pressing concern of rural inhabitants, it merits noting that, after the right of *franc-fief* (mentioned by thirty-three parishes), seigneurial justice was the issue most-mentioned by those *cahiers* with reference to the *seigneurie,* standing ahead of such hated and contentious dues as the seigneurial *corvée* (nineteen *cahiers*) and the tithe (seventeen *cahiers*). Despite the overall low incidence of *cahiers* from Aunis and Saintonge that raised the issue of local justice, then, the *relative* weight of the *cahiers* concerning seigneurial justice established this issue as one high on the list of ways to ameliorate the lives of rural inhabitants (of course, royal taxation attracted the most complaints).

In Tables 17(A) and 17(B) I enumerate the criticisms and suggested reforms of seigneurial justice in the *cahiers* from Charente-Maritime. At the heart of the problem of local justice, according to rural inhabitants, was the proliferation of jurisdictions. As seen in Chapter 1, instead of offering an advantage for rural justiciables by ensuring their proximity to a seat of justice, the large number of seigneurial courts simply added another degree of justice and taxed the already strained pool of competent judicial personnel, which in turn rendered litigation slower and costlier and often diminished its quality. Thus, the most frequently proposed improvement of local justice, cited by twelve parish cahiers and by sixty-five parishes in the *cahiers de réduction,* was the abolition of petty jurisdictions or their union with larger seigneurial courts.[8] The parishioners of St. Herie de Mastas summarized the problem of diminutive jurisdictions and offered their solution in an interesting passage:

> Considering that there exist almost as many different jurisdictions as there are villages, and that it would be difficult to find a judge with a

---

7. Luc, *Paysans et droits féodaux,* 79–101. My own study of the *cahiers* merely adds a qualitative complement to Luc's excellent and painstaking quantitative work, although I did count thirty-four *cahiers* referring specifically to seigneurial justice and another fourteen that vaguely called for judicial reform and that one might categorize as implicit references to seigneurial justice. For example, without explicitly citing seigneurial jurisdictions, the *cahiers* of Chatelaillon and La Couarde both complained of too many degrees of justice. Therefore, my figures for *cahiers* addressing the issue of seigneurial justice are slightly higher than Luc's, especially if one interprets those fourteen calls for judicial reform as a way to criticize seigneurial justice without risking the anger or censorship of the judge or seigneur.

8. *Cahiers de réduction,* or district *cahiers* (which have nothing in common with revolutionary districts) were drawn up by delegates from several parishes who met to select representatives to the *bailliage* assembly. Although these *cahiers* are a step removed from the local level, they are still an

degree who would want to work in such tiny jurisdictions, in which there is no courthouse, where sessions are held perhaps four times per year and where one is obliged to hold them *in the cabaret,* we think that it would be in the public interest—and in order to accelerate the trials that are slowed there—to unite them to the seigneurial justice of their suzerain. The latter [lord] would be required to have graduates as officers who reside in the *chef-lieu* of the jurisdiction. It would be interesting to accord to him the competence to judge definitely up to the sum of fifty livres, which would eliminate a multitude of petty trials that parties undertake *par entêtement* and that lead them to their ruin by taking them by appeal to royal seats.[9]

Similarly, the district *cahier* from Montguyon advocated the suppression of "several seigneurial justices that often contain no other territory than a small fief or a single parish," while that of St. Genis called for the elimination of all courts of middle and low justice.[10] Overall, the *cahiers* from Aunis and Saintonge resound with dissatisfaction over the multiplicity of seigneurial jurisdictions. As the *cahier* from Mauzé stated succinctly, "The numerous degrees of jurisdictions are the shameful remains of feudalism."[11]

One can identify the proliferation of justices as the source of complaints even for *cahiers* that did not explicitly mention it. With an exorbitant number of jurisdictions, few of which could justify or afford their own judges, magistrates frequently held several positions at one time. In addition, they preferred to live in larger towns or seats of royal justice where some practiced law on the side. As a result, the absence of judges from their jurisdictions meant infrequent court sessions, thus thwarting justiciables in their desire for the rapid adjudication of disputes, or sessions held before nondegreed, and hence incompetent, attorneys. When parishes such as Soubise expressed their wish to "require the judge of this principality to reside in this town, to be present at all sessions, and never to let himself be represented by any attorney unless the latter has a [law] degree," they alluded to problems stemming from the large number of seigneurial courts.[12] In all, six *cahiers* lamented the absenteeism of judges and the rarity of court

important source of opinion for areas such as Pons, Montlieu, and Saintes, where few primary *cahiers* have survived.

9. ADCM C 263bis (7).
10. Both from ADCM C 260bis, district *cahiers* of Montguyon and St. Genis.
11. ADCM C 267 (52).
12. ADCM C 263bis, Soubise ville.

TABLE 17A   *Cahiers de Doléance* Concerning Seigneurial Justice in
             Aunis and Saintonge

	Parish Cahiers	Cahiers de Réduction
Complaint		
Multiplicity of justices	6	37
Absenteeism of judges	2	—
Infrequent sessions	4	—
Slowness of justice	4	11
High cost	4	11
Partiality, abuse	3	5
Proposed Improvement		
Competent judges	4	39
Resident judges	1	6
Extension of competence	4	9
Limit competence to seigneurial affairs	2	6
Parties to have choice of royal or seigneurial judge	1	—
Abolish intermediate justices	6	5
Unite small justices to large	6	60
Implicit conservation of seigneurial justice	8	66
Explicit conservation	4	20
Explicit abolition of seigneurial justice	11	10

SOURCE: J.-N. Luc, *Paysans et droits féodaux*, 96.

sessions, while at least five parish *cahiers* (and forty-five parishes in the district *cahiers*) demanded competent, resident judges.

Infrequent court sessions and absent judges, not surprisingly, prompted several parishes to excoriate seigneurial justice for the snail's pace at which it dispensed justice. The inhabitants of Charentenay remonstrated in exasperation that "the most serious and the most pressing" matters lingered for years because of the "imperfection in the exercise of seigneurial justices," where judges residing in distant places rarely appeared in *seigneuries* to convene the court.[13] Indeed, trials originating from lords' juridictions were so lengthy that, in one case, the district *cahier* of St. Aigulin solemnly proposed a three-year limitation on them as an *improvement*.[14]

Although rural inhabitants implicated the proliferation of justices, an issue inextricably linked to the nature of seigneurial justice, as one reason

13. ADCM C 267, parish of Charentenay.
14. ADCM C 260bis, district of St. Aigulin.

TABLE 17B   Cahiers Referring to Seigneurial Justice—La Rochelle

Parish	Comment/Complaint/Improvement of Justice
Andilly	Reform justice system
Angoulins	Cases of lord vs. vassal judged by lords
Charentenay	End plurality of positions, especially judgeships
Chatellaillon	Too many degrees; bring justice closer
Clavette	Cost of justice often exceeds object
Courson	Conserve lords' justice; royal justice expensive
Ferrières	Eliminate degrees of appeal
Forges	Want faster, cheaper justice; better police
La Couarde	Too many degrees of justice
La Laigne	Abolish degrees between seigneurial, royal justice
Le Bois	Length, cost of justice favors rich
Le Cher	Expensive; abolish several degrees
Le Thou	Cost; education of judges; police neglected
Longèves	Reform justice system
Marans	Fewer degrees; enormous costs
D'Aligre	Length; cost; too many degrees
Marsay	Suppression of seigneurial justice
Mauzé	Length; cost; too many degrees
Montroy	Suppression of seigneurial justice
Nieul	Length; chicanery of procureurs
St. Martin/Nuaillé	Bring justice closer to justiciables
St. Cyr	Conserve, but eliminate several degrees
Sainte-Marie	Cost; prefer to have royal seat
St. Ger./Mrcnes	Suppress degrees of justice
St. Marc	Excessive jurisdictions; length; cost
St. Martin de Ré	Too many degrees; want royal seat
St. Médard	Implicit suppression of seigneurial justice
St. Pierre	Partial suppression; length; too many degrees
St. Saturnin/Bois	Suppress minor seigneurial justices
St. Saveur	Suppress subaltern justices; limit competence
Salles	Reduce number; reform abuses in seigneurial rights
Thaire	Reform justice system
Usseau	Reform justice system
Vallans	Reform justice system

SOURCE: ADCM L 267, *sénéchaussée* of La Rochelle.

for the slow adjudication of cases, they also denounced the complicated rules of judicial procedure—which stemmed from the royal administration of justice and to which royal courts were not immune—as exacerbating the problem. Numerous parishes pleaded for the reform of both civil and criminal procedure, which not only delayed cases in the first instance, but also maddened litigants when procedures were repeated during the appeals process. Furthermore, as the district *cahier* of Jonzac noted, underpaid and underemployed seigneurial court personnel could scarcely resist the temptation to profit from a legal system that paid by procedural item and not by case—a strong incentive to prolong litigation.[15]

The slowness of justice caused by royal civil and criminal procedure and the proliferation of petty seigneurial jurisdictions was, according to the *cahiers*, aggravating enough for the denizens of rural Aunis and Saintonge. But when the same combination conspired to render litigation as expensive as it was time-consuming, it brings into question the accessibility of the legal system and even its legitimacy, since access to dispute resolution regardless of one's financial status is inherent in the definition of justice and was a right guaranteed by French judges in their oath of office. According to the ten parishes represented by the district *cahier* of Saujon, litigation over an object as little as six livres or a simple injury could lead to financial disaster for one party because of the "abusive but very favored practice" of courts employing written procedure.[16] Perhaps the parishioners of the Ile d'Elle stated the problem most succinctly, albeit acerbically, when they wrote that "we are ruined as soon as we are obliged to litigate. Is it really necessary to have so much written procedure, to have recourse to so many judges, and for it to cost so much in order to obtain justice?"[17]

Of course, when litigation or an attempt to obtain justice means financial ruin, a legal system's accessibility diminishes, and the doors of justice remain closed especially to a society's poorer members, who have fewer resources to risk on a long and costly trial. By exposing that "the rich drag the poor from court to court," the inhabitants of both Sainte-Marie and Le Bois acknowledged that French local justice favored those people wealthy enough to intimidate opponents into acquiescence by threatening them with the prospect of a ruinous court case.[18] The district *cahier* from Barbézieux also recognized serious social repercussions that resulted from the excessive degrees of justice "considering that the multiplication of the different jurisdictions is an obstacle preventing the poor from obtaining justice."[19] Likewise, the potential for social bias in seigneurial justice was

15. ADCM C 26obis.

16. ADCM C 26obis.

17. ADCM C 267, parish of Ile d'Elle, *sénéchaussée* of La Rochelle.

18. ADCM C 267 (62) parish of Ste. Marie and (39) Le Bois. The similarly worded *cahiers* suggests that one served as the model for the other.

19. ADCM C 26obis.

evident to the people of Angoulins, who contended that judges were not only dependent on the lords who employed them but were also inevitably fiefholders themselves. "Until now all the differences that arise between seigneurs and their vassals have been judged by other proprietors of fiefs, and abuses result from this."[20] In a *cahier* that implicitly indicted seigneurial justice for its inaccessibility to the poor and explicitly cast a dark shadow over its integrity, the inhabitants of Mauzé alleged that "it [seigneurial justice] is the scourge of the countryside and sells too dearly the favors of its protection."[21] Seigneurial justice, in this case, stood as another pillar supporting the French social order against which peasants could not or dared not struggle.

The *cahier* of Saint-Médard echoed the view that justice was a commodity to be sold to the highest bidder. "What person inhabiting the countryside is unaware of how seigneurial justices encourage among the peaceful cultivators the desire—for a certain sum of money (so rare among us)—to press doubtful or unjust claims?"[22] This passage signifies not only that justice was for sale but also that it constituted a game subject to the manipulation of pettifogging practitioners (derogatively called *chicaneurs*) schooled in its recondite rules.

Indeed, the near universal dissatisfaction with chicanery felt by rural dwellers is perhaps the dominant theme concerning justice that one can extract from the *cahiers* of Aunis and Saintonge. Seigneurial jurisdictions, covering several degrees, employing byzantine procedures, dominated by an army of underpaid officers, and removed from the surveillance of the royal bureaucracy, proved fertile terrain for the artful subterfuge of rural *chicaneurs,* as witnessed in the parish of Genouille:

> Another inevitable evil for the said inhabitants is that which subjects the most insignificant contestation to formalities of justice and degrees of jurisdiction that are ruinous to the parties. The peaceful person prefers his [or her] spoliation to his ruin. The *chicaneur,* the swindler commits usurpations with impunity. For an object valued at twenty sols or for a minute slice of land, the parties only receive the [definitive] decision of their differences in a sovereign tribunal located thirty *lieues* from their parishes. A *cause personnelle* ends only after being carried to three

20. ADCM C 267, parish of Angoulins.
21. ADCM C 267 (52), parish of Mauzé.
22. ADCM C 267 (70), parish of St. Médard.

tribunals. The procedure for the trial, whose expenses are unknown to the parties until after the damage has been inflicted, is a scourge for every person unlearned in law and . . . [possessing only] his credulity and his innocence.[23]

The parish of Ranson linked the ubiquity of chicanery directly to the over-abundance of petty seigneurial justices, claiming that "if there were fewer small jurisdictions, there would be fewer *chicaneurs*, fewer of these country attorneys who would disappear because of a lack of clients."[24]

In essence, the net effect of all these ills surrounding seigneurial courts stood the conception of justice on its head. Instead of acting in an idealized version of the role of justice in a society, in which an accessible and blind-folded Justice impartially weighs the merit of opposing arguments, Sei-gneurial Justice removed its blindfold to glance at the respective parties' coffers and weighed their ability to purchase "the favors of its protection."[25] Furthermore, instead of ensuring peace and equilibrium in a society by solving disputes in a way that both parties agreed was fair, seigneurial juris-dictions—by multiplying the stages of justice, by rendering it so costly as to threaten its accessibility, and by subjecting it to the cancer of chicanery—actually prolonged disputes, increased their stakes, and rarely instilled a sense that justice had been served. The inhabitants of Marsay attested to this inversion of the role of justice by remonstrating that seigneurial courts were a cause, rather than a forum for the resolution, of the social tensions that afflicted Old Regime France: "Seigneurial jurisdictions only tend to delay justice, to nourish petty parish squabbles, to obscure the means of defense, to support animosity and resentment, and to encourage a little war between individuals whose worries for cultivation would better serve the state; therefore, the inhabitants of Marsay demand their suppression and the right to bring our contestation to the presidial courts."[26] With such a judicial system for the adjudication of their disputes, it is no wonder that eighteenth-century rural French earned a reputation—corroborated by

23. ADCM C 263bis, parish of Genouille.

24. ADCM C 263bis, parish of Ranson. Interestingly, this *cahier* claimed that chicanery bene-fited debtors (not especially the rich) who, with the aid of slow courts and cumbersome procedure, evaded legitimate creditors.

25. One might object that I have anachronistically thrust a modern conception of justice onto a hierarchical and inegalitarian society with its corresponding conception of distributive justice that treated equals equally and unequals unequally. I think this objection is met by distinguishing between a bias in the law and a bias in the application of the law.

26. ADCM C 267 (50), parish of Marsay.

many *cahiers* as well as the judicial archives—for litigiousness, for lingering social resentment, for endemic violence and revenge.

In summary, the *cahiers de doléance* from Aunis and Saintonge expressed frustration and dissatisfaction with the inutility of seigneurial justice. It is scarcely surprising that village assemblies' criticisms of seigneurial justice focused on reforming this inutility—the number of degrees, the incompetence and abuses of the personnel, the cost and speed—rather than on the principle (more troubling to modern readers) that treated justice as a form of private property.[27] After all, villagers were not jurists, and what concerned them most was the practical effects that a judicial system had upon their time, property, and social relations.

The data in Table 17(A) indicate that more parishes implicitly called for the conservation of this institution than for its abolition and that four parishes wanted an *extension* of the competence of seigneurial jurisdictions. On the one hand, this fact indicates an inability to conceive of any systematic change in the justice system. On the other hand, it is also a reminder that seigneurial justice did provide useful services (especially in *juridiction gracieuse)*, that its promixity was cherished, that it sometimes did settle disputes satisfactorily, and that royal justice was potentially even more costly.[28] However, it would be erroneous to contend that rural dwellers expressed contentment with lords' justice, for even those *cahiers* calling for the conservation of lords' courts attached major conditions for the improvement of justice. Such conditions included competent personnel, swifter justice as a result of fewer degrees and less complicated procedure, and less costly adjudication. Similarly, a call for an extension of seigneurial courts' competence (for example, by allowing them to decide definitively all matters of fifty livres or less) was really an attack on the number of degrees, the slowness, and the expense of local justice as it stood. The Ministry of Jus-

27. More surprising, however, is how few juridical treatises attacked "the property of justice" in eighteenth-century France. Was this because few jurists cared about the peasants most inconvenienced by seigneurial justice? Was it because many jurists profited from lords' justice in their capacity as *feudistes* or rather a result of the timidity of royal officials in asserting the king's role as the source of all justice? On the (limited) public debate over seigneurial justice in the eighteenth century, see J. Mackrell, *The Attack on "Feudalism" in Eighteenth-Century France* (London, 1973).

28. S. Reinhardt argues that seigneurial justice in the Sarladais was often useful to parties of equal social status, but less so for social unequals. He notes, however, that the *cahiers* from the region specified that the most contentious ligitants won cases. See *Justice in the Sarladais*, especially chap. 9, "Seigneurial Justice and Retaliation." Even P. Villard's relatively optimistic study of seigneurial courts recognizes that the vast majority of *cahiers* from the Marche complained about the length and cost of justice. See *Les justices seigneuriales dans la Marche.*

tice, charged with the task of generating a report on the *cahiers'* contents, had no trouble interpreting the meaning of these petitions; its report asserted that the *cahiers* demanded the suppression of seigneurial justice.[29] What would the revolutionaries do to accommodate the *cahiers'* calls for swift, proximate, inexpensive, and simple justice?

THE REVOLUTIONARY PRINCIPLES OF JUSTICE

Seigneurial justice died a quick and quiet death; it was a casualty, along with feudalism, regional particularism, and the principle of venality, of the remarkable Night of August 4. Its abolition generated little discussion and even less opposition, and then only from lords and officeholders hoping for indemnification for their investments—a sure sign that the institution was indefensible on grounds of principle or utility. In fact, the Feudal Committee of the National Assembly saw no need to defend the suppression of seigneurial justice in any of its reports. The deputy Vieillard did compose a report justifying the clause denying lords and officeholders indemnification, but he never presented it to the assembly. The committee had raised the question of indemnification largely out of sensitivity to questions of property and to maintain the value of land that revolutionaries hoped to sell to solve the state's financial crisis. In addition, indemnification allowed revolutionaries to steer a political middle course between radical peasants and potentially counterrevolutionary lords. Ultimately, however, they decided that seigneurial courts were illegitimate usurpations of a public power.[30]

Obviously, in the aftermath of August 4 France required a new institution of local justice. But perhaps unbeknownst to the representatives at the time, the decrees of 4 August necessitated a reorganization of the entire judicial order, for the denunciation of venality attacked nearly every royal judicial officeholder in France, while the criticism of provincialism cast an ominous shadow over the legitimacy of the parlements, which "stood as exemplars of provincial identity and privilege, weighty impediments to the

29. AN B(a) 89, Etats généraux de 1789. Reprinted in E. Séligman, *La justice en France pendant la Révolution*, vol. 1 (Paris, 1913), 489–505.

30. See *Archives parlementaires*, vol. 12, annexe du 5 mars 1790. I thank J. Markoff for explaining this debate to me. Chapter 3 of his work *The Abolition of Feudalism*, contains a detailed discussion of the issue of indemnification for feudal rights in general.

prospect of national unity."[31] From impoverished notaries to the august magistrates of the Palais de Justice, from diminutive seigneurial courts to the powerful Parlement of Paris, no judicial employee or tribunal escaped the fatal blows struck in the revolutionary atmosphere of 4 August 1789.

The National Assembly took advantage of this clean slate to found its new judicial order on what it considered clear and coherent principles, the first of which was an assertion that justice was a public power with the sovereign Nation as its source.[32] In an influential discourse establishing the Revolution's guiding judicial principles, the representative Thouret condemned the corruption of this basic ideal under the Old Regime: "The most bizarre and unhealthy of all the abuses that corrupted the exercise of judicial power, was that corps or simple individuals possessed *patrimonially* . . . the right to have justice rendered in their name; that other individuals could acquire by *heredity* or *purchase* the right to judge their fellow citizens; and that justiciables were obliged to *pay the judges* in order to obtain a writ of justice."[33] In this single passage, Thouret indicated that justice would no longer be the private domain of lords, a powerful tool in the defense of the *seigneurie;* nor would interpretation of the law be the monopoly of a caste of venal magistrates. Rather, the nation became the sole depository of the *pouvoir judiciaire,* and the right to judge derived directly from it.

The election of judges was the logical but quite radical corollary to the idea that the right to sit in judgment of others came from the nation. Revolutionaries decreed the election of magistrates with the hope of inspiring confidence in the new judicial administration by rendering judges responsible to the people rather than their being a corporation separate from, and often parasitical toward, them. At the local level, the election of judges meant that rural dwellers could chose as justice of the peace someone they knew and in whom they had confidence to adjudicate their disputes rather than subjecting their legal problems to the questionable independence of a seigneurial magistrate.

---

31. Woloch, *The New Regime,* 300.

32. Three recent and excellent collections of studies treat the transition from Old Regime to revolutionary principles of justice: R. Badinter, ed., *Une autre justice: Contributions à l'histoire de la justice sous la Révolution française* (Paris, 1989); P. Boucher, ed., *La Révolution de la justice: Des lois du roi au droit moderne* (Paris, 1989); *La Révolution et l'ordre juridique privé: Rationalité ou scandale? Actes du colloque d'Orléans 11–13 septembre 1986* (Paris, 1986). See also J.-P. Royer, *La société judiciaire depuis le XVIIIe siècle* (Paris, 1979) and M. Fitzsimmons, *The Remaking of France: The National Assembly and the Constitution of 1791* (Cambridge, 1994), especially 104–8.

33. *Archives parlementaires,* vol. 12, 344–48 (discours du 24 mars 1790). Thouret's emphasis.

Finally, Thouret considered the *gratuité* of justice a derivative of the principle that the nation constituted the source of all justice, since access to dispute resolution was a right of every member of society; indeed, it was in theory an important reason for the creation of society. Hence, judges became salaried officials of the nation and received no pecuniary benefits from the prolongation or outcome of litigation. While the *gratuité* of justice obviously did not signify that litigation would be completely without cost, the destruction of a system in which the quantity of procedures served as the basis for the quantity of expenses removed the incentives (at least among magistrates) for chicanery and delay and went a long way to satisfy the demands of rural constituents concerning the improvement of local justice.[34]

Besides discussing the principle that the nation was the source of justice, the revolutionaries centered the debate over the new judicial esprit around the role of the lawyer.[35] They strongly distrusted the corporate spirit of *avocats;* and the experience of the Old Regime, in which a veritable swarm of barristers and attorneys manipulated the law to augment its fees, left the legislators in Paris with a pronounced distaste for formal litigation and for the involvement of lawyers in disputes. Thus, the National Assembly removed lawyers altogether from petty civil lawsuits by requiring parties to represent themselves before a justice of the peace. Without lawyers on the scene, the Assembly hoped to eradicate the culture of litigiousness and the lingering ill will—often caused by minor squabbles that became interminable and with disproportionate stakes because of the poor administration of justice—that plagued rural France.

The attempt to minimize the role of lawyers was similarly evident in the revolutionary emphasis on, if not apotheosis of, mediation and arbitration. Whereas lawyers encourage disputants to stand on their rights and judges determine who is right or wrong in a case by looking back to events, mediators appeal to parties' common interests and encourage them to look forward to the consequences of the peaceful resolution of their disputes.[36] In this distinction between formal and informal dispute resolution, revolutionaries hoped not only to increase the utility of justice (since mediation and arbitration are faster and less expensive than lawsuits), but also to "re-

---

34. On this idea, see M. Talon, *Simplification des procédures et réduction des frais de justice* (Paris, 1790).

35. Woloch, *The New Regime,* 321–54.

36. T. Eckhoff, "The Mediator and the Judge," in Aubert, *Sociology of Law,* p. 171–81.

generate" France by inaugurating a more peaceful and conciliatory social climate—a combination of the practical and the idealistic so common to the reforms of the French Revolution. So enamored were the revolutionaries of this principle that they subjected all family disputes to the obligatory arbitration of a *tribunal de famille,* where matters could be settled quickly and privately through the intervention of relatives, friends, or neighbors.[37] Similarly, legislators forbade litigants to pursue civil cases before district civil courts without a prior attempt to mediate their differences before a *bureau de paix et de conciliation.*

The Creation of the Justice of the Peace

The National Assembly created the institution of the justice of the peace to fill the void left by the abolition of seigneurial justice and to conform the institution of local justice to its new judicial principles. Although the source of inspiration for the institution is unclear—some argue that English JPs were the obvious example while others cite the influence of Voltaire's admiration for Holland's "feseurs de paix"[38]—the idea of a local justice of the peace was not confined to the learned discussions of urban salons, for many parishes had already pleaded for such magistrates in their *cahiers.* In an impressively prescient clause, the petition of St. Saturnin de Loubillé called for "the election of a *juge de paix* in the parishes in order to terminate amicably the difficulties that arise among individuals."[39] Similarly, the Ministry of Justice's report on the *cahiers* acknowledged that many parishes desired the establishment of a Conseil de Paix for the adjudication of local matters.

Historians of eighteenth-century French justice have, for the most

37. R. Phillip's work *Family Breakdown in Late Eighteenth-Century France: Divorce in Rouen, 1792–1803* (Oxford, 1980) offers the most in-depth study of the revolutionary *tribunaux de famille* and their emphasis on mediation and arbitration. For a succinct statement on the revolutionary attempt to reform family law, see R. Phillip, "Remaking the Family: The Reception of Family Law and Policy in the French Revolution," in Reinhardt and Cawthon, *Essays on the French Revolution.* S. Desan's recent study of family tribunals makes an important contribution to our understanding of the issue of gender in the French Revolution. See " 'War Between Brothers and Sisters': Inheritance Law and Gender Politics in Revolutionary France," *French Historical Studies* 20, no. 4 (1997): 597–634.

38. On this debate, see C. Ten Raa, "De Oorsprong von de Kantonrechter (les origines du juge de paix en France ainsi que celles du 'Kantonrechter' en Hollande)," (Ph.D. diss., University of Rotterdam, 1970).

39. ADCM C 263bis.

Departments of Revolutionary France

part, treated the justice of the peace as an afterthought, considering it the
realm where mediocre magistrates handled the minor or unimportant affairs of country people. From the standpoint of political drama, one can
scarcely blame scholars for preferring the trials of the Revolutionary Tribunals to the mundane proceedings under rural JPs. But the agenda of French
Revolution historians has been transposed with that of the revolutionaries
themselves, for whom a viable and fair judicial order required a firm basis
at the local level where the majority of disputes originated. Hence, in his
plan for France's new tribunals, Thouret did not present the justice of the

VENDÉE

• Marans

Ars-en-Ré

Courson •

St. Martin •

LA ROCHELLE / • Benon

DEUX-SÈVRES

La Jarrie

• Surgères

• Ciré

Lozay • • Lonlay

ROCHEFORT

• Aunay

St. Pierre

• Tonnay-
Charente • Tonnay-Boutonne

Château d'Oléron •

Soubise

• St. Savinien St. JEAN D'ANGÉLY

MARENNES Port d'Envaux • • Taillebourg

• Pont l'Abbé • Matha

Escoyeux • • Brizambourg

La Tremblade

Le Gua • SAINTES •

Royan • Saujon

Dompierre •

CHARENTE

Coze • • PONS

Gemozac •

Mortagne Archiac •

/ St. Genis •

• St. Fort Jonzac •

Mirambeau • • Léoville •

• Montendre

MONLIEU • Montguyon

St. Aigulin • DORDOGNE

GIRONDE

Seats of Justices of the Peace in Charente-Inférieure

DISTRICT CHEF-LIEU •

Cantonal Seat •

peace as an institution designed to plug the gaps in jurisdiction left by higher and more important courts; rather, he commenced with the justice of the peace as the symbol of the Revolution's commitment to a new type of justice and as the crucial foundation of civil justice in the first degree.

The revolutionaries conceived of the JP as the antithesis of the seigneurial judge. Unlike the lord's magistrate, who was a specialist trained in law and a representative of an urban legal culture, the JP was envisioned by

French reformers as a mediating amateur whose paramount qualifications were intimate knowledge of the problems of rural dwellers and a sense of fairness instead of familiarity with a body of legal knowledge. Hence, legislators allowed all men thirty years of age or older who met the eligibility requirements for any other district or departmental administrative position to become a justice of the peace.[40] In juxtaposition to the questionable independence of seigneurial judges who served as employees of their lords and were subject to dismissal, the JP held his office through the wishes of his fellow citizens. Because the JP was a popularly elected official expected to rule in equity, his *experience* in rural affairs and the *confidence* in his probity that he inspired among country dwellers mattered more than his grasp of "the science of forms and of laws."[41] These conceptual changes in the magistracy constituted part of the Revolution's attempt to move dispute resolution in the first instance from courts of law to the fields—a move to be understood both literally (since JPs often decided cases at the source of contention) and metaphorically, since adjudication in the fields symbolized for revolutionaries a judicial system dominated by rural inhabitants who loved justice, order, and morality and one far removed from the pestilential and obstructionist atmosphere of Old Regime law courts.

The Revolution's ambitious goal of simultaneously ushering in a new social climate in rural France on the back of a reformed judicial system was not lost on local officials in Charente-Inférieure. In a lengthy discourse to the primary assembly of Tonnay-Charente, gathered to select the canton's first justice of the peace, the meeting's president, M. Bargaud, revealed the lofty aspirations he held for this new institution:

> Gentlemen, you must elect a justice of the peace, that is to say a man destined to stop at the source all dissention among citizens of this canton, and as a consequence one who has almost never given occasion to question his private life, always having been a good friend, a good neighbor, and a man of good mores; who, knowing how to respect the rights of others, sometimes backs off of his own [rights] in order to enjoy the advantage he must procure for his fellow citizens: peace; a man who has only acted with honesty . . . and who, as an enemy of trials, has never used that unique tool of base souls—chicanery—which

---

40. *Archives parlementaires*, 18:105. The basic laws pertaining to the justice of the peace were laid out in the laws of 16–24 August 1790 (on the new judicial order), 14 October 1790 (on the procedure before JPs), and 19 July 1791 (on the *police correctionnelle*).

41. Discourse of Thouret, 24 March 1790. *Archives parlementaires*, 12:346.

was employed with so much success in the old tribunals by litigants of bad faith.[42]

Similarly, the mayor of Rochefort went so far as to elevate the JP to the moral position occupied by the local priest in the Old Regime, for the JP would embody the values of the new nation and restore social tranquility to rural France:

> This new magistracy, one of the greatest benefits of our constitution, will become a type of clergy when exercised by men who will link the purest patriotism to sublime virtues such as courage, beneficence, and the forgetting of self for the happiness of all. . . . The protecting laws [*les lois protectrices*] created by the National Assembly have destroyed the abuses of the old ones, and when applied by virtuous and educated men, they will bring peace to families, they will prevent hate and dissention, they will destroy the oppression caused by the barbarous right to crush the weak with gold.[43]

Continuing the religious imagery, one might say that this brief passage damned seigneurial justice for a number of mortal sins: its complicity in internecine battles, its tendency to exacerbate dissension amongst neighbors, and its propensity for social bias. Finally, the mayor of St. Pierre d'Oléron offered the following encomium to the new magistracy: "Through it [the institution of the justice of the peace] the laws will be upheld, through it the widow and the invalid will be protected, through it the poor and the unfortunate will be soothed, through it the insidious [judicial] *corps*, which were responsible for jealousy, calumny, and animosity among good and peaceful men, will be annihilated."[44]

Just as some spiritual leaders fail woefully in fulfilling their heavenly missions, many new magistrates were bound to disappoint those whose lofty aspirations for the justice of the peace included nothing less than a revolution in rural morals and sociability. In fact, some historians would cite these ambitious expectations as another manifestation of the revolutionaries' determination to effect a moral regeneration of the French people.[45] Although much of the rhetoric accompanying the inception of the

---

42. ADCM L 127 (élections), 31 October 1791.

43. ADCM L 604 (élections—Rochefort), 21 January 1791.

44. ADCM L 127, St. Pierre d'Oléron, November 1790?.

45. See, for example, M. Ozouf, "Regeneration," in Furet and Ozouf, *A Critical Dictionary of the French Revolution*, 781–91.

justice of the peace expressed undeniably hyperbolic expectations, the revolutionaries focused less on the utopian vision of altering human nature than on reforming some very practical problems of local justice. Through such practical reforms they exhibited their not unrealistic belief in the power of institutions to influence and change social relations. If, as the *cahiers* of Aunis and Saintonge indicated, the poor administration of local justice under the Old Regime exacerbated or even provoked social tensions in rural France, then there is no reason to denounce as naive or dangerous the hope that justice expedited swiftly and inexpensively by a popularly elected member of the rural community would result in improved peasant relations. To be sure, institutional changes were no social panacea; a poor laborer's hatred of a well-to-do cultivator had deeper roots than the maladministration of justice. Still, a justice system could influence both the extent and the expression of that hatred. Behind all the talk of new men and regeneration to which the revolutionary fervor gave rise stood the very practical judicial reforms of French legislators.

Revolutionary legislators focused on four issues in their reforms aimed at improving the utility of local justice: geographical organization, jurisdiction, appeals, and procedure.[46] As noted in Chapter 1, an essential qualification of a system of local justice is its proximity to those requiring its services. In theory, the approximately five hundred seigneurial courts of Aunis and Saintonge ought to have admirably satisfied this qualification, since nearly every parish had its own tribunal. In practice, however, this plethora of local courts only multiplied the degrees of justice and led to an enormous but often unqualified body of legal personnel that squeezed justiciables in order to eke out a living. Paradoxically, by fulfilling too well one requirement of local justice—proximity—seigneurial tribunals neglected other equally essential requirements—speedy and inexpensive dispute resolution.

The revolutionaries used their administrative rationalization of France (in which eighty-three similarly sized departments contained several districts, each district several cantons, and each canton several communes) as the framework for their reorganization of local justice by making each canton a seat of a justice of the peace. For Charente-Maritime, this meant that fifty-three JPs took over responsibility for local justice from roughly five

---

46. To follow legislation on JPs throughout the revolutionary period and the restoration, consult Métairie, *Le monde des juges de paix de Paris*.

hundred seigneurial jurisdictions.[47] Previously, one seigneurial court had served approximately every 766 people in Aunis and Saintonge; now each justice of the peace constituted the tribunal of first instance for more than 6,500 justiciables (see Table 18).[48] While denied a seigneurial tribunal that was practically right outside the front door, rural inhabitants still benefited from proximate courts located no farther than one of the neighboring parishes. The advantages of this tradeoff were enormous, however, for instead of litigating at seigneurial courts that convened perhaps once a month (and then often without the judge), peasants now traveled a few miles within their cantons to seek justice before JPs who could be found at fixed times several days per week. For the lawmakers in Paris, the canton was their solution to that delicate problem of local justice—namely, how to guarantee proximity in light of limited qualified personnel and without creating the type of bloated mass of legal employees that resulted in so many abuses during the Old Regime.

After laying the geographical foundations for the new judicial structure, the Constituent Assembly turned its attention to the jurisdiction of the JP. The resultant laws of 16–24 August 1790 and 19–22 July 1791 assigned the JPs four essential duties. First, JPs, like their predecessors in the seigneurial magistracy, exercised a paternalistic role in *juridiction gracieuse*

TABLE 18   The Administrative Organization of Charente-Inférieure

District	Cantons	Communes
Saintes	9	97
La Rochelle	6	57
St. Jean d'Angély	9	126
Rochefort	5	56
Marennes	7	44
Pons	6	98
Monlieu	5	60
	47[a]	538[b]

SOURCE: *Ephémerides du département de la Charente-Inférieure* (1792).
[a] There were also JPs in the towns of Marennes, Pons, Saintes, La Rochelle (two by 1793), St. Jean d'Angély, and Rochefort, giving the department a total of fifty-three justices in 1791.
[b] Charente-Inférieure had 345,400 inhabitants and an area of 360 square *lieues*.

47. In 1791 Charente-Inférieure had forty-seven cantons plus six urban JPs from Marennes, Saintes, La Rochelle, St. Jean d'Angély, Rochefort, and Pons.
48. *Ephémerides du département de la Charente-Inférieure* (La Rochelle, 1792).

by protecting the interests of minors and absent persons. This important and time-consuming function made JPs responsible for affixing and raising judicial seals, for naming tutors and trustees, for emancipating minors, and so on. Second, JPs became judges of certain cases of civil litigation; in property disputes, legislators limited the jurisdiction of JPs to cases of mobile property whose value did not exceed one hundred livres. Importantly, there was no appeal of a JP's decision in cases of mobile property worth fifty livres or less. Justices of the peace also had cognizance of other civil cases regardless of the lawsuit's value (although subject to appeal in a district court if more than fifty livres). Such categories included disputes over damages to property by persons or animals, over boundaries or usurpation of property, between proprietors and tenants over repairs to property or for breach of contract, between masters and workers or servants over wages, and for verbal injuries and assault not pursued in criminal court. Third, these laws also made JPs mediators, for no plaintiff could bring a civil case to a district court without a certificate, granted by a *bureau de paix et de conciliation* over which the JP presided in rural areas, attesting to a prior attempt at conciliation. Finally, the laws of 19–22 July 1791 required the JPs to don a fourth cap—that of the police officer—by granting them a penal role as members of the *tribunal de police correctionnelle* (responsible for misdemeanors) and as judicial police officers who made arrests and investigations (but did not prosecute) in more serious crimes.[49]

Rural dwellers' denunciation of the multiplicity of degrees of justice, which meant that financial ruin often accompanied protracted litigation, did not go unheeded by the Parisian lawmakers. Their refusal to allow appeals of JPs' judgments in cases worth less than fifty livres was a stark manifestation of their vow to terminate trials at the source. Indeed, one might even argue that the inability to appeal such cases was patently unfair to the poor, for an object of fifty livres has as much relative significance for an indigent sharecropper (*métayer*) as has a lawsuit of five thousand livres for a successful bourgeois. Why should the latter but not the former have recourse to an appeal if he or she thought that justice had not been served? Here it seems that the revolutionaries could only bow to reality by recognizing the latter's ability to pay for the appeals process. If denying appeals in some cases was theoretically unjust, the revolutionaries thought that at least it spared people from the disastrous financial path so common in the

---

49. More detailed studies of the role of JPs in civil justice, conciliation, and penal matters are the subjects of Chapters 6, 7, and 8, respectively.

Old Regime. Furthermore, the limited jurisdiction of the JPs—they did not decide cases of real property, which often involved massive sums and complicated points of law—ensured that the nature of cases before them (dealing with points of fact and involving minor sums) were amenable to quick resolution and did not require an appeal. In any event, appealed decisions of JPs went to the district court, rarely located more than ten miles from any cantonal seat, which adjudicated them definitively.[50] Limiting the degrees of justice to two (and to one in minor cases), with its significant implications for the cost and speed of adjudication, must certainly have been a reform enthusiastically celebrated by rural dwellers.

The final reform of local justice that revolutionaries deemed necessary if they were to satisfy the demands of rural constituents and to improve social relations in the countryside centered on the issue of procedure. Most important, the new laws prohibited not only the use of counsel in cases before a justice of the peace, but also that useful tool of lawyers: written testimony. Instead, disputing parties arrived unaccompanied before the JP either voluntarily or upon reception of a citation issued after an initial complaint. There, in a simple public space unadorned by the accoutrements that normally served as reminders of the majesty of justice, without a lawyer, the parties simply stated their own cases.[51] The JP, assisted by two elected but unpaid *assesseurs,* could often decide the case on the spot. If the case required further investigation, the JP and his assistants could call for proof (for example, to look at account books), hear the oral testimony of witnesses or experts, demand that one party swear an oath to the veracity of his or her claim, or descend to the site of contention itself (for example, in frequent boundary disputes). Significantly, these investigations, usually carried out only a few days after the parties' initial appearance, were almost always limited to one day. Thus, the JP, who was not required to elaborate upon his reasons for a decision—a time and cost saver, to be sure, even though unfortunate for the researcher—dispensed with all cases either immediately or within a few weeks.

50. Civil cases beyond the jurisdiction of JPs were first heard in a district court (after a required prior attempt at conciliation) and went on appeal to any other of the nearest seven district courts. A superior court in Paris, the Cour de Cassation, guarded the uniformity of French jurisprudence and maintained the right to overturn decisions from district courts for excess of power or violation or false application of the law.

51. The JP in 1791 had no special uniform; he simply carried a blue and red insignia reading "La Loi et la Paix." In 1795 JPs were in theory supposed to carry a symbolic olive branch made of metal. In 1802 JPs began to wear the black toga required of all civil judges.

Although the extremely simplified procedure before the JPs may strike modern judicial positivists as an affront, it stands as a testimony to the revolutionaries' belief that certain cases could be decided quickly, inexpensively, and without bitter recriminations if lawyers were removed from the process. Hence, the restriction of the jurisdiction of local justice—to minor deals gone bad, to cases of disputed boundaries, to questions of who must repair a shared wall, to the numerous insults and fisticuffs among neighbors—was inextricably linked to the simplification of procedure. Not only were these cases most susceptible to swift adjudication (centering mostly on disputed facts and not on complicated points of law, which the JP, as an amateur, was not qualified to handle), but they were also the most needful of quick resolution, for every unresolved minor local dispute could escalate into something far more sinister and destructive. These reforms of the jurisdictions, procedure, and degrees of local justice, then, aimed at rectifying both the inutility and the socially deleterious effects of seigneurial justice while preserving the cherished proximity of local tribunals. How well the institution of the justice of the peace succeeded will constitute the focus of the following chapters.

PERSONNEL

If some revolutionaries actually expected voters to select their cantons' paragons of morality, selflessness, and personal stability for the position of justice of the peace, then for them the elections of 1790 must have served as a monument to the upstanding character and moral superiority of notaries (Tables 19[A] and 19[B]). Actually, the high incidence of notaries as JPs is not surprising and can be explained by looking at both the social status and the function of this profession in the Old Regime. As local notables whom rural clients sought out to prepare documents concerning many of the most important transactions of their lives, notaries were indispensible and by-and-large trusted participants in the personal business of local inhabitants. Because both parties to a contract agreed upon a notary who merely documented and witnessed the transaction, the notary rarely provoked the animosity of clients.[52] Legal professionals, on the other hand, either disappointed their own clients if they lost a case or stirred the wrath

---

52. See Reinhardt, *Justice in the Sarladais,* 158–59.

of the parties whom they defeated in court, thus increasing the likelihood of a group hostile to their election as JP. Although the idyllic vision of simple yet equitable rural cultivators serving as JPs and mediating amicably the disputes of their neighbors never became reality, notaries were well-qualified candidates for the role of JP. They were familiar with the affairs of their constituents, they enjoyed the trust of rural dwellers, they possessed some knowledge of law while avoiding the taint of chicanery that plagued lawyers, and their jobs naturally positioned them as disinterested mediators, symbols of the revolutionary judicial order.

Unlike their counterparts in the counterrevolutionary West and in politically charged Paris, the JPs of Charente-Inférieure were relatively immune to vicissitudes of the political climate.[53] Even Lequinio, the redoubtable, zealous representative-on-mission who was instrumental in organizing Rochefort's Revolutionary Tribunal, seemingly found little need to purge the ranks of the JPs in the Year II.[54] This relative immunity allowed for a high degree of continuity among JPs; for example, François Riguet, Denis Prieur, and M. Poullet remained as JP of the town and canton of Saintes and the canton of Courson, respectively, from 1790 through the Year VII, while Antoine Jonon sat at Marans from the institution's inception until the Year VI. Significantly, all five JPs in the district of Monlieu won reelection in 1792.[55] When turnover in the ranks of JPs occurred, it was as often the result of a JP's desire to step down as it was the case of voters expressing dissatisfaction with an incumbent. In the district of Saintes in 1792, six of nine JPs were returned to office; of the three new JPs, two won vacant seats while only one defeated an incumbent.[56] In all, of fifty-three seats of justices, only eleven saw changes in their JP from

53. In the West, JPs were often targets of *chouan* activity, while from 1792 to 1794 Parisian artisan or merchant activists replaced the legal professionals elected in 1790. See, respectively, J. L. Debauve, *La justice révolutionnaire dans le Morbihan, 1790–1795* (Paris, 1965), and Andrews, "The Justices of the Peace of Revolutionary Paris."

54. In Marennes, for example, Lequinio gathered the popular society in the Temple of Truth and invited them to denounce those JPs in the area whose "qualifications" (presumably patriotic) were suspect. He later departed without making changes, although he did authorize the *agent national* to replace *assesseurs* (the JPs' unpaid but elected assistants) if necessary (ADCM L 867, 3 pluviôse II).

55. ADCM L 127 (élections).

56. E.-J. Guérin, *Les justices de paix de Saintes depuis 1790 jusqu'à nos jours* (La Rochelle, 1915), 18–19. My figures reflect M. Edelstein's research on the elections of JPs in Côte d'Or. See "Le bonheur est dans la conciliation: Les élections des juges de paix en Côte d'Or (automne 1790–brumaire an IV)" (forthcoming). Edelstein found that voter turnout was consistently higher during elections for JPs than those for national representatives. On revolutionary elections in general, see P. Guéniffey, *Le nombre et la raison: La Révolution française et les élections* (Paris, 1993).

TABLE 19A The Justices of the Peace in Charente-Inférieure in 1790

District	Canton/Town	JP	Occupation
Saintes	Saintes ville	Riguet	Procureur
	Saintes canton	Prieur	Bourgeois
	Dompierre	Ardouin	Notaire
	Ecoyeux	Godet	Notaire
	Pont l'abbé	Desnaules	Bourgeois
	Port d'envaux	Gaillard	Notaire
	Saujon	Duplex	Avocat
	Cozes	Tourneur	Notaire
	Mortagne	Gorry	Avocat
	Gemozac	Magistel	Notaire
Monlieu	Monlieu	Rocher	—
	St. Aigulin	Vigent	Propriétaire
	Montendre	Morineau	Avocat
	Léoville	Ranson	Notaire
	Montguyon	Mauget	Notaire
Pons	Pons ville	Quantin	Avocat
	Pons canton	Gout	Avocat
	Jonzac ville	Flornois	Avocat
	Jonzac canton	Sauvaistre	Bourgeois
	Archaic	Dusault	Avocat
	Mirambeau	Bascle	Notaire
	St. Fort	Robert	Practitioner
	St. Genis	Ligs	Cultivateur
Marennes	Marennes ville	Fontenelle	—
	Marennes canton	Marguard	—
	Royan	Vallet	—
	Le Gua	Crochet	Mtre/Chirurgie
	La Tremblade	Rousseau	Notaire
	St. Pierre	Godeau	—
	Château	Bernard	Notaire
	Soubise	Bourgeois	—
Rochefort	Rochefort ville	Gaultier	Notaire
	Rochefort canton	Gouffet	Huissier
	Tonnay-Charente	Girardières	Propriétaire
	Surgères	Mestadiers	Notaire
	Benon	Petit (1792?)	Notaire
	Ciré	Pinaud	Notaire
La Rochelle	La Rochelle ville	Giraud	Homme de loi
	La Rochelle canton	Leconte	Avocat
	La Jarrie	Lambert	—
	Marans	Jonon	—

District	Canton/Town	JP	Occupation
	Ars-en-Ré	Bourgeois	—
	St. Martin	Saintmont	Notaire
	Courson	Poullet	Homme de loi
St. Jean	SJ d'Angély ville	Binet	—
d'Angély	SJ d'Angély canton	Marchant	—
	Brizambourg	Charrier	—
	Matha	Loizeau	—
	Taillebourg	Roquet	—
	St. Savinien	Charrier	—
	Aunay	Guerin	—
	Lonlay	Duvergier	—
	Lozay	Charrier	—
	Tonnay-Boutonne	Carville	—

TABLE 19B   The Occupations of Justices of the Peace in 1790

Notaire	6
Notaire royal	9
	—
	15
Avocat	3
Homme de loi	6
Avocat au parlement	1
Procureur	1
Practitioner	1
Huissier	1
	—
	13
Bourgeois	3
Cultivateur	1
Propriétaire	1
Propriétaire/négociant	1
	—
	3
Maître en chirurgie	1
	—
	34

SOURCE: ADCM L 604, L 127 (élections); *Ephémerides du département de Charente-Infèrieure* (La Rochelle, 1793). The lacunae represent a paucity of documents for several cantons.

1791 to 1793, meaning that the vast majority of magistrates won reelection after their first term.[57] The sparse election records from 1792 prevent one from commenting on whether reelection stemmed from voter apathy or satisfaction with JPs, but without a doubt the continuity of these elected officials stabilized the practice of local justice and helped legitimize the institution.

Perhaps the single most important reason for personnel changes among the JPs of Charente-Inférieure was the incompatibility of that office with other professions or administrative functions. Already in 1791 the position was incompatible with that of mayor or registered attorney, and the law of 1 brumaire II forbade JPs to operate simultaneously as notaries. This unfortunate law precipitated massive resignations from JPs for whom no-tarial work was financially more lucrative than the stingy wages (six hun-dred livres, raised to nine hundred in 1793) offered to them for their exhausting service. In the district of Rochefort during the Year II, four of five JPs—Petit of Benon, Mestadier of Surgères, Pinaud of Ciré, and Gaultier of Rochefort—preferred to remain notaries rather than JPs, re-quiring the Conseil du district to designate replacements.[58] The expanding list of functions incompatible with the office of JP diminished the pool of qualified and interested candidates to adjudicate among their fellow citi-zens. Although at the local level it is difficult to detect dissatisfaction with the quality of JPs, legislators in Paris increasingly grumbled about the dif-ficulty (one of their own making) of ensuring competent people for the position of JP.[59] Ultimately, the Tribunate decided to reduce the number of cantons in 1801 in order to weed out the more incompetent local judges.[60]

In another move from 1801 aimed at improving the quality of personnel associated with local justice, the Tribunate abolished the position of *asses-seur*.[61] Every municipality had elected four of these unpaid assistants, two of whom aided the JP in making decisions at any given time. The *assesseurs* originally symbolized the Revolution's vision of local justice, in which re-spected community members adjudicated disputes among their neighbors.

---

57. *Ephémerides du département de la Charente-Inférieure.*

58. ADCM L 371, Rochefort, 28 prairial II. To their credit and to the benefit of the judicial administration, Petit, Mestadier, and Pinaud agreed to work as unpaid *assesseurs* in their cantons.

59. See, for example, the lingering debate in the Year IV over the problem of filling vacant seats because of resignations or the refusal of elected persons to serve as JPs. *Réimpression de l'ancien Moniteur* 26.

60. I. Woloch follows this debate in *The New Regime,* 317–20.

61. Law of 29 ventôse IX (20 March 1801).

Indeed, the judicial archives offer testimony to the helpful services, including gathering information and assessing damages for certain cases, that they performed as auxiliaries of the JPs. In practice, however, the required participation of two *assesseurs* in every civil case and attempt at conciliation at times burdened the justice system. On the one hand, many rural communes simply lacked qualified candidates for the position, which was potentially injurious to judicial decisions, because *assesseurs* could outvote JPs by a margin of two to one. On the other hand, the severe but unremunerated constraints on assistants' time sometimes left qualified notables uninterested in the position or rendered them frequent no-shows when duty called.

The importance of the position of *assesseur* as well as the quality of the personnel apparently varied significantly from canton to canton. For example, in the canton of La Rochelle, both Jean Monneron, the mayor of Dompierre, and Sieur Fillonneau, the curé, served as assistants to the JP. At Brizambourg, Pierre Poitevin, the commander of a battalion of the National Guard, sought and won election for the job of *assesseur*. In other words, it seems likely that these notables maintained their roles as local power brokers by becoming *assesseurs,* from which position they could learn of and regulate local problems and disputes. Similarly, three former JPs were working as *assesseurs* in Gemozac in the Year IV, just as three of the four JPs from Marennes who resigned in the aftermath of the law of 1 brumaire II remained as assistants to their replacements. Thus, the position of *assesseur* was frequently held by qualified and conscientious persons, which was doubtless instrumental in gaining both stability and respect for the new institution of local justice.[62]

For the most part, the sparse evidence concerning the social status of the *assesseurs* reveals that most who occupied that modest position ranged from merchants to cultivators. One can only speculate about what this meant for their intellectual and moral capacity to assist in dispensing justice. Was the deputy Faure exaggerating or stating a widely accepted opinion when he lamented in 1801 "how much the lack of enlightenment among the *assesseurs* is harmful to justice"?[63] How representative was the case from the canton of Saujon, where four parishes united to elect *assesseurs* in 1790

62. ADCM L 984, La Rochelle; L 796.3, Brizambourg; L 1447.3, Gemozac.
63. Cited in Guérin, *Les justices de paix de Saintes,* 23. Such opinions might have reflected the legal professional's disdain for the amateurs of the justice of the peace more than popular discontent with the personnel of local justice.

but were unable to find any notables who could fulfill the National Assembly's decree that candidates must be able to read and write?[64] In the parishes of Près and Loire (canton of Rochefort), only five electors assembled in 1792 to select eight *assesseurs*—circumstances hardly conducive to ensuring the highest-quality personnel.[65] Such issues attained great importance during the commonplace albeit brief absences of the JPs, usually because of illness, since *assesseurs* served as replacements. Here, of course, the Old Regime problem of the magistracy devolving on incompetent subordinates had the potential to replicate itself under the new institutions of local justice. It is true, however, that since JPs held only one (salaried) office and were required to hold court on fixed days every week, the structural and financial causes of this problem were largely solved. Hence, the replacement of JPs by *assesseurs* remained brief and localized, except perhaps in the aftermath of the law of 1 brumaire II.

Because it is difficult to determine the moral and intellectual character of the *assesseurs*, it is also difficult to say what effect, if any, their personal qualities had on the quality of local justice in Charente-Inférieure.[66] In any case, one can state with certainty that the position of *assesseur* was simply too time-consuming, thus requiring JPs to cancel sessions for lack of a quorum or to ask litigants to bind themselves to decisions despite the absence of the auxiliaries' input.[67] At Ars-en-Ré in the Year III, four *assesseurs* simply informed the JP that, because their "multiple and daily affairs prevented (them) from assisting at all sessions," they were limiting their involvement to two séances per *décade* (ten-day period).[68] By 1801, then, the revolutionaries had learned an important lesson of state formation: that local justice needed more than just patriotism and the good intentions of

64. See P. Ferchaud, *Saujon le Gua (1789–An III): La Révolution dans deux cantons ruraux* (Saujon, 1988), 34.

65. ADCM L 127.

66. Unfortunately, the institution's emphasis on simplicity of procedure, which excused JPs from giving the reasons for their decisions, renders it impossible to get a sense of the dynamics between JPs and their auxiliaries.

67. Such occurrences were rather common. For example, in the canton of La Rochelle on 16 March 1791, the apothecary Guinière sued the *fille majeure* Crozet for fifteen livres worth of medicine. The JP claimed that he was unable to assemble the obligatory *assesseurs*, at which time the parties requested the JP's decision anyway and agreed to abide by it. ADCM L 894.

68. ADCM L 792; Ars-en-Ré, 22 nivôse III. Curiously, on 25 nivôse two of the *assesseurs*, Etienne Brumet and Mathieu Mercier, appeared before the *bureau de paix et de conciliation* as litigants over a grain sale. They settled the dispute amiably, but it points out the significance of interpersonal dynamics for the functioning of local justice.

simple people; it required both educated citizens and money to attract them (something lords had known all along). Was the door open for the return of legal professionals?

The Activity of the Justices of the Peace

Table 20 contains a list of the activities that occupied the energies of rural JPs. Since these activities constitute the focus of the remaining chapters, I will make only a few general comments here. First, the magistracy maintained its crucial role in the realm of *juridiction gracieuse*, for a large percentage of its time consisted of protecting the interests of minors. As such, the JP fulfilled the same paternal role as the fiscal procurator once had, with the significant difference that the people (really the adult males) now selected and held accountable their own paternal figure rather than submitting to the choice of the lord. Whether assembling the family of Jean Ridoret, whose madness rendered him prone to violence and incapable of speaking, reasoning, or taking care of his most basic needs, or whether naming a trustee to oversee the property of a minor, the JP stood as both the protector of the community and the defender of those incapable of exercising their rights.[69]

Second, in comparison to the extremely high ratio of procedural items to decisions under seigneurial justice, nearly every entry in the registers of the justice of the peace corresponded to a judgment.[70] For example, of the 147 civil judgments from Jonzac in 1792, only twenty-four were *jugements préparatoires*, which required a visit to the source of contention or that one party offer proof of its claim.[71] Hence, JPs decided the vast majority of cases on the spot, without hearing from lawyers, reading briefs, or following procedural formalities, with obvious effects on the time and cost of local justice, especially since court personnel were no longer paid by the procedural item. Moreover, nearly every one of the twenty-four cases requiring further inquiry was adjudicated within a week.

A final general comment about the activity of the JPs is that the year 1791 witnessed an explosion in the number of justiciables seeking the ser-

69. ADCM L 789, Ars-en-Ré, 3 fructidor VI.

70. Under seigneurial justice, there were approximately ten procedural hearings per every civil decision rendered. See Chapter 1.

71. ADCM L 825.

TABLE 20   The Activity of Various Justices of the Peace (number of judgments)

Canton	Civil	Conciliation	Juridiction Gracieuse	Police
Marennes 1791	318	39	45	—
Marennes an II	125	—	99	11
Marennes an V	170	—	136	69
Marennes an VI	104	65	111	65
Ars-en-Ré 1791	119	—	—	—
Ars-en-Ré 1792	59	—	—	—
Ars-en-Ré an IV	83	—	—	—
Ars-en-Ré an V	—	45	—	—
Ars-en-Ré an VI	46	—	37	—
Jonzac 1792	147	—	—	—
Jonzac an II	125	—	—	—
Gemozac 1793	—	—	—	20
Gemozac an III	—	—	—	31
Gemozac an IV	—	117	—	—
Marans 1791	60	—	50	—
Marans 1793	—	—	108	—
Marans an V	—	—	72	—
Cozes an VI	63	112	20	22

SOURCES: ADCM L 842 and L 867, Marennes; L 787, L 788, and L 793, Ars-en-Ré; L 826.1 and L 826.2, Jonzac; L 1447.1, L 1447.3, L 1435.2, L 1436.2, Gemozac; L 837, Marans; L 1411, Cozes.

vices of local magistrates. The JP of Marennes handled 318 civil cases, that of Ars-en-Ré judged 119 suits, and the JP of the canton of La Rochelle issued an astounding 635 judicial acts in that year.[72] The year 1791, then, represents the quenching of rural dwellers' thirst for justice and reflects the inaccessibility of the lords' courts. Although the new jurisdictions consisted of the union of several seigneurial jurisdictions, it is inconceivable that the latter would (or could) have collectively adjudicated so many cases in a single year. Herein lies a paradox of the new judicial system: by reforming the abuses of the seigneurial tribunals, partially in the hope of rendering

72. ADCM L 842, Marennes; L 787, Ars-en-Ré; L 894, La Rochelle canton. Ideally, one would determine all the seigneurial jurisdictions corresponding to a revolutionary canton, count the number of civil cases in these courts that would have fallen under the jurisdiction of the JP (recall that seigneurial tribunals had far greater jurisdiction than JPs in terms of amounts and types of cases), and then decide if people were actually more or less litigious during the Revolution than under the Old Regime. In reality, even if one succeeded in completing the enormous geographical exercise, one's reward would simply be a paucity of documents considering the sporadic nature of the archives for both seigneurial justice and the justices of the peace.

rural society less litigious, revolutionary lawmakers created a system of local justice so accessible that it probably encouraged more litigation.[73] Of course, there was a crucial qualitative difference in the litigiousness of the Old Regime, in which minor disputes assumed major repercussions during long and expensive trials, and the litigiousness of the new order, in which cases were handled quickly and inexpensively. As long as the social, economic, cultural, and psychological bases for conflict existed, the greatest benefit of a justice system would consist of providing a trusted forum for the speedy resolution of those conflicts instead of contributing to them in the ways that seigneurial justice had.

The best means of attaining a sense of both the activity of the JPs as well as the new style of justice is to follow these magistrates in action. For cases in which parties agreed on the facts concerning the object of contention, JPs and their *assesseurs* offered immediate decisions. If litigants differed in their *dires,* JPs often accepted a defendant's oath as grounds for dismissing a suit if it did not lend itself to further investigation. For cases where further information could aid magistrates in their decisions, JPs often ordered a visit (limited to one day, almost always one week after the parties' original appearance) to the source of contention, where they could make their own assessments (in disputes over passages, property boundaries, and so forth), speak to witnesses (but without taking costly and time-consuming depositions), or listen to the advice of "experts." At other times, the JP requested the plaintiff to document a claim with a title, a bill of lading, or an account book. The style of local justice, then, emphasized procedural simplicity and celerity in its minimization of paperwork and in the JPs' freedom from prescribed restraints in arriving at decisions.

Besides revealing the simple and expeditious nature of local justice under the new magistracy, the judicial archives also give evidence of the important conceptual shift toward equity and conciliation in official dispute resolution.[74] In 1793 at Jonzac, the *cultivateur* Brivet claimed that the locksmith Allongue owed him forty livres for the sale and delivery of wine.[75]

---

73. The desire to make litigation more difficult in part fueled the movement to reduce the number of cantons in 1801.

74. Undoubtedly informal conciliation was practiced under the Old Regime, sometimes simply out of necessity when official justice proved inaccessible in civil matters or uninterested in pursuing criminal complaints. S. Reinhardt makes the most elaborate case for infrajudicial dispute settlement in *Justice in the Sarladais,* 118–60. The Revolution appears to have institutionalized a practice already used by peasants, which certainly contributed to its acceptance after 1789.

75. ADCM L 829 (182).

The problem was that Brivet had lost a signed purchase order. For Allongue's part, he admitted that he had received the wine but lamented that he had misplaced his receipt of payment for the goods. Confronted with "the impossibility of knowing the facts" (apparently there were no witnesses to the deal), the JP and his auxiliaries, instead of referring to laws that placed the burden of proof on the plaintiff, ordered Allongue to pay Brivet twenty livres—a decision that could not be appealed. In a similar case from Cozes, the widow Marie Chevallier inherited a purchase order worth 116 livres for the sale of a boat to Jean Genereau.[76] Jean did not deny the debt, but he stated that the responsibility for payment fell on his brother Antoine, a mariner who had taken de facto possession of the boat. In light of the brothers' continued disagreement over the issue, the JP made them split the cost of the boat. Again, in La Rochelle a municipal officer sued a woman over "reparations for violence," while the woman countersued for "excesses committed." Instead of taking the depositions of many witnesses and then assessing blame, which under seigneurial justice would have led to an expensive trial and most likely an appeal, the JP listened to their respective versions of the story, chided them both for mutual provocation, and sent them home.[77] Unlike the court personnel under seigneurial justice, no financial incentive existed to allow the pursuit of probably spurious cases.

None of the preceding decisions was liable to please everyone; on the contrary, each risked upsetting nearly every party involved. But they signaled the Revolution's commitment to a more conciliatory justice at the local level, and conciliation means getting people to back off of their presumed rights. To be sure, JPs' decisions often assigned right and blame. After all, a debt is simply a debt and is not amenable to conciliation; it must be paid. Yet even in these cases, JPs endeavored to convince litigants to be more flexible and conciliatory in demanding their rights. In the canton of La Rochelle, for example, the harsh winter of 1791 produced scores of cases in which creditors sought payment for having furnished bread or flour to customers. Instead of merely condemning the defendants to fulfill

---

76. ADCM L 1411.1, 21 fructidor VI.

77. ADCM L 894, canton of La Rochelle, 1791. This is not to imply that JPs always ordered a splitting of the object in contention. In fact, for cases in which parties disagreed over facts and when there was no way (through witnesses, experts, account books, and so on) of ascertaining the truth, JPs usually accepted a defendant's oath as sufficient grounds to dismiss a suit. These examples simply demonstrate the wide latitude given to the JP to operate from a sense of fairness rather than from strict legal forms.

their obligations, the JP Leconte almost always succeeded in working out
a payment schedule—a debt of thirty-nine livres would be repaid in three
installments of thirteen livres from 1792 to 1794. Significantly, both Leconte
and the JP of Marennes, Marquard, convinced creditors to avoid requests
for interest payments in these schedules. In return for the debtor's immediate recognition of the debt and a partial repayment, the creditor accepted
the delayed fulfilled of the obligation and relaxed his or her claim to collect
interest. Another of Leconte's preferred tactics was to substitute labor for
cash payments. On 17 January 1791, the *laboureur* Belineaud filed a suit for
fifty livres against the *vigneron* Turpeau. Leconte stated: "With the consent
of the plaintiff, we have ruled that the payment will be made by means of
one day of labor per week that he [Turpeau] will give to said plaintiff."[78]

Finally, JPs sometimes employed moral suasion to convince parties to
accept their judgments even in cases far outside their jurisdiction, thereby
saving litigants the time, money, and bitterness accompanying a formal
lawsuit in a district court. When this moral suasion worked, it was almost
always for disputes over which the parties appeared voluntarily before the
JP, a signal that they were already predisposed to avoiding a long trial. On
15 January 1793 the JP of Jonzac, Sauvaistre, settled two disputes beyond his
competence (one was for 250 livres) after the parties promised "to put up
with [*s'en passer par*] and submit to our [the JP's] decision."[79] At La Rochelle in January of 1791 the *vigneron* Rolland and the *laboureur* Cerclet
voluntarily sought Leconte's judgments in two disputes, one for 411 livres
and the other for twenty-nine years' arrears of a *rente* of twenty-five livres
per year, both significant sums exceeding the jurisdiction of the justice of
the peace. Leconte wrote concerning the latter case:

> After having remarked to the parties that the sum sought by the plain-
> tiff and the principal of the *rente* greatly exceed our jurisdiction, they
> said they wanted a decision and would leave things to us [*s'en rapporter
> à nous*]. . . . Having equally asked Rolland if he had some document,
> paper, or title upholding his claim . . . [he responded] that he had no
> such thing; only that he knew in his soul and in his conscience that he,

---

78. ADCM L 894, La Rochelle; L 842, Marennes, 1791. These good intentions of JPs could
backfire, since the devaluation of the assignat sent creditors back to the courts to demand payments
in hard currency or in kind.

79. ADCM L 829. Such activity differed from that of JPs' work on the *bureaux de conciliation,*
because here they offered judgments, not attempts at mediation. In other words, parties did not want
a settling of their differences; they sought a determination of who was in the right.

Rolland, spoke the truth; to which Pierre Cerclet responded that he was ready to take an oath that he owed Rolland nothing.[80]

Leconte released Cerclet from his adversary's demands.

Although such decisions were not legally binding until notarized as contracts, the extraction of promises from the litigants, whose voluntary appearance signaled both their good faith and their respect of the JP's authority, often sufficed to bind them morally to a decision. Significantly, all cases in which adjudication was sought voluntarily were handled without expenses. Thus, even though Rolland could still take his case to a district civil court, he received before the JP a free indication of how he might expect to do there. Under seigneurial jurisdictions, Rolland's options would have been to pursue a long and expensive lawsuit or, fearing this, to harbor his resentments or to take revenge on Cerclet. Under the new system, all of these options still existed, but the presence of the justice of the peace provided for a quick, cost-free and official designation of right. As such, it most likely minimized Rolland's claim to take justice into his own hands. The revolutionary system of local justice, of course, could not solve France's social problems, but at least now it did not exacerbate them.

CONCLUSION

"We are ruined as soon as we are obliged to litigate." In one brief line the parishioners of the Ile d'Elle undermined the legitimacy of one of France's ancient institutions. Contemporary inhabitants and revolutionary elites alike condemned Old Regime local justice for its failure to fulfill its perceived role in society. They identified myriad problems associated with seigneurial justice, some stemming from the usurpation and hence proliferation of seats during feudal times with others resulting from the royal administration of justice (especially procedure), that taken together left justiciables unconvinced that justice had been served when the justice system had been used. Seeking justice was such a long and costly process and it included so many legal formalities that justiciables wondered whether the entire process was meant to maintain the power of lords and pay the salaries of legal administrators rather than guarantee harmony in society. Since a society's cohesion and legitimacy rest to a large degree on peoples'

80. ADCM L 894, canton of La Rochelle, 4 January 1791.

belief that justice is in fact just, the questioning of local justice in the eighteenth century constituted a blow to the sanctity of an important institution of Old Regime France. Here, rural justiciables take their place alongside Grub Street journalists, pornographic critics of royalty, enlightened nobles, and other groups who, by attacking the legitimacy of Old Regime ideas and institutions, prepared the path for the acceptance of the Revolution.[81]

Complaints by justiciables of Aunis and Saintonge about the proliferation of jurisdictions, the quality of personnel, the procedural complications, and the degrees of justice all pointed to the fact that adjudication was too expensive and too slow, which rendered it inaccessible for many people and invited chicanery. The revolutionary solution to these problems was to implement the institution of the justice of the peace in the cantons, which cut down on the number of local tribunals while preserving the cherished principle of proximity. In addition, the revolutionaries radically simplified the procedure of local civil justice. The problem of numerous degrees was solved by their reduction to two in most cases and even by the prohibition on appeals in certain cases. Finally, through a series of decisions, including the diminution of the number of jurisdictions, the limitation of the jurisdiction of justices of the peace to "simple" cases, and the commitment to the principle of election, Parisian legislators endeavored to rectify the problems of personnel surrounding local justice.

One of the ironies of the justice of the peace is that, in their commitment to a new type of local justice, the revolutionaries in some ways relaxed their commitment to the Enlightenment principle of rationalization (a principle seen in the administrative reorganization of France, for example). To be sure, revolutionaries "rationalized" local justice by rendering the justice of the peace a uniform institution, with each seat responsible for roughly the same amount of territory and the same number of justiciables and guided by the same rules. But within each seat, the JP was given free reign to restore tranquility and harmony in his territory. He was free to

---

81. On the ways in which these groups contributed to a sapping of the legitimacy of Old Regime institutions, see R. Darnton, *The Literary Underground of the Old Regime*, especially chap. 1, "The High Enlightenment and the Low Life of Literature" (Cambridge, Mass., 1982); L. Hunt, *The Family Romance of the French Revolution* (Berkeley, 1992); G. Chaussinand-Nogaret, *The French Nobility in the Eighteenth Century: From Feudalism to Enlightenment*, trans. W. Doyle (Cambridge, 1985). For detailed studies of the climate of opinion in Old Regime France and the origins of the French Revolution, see R. Chartier, *The Cultural Origins of the French Revolution*, trans. L. Cochrane (Durham, N.C., 1991) and R. Darnton, *The Forbidden Best-Sellers of Pre-Revolutionary France* (New York, 1996).

rule in equity instead of being tightly bound by "the science of laws"; he did not have to cite reasons for his decisions; his decisions were immune to appeals on procedural grounds; in fact, many of his decisions could not be appealed at all.[82] Did the revolutionaries grant the JP a potential arbitrariness in adjudicating—an arbitrariness checked only by the occasionally appealed decision and by biannual elections—thereby undermining their principle of rationalization? If so, in the eyes of revolutionaries this potential arbitrariness posed less of a threat to the harmony of rural France than did the intervention of lawyers in local disputes. To meet the demands of constituents concerning local justice, Parisian lawmakers preferred their symbol of the enemy of trials, the justice of the peace, to that symbol of trials par excellence, the lawyer.

82. In this emphasis on equity and the drift from legal positivism, readers may see similarities between the revolutionary justice of the peace and Khadi justice, described by Max Weber. See G. Roth and C. Wittich, eds., *Max Weber: Economy and Society*, 2 vols. (Berkeley, 1976), 2:976–78. Of course, the JP's authority derived from his status as a trusted and elected member of the rural community rather than his religious position.

CHAPTER 6

The Amateurs at Work

Civil Justice Under the JPs

The records of civil justice under the *juges de paix* of Charente-Inférieure are a powerful soporific. The cases strike one as petty, almost banal, as every sharecropper with a claim to a few pockets of grain and every servant with a claim to a few livres in wages sought redress before their elected magistrates. The documentation of the cases is minimal and unspectacular, those recording them routinely offering a brief description of the issue before remarking that the JP and his assessors deliberated privately and then stated their decision. After examining hundreds of cartons of records and thousands of civil cases adjudicated by justices of the peace, I was struck by a sense of the routinization and banalization of justice.

These findings troubled me for quite some time. Given the nature of civil justice under the justices of the peace, one might empathize with the scholar's trepidation about writing a chapter as conducive to sleep as the records on which it was based. But all the while I was really missing the crucial point. The simplicity of the proceedings, the humble origins of many of the litigants, the nature of the plaintiffs' demands, and the expeditious and informal manner in which JPs handled contentious issues constituted the essence of the new institution. The simplicity of civil adjudication meant that justice was a burden on neither the finances nor the time of rural inhabitants, which rendered recourse to official justice accessible to people hitherto excluded from the courts. And the routinization of justice signified the degree to which JPs terminated with celerity the disputes that plagued rural areas. Of course, the new adminstration of justice could not alter the social structure, property relations, and commercial tensions that served as the source of disputes, but it could defuse the disputes by resolving them rapidly and by minimizing the stakes involved. In doing so, did it not also alter the psychology that prolonged quarrels and contributed to their acerbic flavor? As one early study of the justices of the peace rightly concluded, the administration of local justice no longer exacerbated the social tensions of rural France.[1]

In this chapter, I document the effects of the revolutionary changes in local civil justice and then speculate on the significance of those effects on the relations between the state and rural society.[2] Although one can easily ascertain that justice became faster and cheaper under the revolutionary creation, the meaning of these changes remains more difficult to assess. Can one argue that the improvements in local civil justice, by granting people a largely trusted and inexpensive forum for the resolution of conflicts, helped pave the way for the acceptance of the modern French state? Was not the willingness of rural inhabitants to subject their disputes to official channels instead of exacting private retribution a triumph for the architects of the state, whose goal was the penetration of rural areas?

THE PRACTICE OF REVOLUTIONARY LOCAL CIVIL JUSTICE

A succinct recapitulation of the three factors that distinguished revolutionary local justice from seigneurial civil justice highlights the distinctive nature of the new institution. First, justices of the peace were popularly elected and state-salaried magistrates. On the one hand, this signified that JPs enjoyed a modicum of justiciables' trust and contributed to the institution's legitimacy. On the other hand, the receipt of a state salary removed the temptation to prolong cases that had proved so irresistible to impecunious officials under the Old Regime; the remuneration of JPs remained completely independent of the cases they adjudicated. Second, revolutionary legislators limited the jurisdiction of justices of the peace to seven categories of disputes.[3] Essentially, they restricted the JPs' powers to those cases

---

1. V. Jeanvrot, *Les juges de paix élus sous la Révolution* (Saintes, 1883), 11.

2. I am aware of only one in-depth study of local civil justice during the Revolution. See D. Bouguet, "La sociabilité conflictuelle dans le canton de Loches d'après les archives de la justice de paix (1790–an III)," *Histoire moderne et contemporaine* 1, no. 2 (1986): 159–70. Two other studies treat civil justice in more cursory fashion. See J. Bart, "La justice de paix du canton de Fontaine-Française à l'époque révolutionnaire," and Debauve, *La justice révolutionnaire dans le Morbihan.* See also C. Coquard and C. Durand-Coquard, "Société rurale et Révolution: L'apport des actes de deux justices de paix de l'Allier (1791–fin de l'an VI)" (Ph.D. diss., Université de Borgogne, 1998).

3. The categories, defined by the laws of 16–24 August, 1790, were (1) *causes personnelles et mobilières* (debts, *rentes*, broken commercial conventions), to fifty livres without appeal and to one

amenable to resolution through fairness, good sense, and visits to the site of contention (particularly instances involving simple debts, boundary disputes, and verbal quarrels), rather than cases following rigorously prescribed legal forms. The distinction between cases requiring a corroboration of facts (cases before nonspecialist JPs) and those requiring an interpretation of law (cases handled by legal specials in district courts) enabled revolutionaries to implement the style of local justice they envisioned for rural France. Third, civil procedure under the JPs was radically altered to protect "the truth" from the manipulation of lawyers and the morass of legal formalities. Most important, revolutionary laws forbade the appearance of lawyers and written testimony from cases before the JP. In addition, the new procedure countenanced on-site inspections and questioning of witnesses in an effort to speed up and decrease the cost of civil justice.

The law of 14 October 1790 is remarkable for the simplicity of the procedure before justices of the peace. The brief rubric "On Expenses" authorizes the charging of minor sums for only a few items: One livre for the issuing of a summons (and ten sols for each subsequent summons delivered by a clerk to a separate domicile) and the service of a judgment; one livre for the delivery of a definitive judgment; ten sols for each preparatory judgment and *procès-verbal* of a visit (both of these acts were necessary only for cases that could be appealed); fifteen sols for the delivery of a preparatory judgment against a defaulting party; one livre for the clerk accompanying a JP to an on-site visit; one livre ten sols for a half day's employment of an expert, or three livres for a full day. As the deputy Thouret indicated, adjudication would literally be without cost if two parties arrived before the JP voluntarily (which often occurred) and did not require a delivery of the judgment.[4] In any event, Thouret hoped, simple cases in which litigants arrived after a summons and that required nothing besides the perusal of an account book or the verification of a debt's authenticity would cost only three livres. The most complex cases under a JP's jurisdiction, those necessitating the questioning of witnesses, the opinions of experts, the visit to

---

hundred livres on appeal; (2) cases concerning damages done by humans or animals to fields, harvests, or produce; (3) usurpations of land, trees, etc. and boundary disputes; (4) repairs by renters to houses and farms; (5) indemnification to proprietors by leaseholders for failure to cultivate or for allowing property to deteriorate; (6) disputes over the payment of wages to workers or domestics and the fulfillment of obligations between masters and employees; (7) cases of verbal threats, libel, slander, and physical assault not pursued by the authorities of criminal justice.

4. *Archives parlementaires*, 19:605.

the place of contention, or a combination of these could scarcely exceed ten or twelve livres, in Thouret's opinion.

The records of the justices of the peace of Charente-Inférieure confirm Thouret's optimistic scenario about the cost of litigating before the new magistrates. In a random sample of sixty cases from Marennes in 1791, the expenses of forty-seven judgments survive.[5] Of those forty-seven judgments, twenty-one cases cost a mere three livres six sols, while another thirteen cost three livres fifteen sols (as noted in Chapter 2, the value of one day's labor was assessed at one livre in 1789). Only three cases involved expenses exceeding five livres, with the most expensive trial generating seven livres nineteen sols in court costs. A case of *trouble de possession*, which included a preparatory judgment ordering the plaintiff to prove his case with witnesses, cost six livres four sols. Importantly, four cases were absolutely free, since they involved the reconciliation of parties who presented themselves voluntarily before the justice of the peace despite the fact that the source of contention stood outside his jurisdiction.[6] Sixteen cases from Brizambourg in 1792 averaged just less than four livres in litigation expenses.[7] Thirty-six cases adjudicated by the JP of Jonzac in 1792 averaged five livres per decision.[8] The most expensive case cost nineteen livres and included an original judgment in which the defendant defaulted, an appeal of the original decision, followed by a visit to the site in contention (the case concerned payment for damaged cherry trees) and the interrogation of six witnesses. Such sums were unlikely to frighten country dwellers from subjecting their disputes to official channels of justice and were certainly not going to ruin the parties financially.

To compare the average cost of a case under revolutionary justices of the peace to that under seigneurial tribunals (see Chapter 2) is, in a sense, like comparing apples and oranges, given the vastly greater jurisdiction of the latter courts. But the direct comparison of the expenses of similar cases under both systems of justice clearly demonstrates how inexpensive civil disputes became under JPs. At Brizambourg in 1788 a conflict over the sale and delivery of twenty livres of wine cost twenty-six livres; under the JP of Brizambourg in 1792 a conflict over the sale and delivery of sixty livres of

5. ADCM L 842. The JP handled more than three hundred civil cases in 1791.
6. Three cases for the regulation of accounts involved sums of more than one hundred livres; the object of the fourth case was the use of a marsh.
7. ADCM L 796 (3).
8. ADCM L 826 (2).

wine cost less than three livres.[9] In the same jurisdiction in 1787, a merchant's victorious request that a cultivator cease passing with his cattle resulted in forty-five livres in court expenses. When two cultivators from
Brizambourg litigated before the JP for the exact same reason in 1792, the
case was adjudicated for eight livres.[10] At Jonzac in 1788, an entrepreneur's
demand of *defense de passer* against a day laborer somehow cost fifty-five
livres despite the fact that the defendant defaulted. A request of *defense de
passer* from Jonzac in the Year II in which the defendant did not default
generated less than eight livres in expenses, which included the calling of
witnesses.[11]

As striking as the preceding examples of the inexpensive nature of civil
justice are, perhaps the greatest benefit of civil justice under the JPs for
people of the French countryside was the speedy termination of disputes.
Besides the obvious advantage of quick trials in allowing cultivators and
workers to dedicate their time to more productive endeavors, they also
contribute greatly to the individual's peace of mind as well as society's tranquility by rectifying injustices quickly and returning things to their rightful
relationship. The longer the status of someone's property, honor, or enjoyment of rights is in question, the longer it takes for a dispute to see its
resolution through official and accepted channels, the greater the likelihood
that the conflict will escalate, possibly into violence.

The importance of a conflict's quick resolution highlights the data on
the length of time it took JPs to adjudicate cases in revolutionary Charente-
Inférieure. In Jonzac, for example, the JP issued a total of 147 civil judgments in 1792.[12] Of those 147 judgments, 24 were preparatory, meaning that
a case's definitive termination awaited the presentation of some form of
proof (such as an account book), the interrogation of witnesses, or the
examination of the contentious site. The remaining 99 cases[13] witnessed
the following judgments: one case was thrown out of court, 6 cases were

---

9. ADCM B 2812 and L 796 (3), 2 September 1788 and 18 September 1792. Of course, the cases
are not exactly alike, and one may have involved witnesses. But the point is that they are similar
enough—both over a simple debt stemming from the sale and delivery of wine—to highlight how
the procedural differences resulted in wildly different costs.

10. ADCM B 2811 and L 796 (3), 3 August 1787 and 25 October 1792.

11. ADCM B 3088 and L 826 (2), 7 September 1788 and 3 sans-culottides II.

12. ADCM L 825.

13. The calculations, although not obvious at first, are quite simple: 147 total judgments minus
48 decisions for the 24 cases with preparatory judgments (such cases had a preparatory and then a
definitive judgment in the registers, or a total of 48 decisions) leaves 99 other cases.

forwarded to the appropriate jurisdictions (2 to district civil courts and 4 to family tribunals), 8 cases ended in the parties' conciliation, and 84 cases received adjudication on the spot. Combining definitive judgments with conciliations, 92 out of 123, or 75 percent, of disputes ended the very day the litigants entered the office of the justice of the peace in Jonzac. At Arsen-Ré, the JP adjudicated 99 of 111 cases on the spot in 1791 and 58 of 64 cases on the spot in 1792.[14] Here, the quickness of adjudication benefited from the practice of requesting that litigants appear with their proof at the initial court appearance, obviating preparatory judgments that called for the interrogation of witnesses or the presentation of evidence. It does not take a stretch of the imagination to remark that a peasant could expect to witness the resolution of a grievance the day he or she stepped into the JP's spartan office.

Even those cases not decided immediately by justices of the peace almost always experienced their definitive adjudication within a week or two after a second court date scheduled before witnesses or at the site of a property dispute. The researcher would be hard pressed to discover a case before the JPs of Charente-Inférieure not judged definitively within a month. At Jonzac in the Year II, a merchant's lawsuit against a cultivator requesting the reintegration of a path with his property began on 2 frimaire.[15] After a transport to examine titles and observe the path in question, the JP rendered his decision four days later, on 6 frimaire. A rather complex case on 14 nivôse in which one cultivator sued for the value of items left in a building sold to a second cultivator received its definitive resolution on 21 nivôse. A lawsuit begun 21 nivôse demanding the return of cut trees received its final adjudication after the plaintiff proved her case with witnesses on 28 nivôse. In a rare case requiring three sessions—the initial appearance of the parties on 8 germinal in which they stated their cases, the second in which witnesses testified for the litigants, and the third on 20 germinal in which the magistrate visited the disputed terrain—the JP still took less than two weeks to issue a decision.

The preceding examples, which one could multiply almost endlessly,

14. ADCM L 786 and L 787. These figures reflect the nature of the cases before the JP, the overwhelming majority of which involved debts or broken commercial conventions. Although one might be tempted to argue that the immediate adjudication of cases points to the high incidence of defaulting (since a judge could, and often did, issue a judgment by default after requiring the plaintiff's oath of the veracity of his or her claim), the records do not support this assertion. Only 37 of 111 cases were judged by default in 1791, and only 13 of 64 in 1792.

15. All cases in this paragraph are from ADCM L 826 (2).

suffice to suggest a general rule regarding the length of civil cases handled by justices of the peace: the overwhelming majority of *causes personnelles et mobilières* (themselves the majority of civil cases; see Table 21) witnessed immediate decisions; the vast majority of property disputes or complaints about damages terminated within a week or two of the initial court date after a visit to the site or the examination of witnesses. One scarcely needs reminding of the comparison with seigneurial courts, where even those simple local disputes that would have fallen under the JP's jurisdiction languished for months and often years.

Speedy and inexpensive justice under JPs, though certainly a desideratum of rural French people, was meaningless if the decisions of the new magistrates failed to terminate disputes. Thus, it is important to inquire about the quality of justice under JPs. If their decisions left a large number litigants dissatisfied and intent on appealing, then the new institution of local justice risked being insignificant at best (since people would have sought definitive judgments in district civil courts) and at worst an annoying waste of time and money. Under such circumstances, the revolutionary institution would have conspicuously resembled the system of local justice it was intended to replace and would have suffered from the absence of legitimacy and acceptance in the eyes of justiciables. After all, one of the most notable complaints about seigneurial justice was that the nearly universal practice of appeals rendered lords' courts a lengthy and costly, yet ultimately useless, obstacle to a conflict's final resolution.

Although determining the "quality" of justice is a difficult and inexact endeavor, at least one piece of evidence exists to suggest that the decisions of JPs satisfied most litigants, signifying that these magistrates did in fact put an end to the disputes before them. From 5 December 1791 through 18 March 1793 the District Tribunal of Marennes adjudicated 1,222 cases, including 153 cases on appeal.[16] The original tribunals of the cases appealed to the district court were as follows: 64 cases appealed from various seigneurial tribunals, 39 from former royal courts, 19 from justices of the peace (including 4 cases before the *police correctionnelle*), 7 from other district tribunals, 15 from family tribunals, 5 from *tribunaux de commerce*, and 4 from municipal police courts. That the decisions of seigneurial courts still clogged district courts well into 1793 reflects in part the complicated nature of the cases within those jurisdictions, but it may also hint at the quality of

16. ADCM L 479, L 480, and L 481.

TABLE 21 Civil Cases Before Justices of the Peace

	Ars-en-Ré 1791	Marans 1791	Marennes 1791	La Rochelle 1791	Brizambourg 1792	Ars-en-Ré 1792	Jonzac 1792	Marennes An II	Marennes An VI	Cozes An VI	Total
Debts/*Rentes*	76	44	39	186	46	40	59	49	64	45	548 (64%)
Property damages	2	—	2	17	2	2	10	22	5	1	63 (6%)
Boundary disputes	3	5	6	19	3	4	30	16	12	5	103 (10%)
Tenant repairs	3	1	3	2	3	1	2	2	1	1	19 (2%)
Failure to cultivate	—	—	1	7	—	—	—	4	1	—	13 (1%)
Salary disputes	14	1	6	18	12	4	7	11	5	5	83 (8%)
Assault & slander	9	4	2	30	9	6	12	13	6	a	91 (9%)
Total	107	55	59	279	75	57	120	117	94	57	920

Sources: ADCM L 894, La Rochelle, 1791; L 837, Marans, 1791; L 793.3 Brizambourg, 1792; L 786 and 787, Ars-en-Ré, 1791 and 1792; L 825, Jonzac, 1792; L 1411.1, Cozes, an VI; L 842, Marennes, 1792; L 867, Marennes, an II and an VI.

a The JP of Cozes handled all cases of assault and verbal injury through the *police correctionnelle*.

the justice in subaltern tribunals. More important, the figures here denote that few litigants appealed JPs' decisions. Considering that the justice of the peace of Marennes alone issued close to three hundred civil decisions in the year 1791, the fact that only fifteen civil decisions were appealed from seven cantons in a sixteen-month period testifies to the effectiveness of JPs in terminating disputes.[17] Of those fifteen appeals, five originated in Royan, three in Le Gua, three in La Tremblade, two in St. Pierre d'Oléron, and one in Soubise. Impressively, only one appellant came from the canton of Marennes despite the whirlwind of activity from that JP, and not a single litigant challenged a decision of the JP from Château d'Oléron, Bernard. For the most part, then, rural dwellers accepted the decisions of their local magistrates, which suggests that quick and inexpensive justice did not compromise quality.

The most tangible result of fast and inexpensive justice was that few people, regardless of their social status, were dissuaded from seeking redress of their grievances or from defending themselves before justices of the peace. Table 22 provides a list of the occupations or social status of litigants from four cantons in 1791.[18] Because of lacunae in the judicial records from Charente-Maritime, a direct comparison of the social status of litigants in seigneurial and revolutionary courts was not feasible, so the import of those figures remains clouded; in any case, the data probably suggest that more people from all social groups litigated before justices of the peace.

Although the mother lode of evidence that would have most obviously demonstrated the accessibility of the new tribunals of local justice—namely, a massive, downward shift in the social status of plaintiffs from 1788 to 1791—proved elusive in the face of archival lacunae, several more indirect, albeit still weighty, pieces of evidence point to the same conclusion. First, defendants' habit of defaulting, which was so marked in sei-

17. I do not know the total number of cases adjudicated by the JPs in the district of Marennes, but a very conservative estimate of fifty cases per canton would total six hundred cases per year when added to those from Marennes, or approximately 800 cases over a sixteen-month period. To be sure, the law forbade appeals for *causes personnelles et mobilières* of less than fifty livres. By including cases from June to December of 1791, the number of appealed civil decisions from justices of the peace to the district of Marennes was only seventeen for the twenty-two-month period covering June 1791 through March 1793.

18. After 1791 the Revolution's egalitarian strain compelled people engaged in agriculture to identify themselves as cultivators rather than according to the hierarchy of Old Regime rural society, which ran from *fermiers* to *laboureurs à boeufs* to *laboureurs* to *laboureurs à bras*. In addition, many people identified themselves simply as "citizen." Thus, the year 1791 is a brief window from which to observe the social status of litigants.

TABLE 22   The Social/Legal Status of Frequent Litigants

Status/Occupation	Plaintiffs	Defendants
Agriculture		
Fermier	6	3
Laboureur à boeufs	2	5
Cultivateur	66	46
Laboureur	39	65
Saunier	33	57
Laboureur à bras	11	4
Journalier	8	23
Doméstiques	12	4
Women		
Veuve	34	40
Femme/fille	8	15
Military/marine		
Soldat	0	2
Marinier	2	9
Artisans/merchants/shopkeepers		
Négociant	5	3
Merchant	41	42
Farinier/boulanger	39	27
Meunier	6	4
Charpentier	19	11
Aubergiste/cabaretier	17	5
Bourgeois/professionals		
Procureur/avocat	9	0
Bourgeois	8	11
Notaire	11	5
Propriétaire	8	8
Chirurgien	9	0

Sources: ADCM L 825, Jonzac, 1792; L 837, Marans, 1791; L 796.3, Brizambourg, 1792; L 842, Marennes, 1791; L 894, La Rochelle (canton), 1791; L 786 and L 787, Ars-en-Ré, 1791.

gneurial courts because of the fear of the costs associated with hiring a lawyer and the time requirements of litigating, ceased under justices of the peace. This meant that, whereas previously plaintiffs could often intimidate their opponents into submission by initiating a lawsuit, defendants could now appear in court and defend themselves against complaints. Hence, the use of litigation as a form of social control stopped, returning justice to its true function: to weigh the competing claims of equal parties. At La Rochelle in 1791, only 45 of 279 (16 percent) of civil decisions were issued by default.[19] Tellingly, whereas 77 percent of cases ended in default in the seigneuries de Ré in 1776, only 28 percent of defendants defaulted at Ars-en-Ré in 1791 and 1792.[20] People who had previously complained about "never peacefully possessing what is ours,"[21] whether because civil lawsuits were interminable or even too risky to undertake in the first place, could now rest assured that they could protect their rights and property in a court of law.

Second, the proliferation of civil cases in 1791, already mentioned in the previous chapter, signaled the opening of official channels of justice to people who had once been wary of taking their disputes to court. The JPs of both Marennes and La Rochelle adjudicated close to 300 civil cases in that year—quite remarkable feats. Whereas the seigneurial judge had rendered 8 decisions in 1765, 9 in 1771, 10 in 1776, 8 in 1785, and 7 in 1788, the JP of Jonzac issued 144 judgments in 1792 and another 125 in the Year II.[22] More extraordinary than the figures themselves is the fact that very few of the cases decided by seigneurial judges would have fallen under the jurisdiction of the justice of the peace. In other words, those same cases that JPs adjudicated by the dozens if not the hundreds never appeared on the dockets of seigneurial courts. For example, according to the register of sentences from the comté of Jonzac, only one case in 1785 and two cases in 1786 in that jurisdiction would have fallen into the JP's area of competence.[23] Thus, the revolutionary period witnessed the opening of justice to those simple disputes—especially broken commercial conventions among humble people involving minor sums—that had once remained outside official courts.

Finally, the proposed reforms of the justice of the peace in the revolu-

19. ADCM L 894.
20. ADCM B 2149, L 767 and 787.
21. ADCM C 26obis, *cahier* of parish of Conlonge.
22. ADCM B 3070, B 3076, B 3084, B 3087, B 3088, L 825, and L 826 (2). Of course, the canton of Jonzac would have included several former seigneurial jurisdictions (not just the comté of Jonzac), so one ought to multiply the number of cases judged prior to 1789 by a factor of, say, six or seven (allowing for one seigneurial court for every 1.5 communes). On the other hand, the jurisdiction of seigneurial courts was vastly more extensive than that of JPs, which means that they ought to have adjudicated many more cases than their revolutionary counterparts. The fact that, given roughly the same territory, JPs handled many more cases than seigneurial judges despite having jurisdiction over only a fraction of the latters' cases lends weight to the argument for the accessibility of justices of the peace.
23. ADCM B 3087. This fact explains the hesitance to compare directly, or to give too much weight to a direct comparison of, the civil cases before seigneurial and revolutionary courts of local justice. To simply compare the time and length of cases tells one little when the nature of cases differ.

tionary decade centered around many legislators' and jurists' belief that justice was *too* accessible under the new institution.[24] In an effort to frustrate habitual litigants and to prevent apparently insubstantial disputes from wasting magistrates' time (and to improve the quality of justices of the peace), some legislators proposed a diminution in the number of justices of the peace. Although such proposals raised questions about the benefits of accessible justice, they underscore the fact of the accessibility of justice under the new institution.[25]

THE MINIMIZATION OF STAKES

An analysis of a typical case of property usurpation from the canton of Ars-en-Ré in the Year IV demonstrates the significance of revolutionary changes to local justice.[26] In a summons issued on 3 frimaire, Charles Bourgeois constrained three cultivators—Benjamin Lebon, Etienne Deniot, and Charles Lagord—to appear before the JP in order to have them condemned to cease reclamation of a marsh property that Bourgeois claimed from an inheritance. The parties gathered before the JP, Jean-Baptiste Ventijol, and his assessors on 5 frimaire, but remained opposed in their respective *dires*. Unable to render a decision under such circumstances, Ventijol scheduled a visit to the *"lieux contentieux"* for 11 frimaire. Reassembled on that day with the four litigants and four *assesseurs*,[27] the JP explained the sequence of procedures leading to the decision:

> We proceeded with the visit and recognition of the property in dispute; we listened to their presentations and examined the title presented to us by Citizen Bourgeois, granted by the will of François Marie Bourgeois, his father, (with said title) signed by de la Fleutrie, *procureur*

24. See the discussion in Woloch, *The New Regime*, 318–19.

25. My view is that accessibility to justices of the peace was not harmful, because the cases ended quickly and with minimal costs. Hence, the accessibility of justice contributed to the rapid resolution of disputes but without straining the finances of litigants or distracting them from their ordinary business. A separate, more difficult issue is whether accessibility was a double-edged sword for the poor. Although it offered greater access to courts (for both plaintiffs and defendants), did it not also make it easier for creditors to force payment of legitimate debts for cases they had previously not bothered to pursue?

26. ADCM L 788 (5 and 11 frimaire IV).

27. Normally, only two assessors assisted a JP. I suspect that the other two accompanied Ventijol in this instance because of their surveying expertise.

général of the defunct Collège Mazarin and dated 27 May 1739. After having walked around and examined the property . . . we realized that the territory . . . appears entirely foreign to his [Bourgeois's] title, since the property spelled out in his lease comprises 1581 *arpents* but would be at least 2085 *arpents* including the disputed area. . . . We also observed that the portion of property taken by Lebon and the others has always been uncultivated as far as we could tell, which gives us reason to believe that the plaintiff's father never regarded this portion as a property included in that land conceded to him by the aforementioned title. And after all these considerations, we, justice of the peace, joined by the assessors signing below, declare Citizen Bourgeois unfounded in his claim of restitution.

Largely because of the procedural informality of revolutionary civil justice, a not insignificant conflict between four proprietors was resolved within eight days of the original summons. The beauty of justice in the fields, or *sur les lieux contentieux,* lay in more than just the rhyme; it allowed a JP, accompanied by unpaid but often expert assessors, to adjudicate a case quickly, inexpensively, and seemingly fairly.[28] Bourgeois may have been disappointed in the decision, but at least he was not ruined, nor had he wasted several years of his time. As for the victorious defendants, they may not have risked defending their position under the Old Regime, depending on their economic status. If they had chosen to litigate, would the justice of their cause or the quality of Bourgeois's legal team have been the crucial variable in the judge's decision?[29]

28. The decision does not list the expenses, which would have been greater than for most cases under justices of the peace because they would have included payment for the voyage of the JP, his clerk, and four assessors (for upkeep of their horses, the equivalent of mileage allowances today) as well as the cost of the summons and the paper. Still, the cost would have been greatly inferior to that of the same case under the Old Regime: no fees for lawyers, no written depositions, no payments to expert witnesses, no *épices* for the judge, no stream of legal documents resulting in massive paper costs. Even if the expenses had been listed for the case, the devaluation of the assignats would have made the figures difficult to interpret.

29. As other historians have noted, litigation was often an act of provocation in a dispute. See, for example, Greenshield, *An Economy of Violence in Early Modern France.* G. Brunelle has argued that commercial litigants used regular courts to pursue vendettas but Rouen's commercial court (*juridiction consulaire*) when they sought rapid, cheap, and high-quality justice. See "To Beggar Thy Neighbor or Not? Mediation Versus Vendetta in Commercial Disputes in Early Modern Rouen" (forthcoming). There are striking similarities between the Old Regime commercial courts and the revolutionary justices of the peace in terms of rationale (cheap and speedy justice), procedure (informal, with a prohibition on lawyers), and appeal (emphasis on mediation).

The function of adversarial civil litigation is to declare a winner and a loser in a dispute, to determine whose rights have been violated by ascertaining the truth surrounding a case (through the collection of facts) and applying the relevant laws. As such, any decision is bound to disappoint the losing party. But the rendering of a civil decision often does not signal the end of a dispute—in fact, it can add fuel to the fire—if the parties cling to the belief that the process of adjudication was unfair. Persisting in the idea that the judicial process is unjust, parties frequently execute justice themselves, with subsequent enormous consequences for social order.

Specifically, the main variables that contribute to a sense that the judicial process is unfair are a partial judge, the advantages conferred by wealth, and the obfuscating effects of pettifoggery employed by the lawyers of parties of bad faith. JPs, whose election represented a certain degree of public trust and whose salary eliminated the nefarious practice of accepting *épices*, were by and large immune to complaints about partiality in Charente-Inférieure. In any case, parties had the right to ask judges to recuse themselves from cases and could appeal most decisions in which they questioned the judge's impartiality. Furthermore, the presence of two elected *assesseurs*, wholly independent of the JP, aimed to ensure the impartiality of the magistracy, since they could and sometimes did outvote the justice of the peace.[30] The advantages of wealth were minimal before justices of the peace, since the low cost of litigating rarely dissuaded anyone from avoiding a session before a JP out of financial concerns. A trip to the local judge no longer required massive overhead or an intrepid (or foolish) peasant. Finally, the absence of opportunities for parties or their lawyers to manipulate judicial formalities guaranteed that the facts of a case could surface easily and that these facts would be the centerpiece of a judge's decision. Significantly, the absence of lawyers and judicial formalities made the parties themselves responsible for their own cases. Although clever people can always outwit less intelligent or less eloquent opponents, few litigants could now complain that their adversaries had somehow manipulated the judicial process to their advantage.

The practice of revolutionary local justice contributed to a phenome-

---

30. Legislators' biggest concern about the impartiality of JPs surrounded cases involving the kin of these officials. They also voiced concerns about the bias of JPs for people from their own communes. Problems of impartiality also existed in places with competing factions. In Jonzac, for example, there is evidence of a violent quarrel between the cliques of Ribeyron and Messin. Election records, should they be found, might shed light on the existence of local factions as well as their impact on the elections and functioning of justices of the peace.

non that may be called the minimization of stakes. Consistent with the nature of adversarial litigation, most revolutionary civil disputes ended with a winner and a loser (although JPs did try to find some middle ground, as is pointed out in the preceding chapter). However, unlike lawsuits under the Old Regime, which entailed serious investments of time and money, cases under justices of the peace witnessed their resolution quickly, inexpensively, and perhaps most important, in a manner that the parties deemed fair. Hence, a JP's legal decision involved minimal anxiety for litigants, it could scarcely ruin the losing party, and it tended to finalize the outcome of the dispute. Prior to 1789 a lawsuit often constituted a veritable declaration of war in a dispute—an attempt to destroy or intimidate one's opponent—and a maximization of the stakes involved in a conflict. With the inception of the revolutionary institution, a lawsuit, rather than being an "upping of the ante," represented a desire to protect one's rights, to restore things to their proper relationship. Thus, one witnesses a *journalier* in the canton of La Rochelle suing for forty sols (a highly unlikely occurrence under seigneurial justice) not from a burning hatred of an adversary but simply to claim legitimate wages due to him.[31]

Nowhere was the minimization of stakes more evident than in cases of *injures verbales* or *reparations d'honneur* before justices of the peace. In seigneurial courts, the involvement of lawyers in such cases led to the submission of voluminous legal briefs and exaggerated claims of injury as plaintiffs demanded massive, often outrageous, damages. In turn, the accompanying expenses and investment of time conspired to turn a minor verbal dispute, perhaps precipitated by a fit of anger or bout of drinking, into an affair with important consequences for a family or a neighborhood. Under justices of the peace, cases of slander usually ended quietly with a public apology, sometimes a small fine whose proceeds went to the poor, with a warning to avoid recidivism. The paltry expenses encouraged apologies, and the civil procedure offered no opportunity for a party of bad faith to manipulate the legal process by delaying a case or by threatening to make it too expensive for an opponent to pursue a grievance.

At Jonzac in 1793, for example, Marie Heard sued Pierre Chefnorry for *reparations d'honneur* and asked for fifty livres in damages and the publication of a favorable decision.[32] The case ended that very day when Chefnorry, accused of calling Heard a bitch and *une vilaine*, admitted that "[I] had the

31. ADCM L 894, 13 March 1791.
32. ADCM L 829, 30 October 1793.

weakness to utter the alleged offences, but [I] repent and offer my very humble apologies." Heard, "having declared that she didn't want to consume Chefnorry with expenses," agreed with the JP's request that she forego damages and accept the public exhibition of a single copy of her adversary's apology. Chefnorry then paid the twenty-five sols in expenses. At Ars-en-Ré in 1791, the merchant Joseph Amelineau sued Magdeleine Lapeau for accusing him of urinating on her wall.[33] He won his case, but the JP rightly saw no reason to award damages; Lapeau apologized and paid two livres for the expenses. The next year also in Ars-en-Ré, Michel Panchevre and Hughes Lamatte, representing the municipal officers and mayor of Les Portes, denounced the *fille* Homeneau for the "atrocious injury" of having called them *coquins*.[34] As is normal in such cases, the plaintiffs considered the offense very grave indeed, especially in the turbulent political climate in which public officials perceived all criticism as detrimental to their authority. Their complaint expounded on the respect they deserved when assembled to carry out their public charge, and they demanded that "she be punished according to the rigor of the law," which included a call for fifty livres in damages. In her defense, Mlle Homeneau admitted that she had used the insult in question, but that she had directed it to the workers who were installing a new window in a building owned by her mother (who rented it to the commune of Les Portes). Thus, she explained, a misunderstanding ensued when she reacted with an epithet to the high price of the window, since the communal officers thought she had referred to them. Homeneau then affirmed publicly her respect for the communal authorities. The JP accepted her story without the verification of witnesses, but fined her three livres (payable to the commune's poor) for using improper and indecent terms in front of the municipality. In this example, who won and who lost? The case is typical of how JPs handled verbal quarrels: the complainant received satisfaction in the form of a verification of respectability, yet the defendant was not punished excessively for a first offence. This defusing of quarrels, or the minimization of stakes, was a hallmark of the civil adjudication practiced by revolutionary justices of the peace.

Conclusion

The fundamental questions guiding the study of both Old Regime and revolutionary local civil justice in France have simply been, Who used the

33. ADCM L 786 (109).
34. ADCM L 787 (59).

system of justice and for what purposes? and, What was the process of adjudication like? Under justices of the peace, the answer to the first query is that anyone with a debt to collect, a claim of unpaid wages owed, a complaint about usurped or damaged property, or a grievance about a slight to one's honor—in other words, anyone with a perceived threat to his or her rights or with a complaint about a broken contract—hurried to the nearest cantonal seat to seek justice before the elected magistrate. Once suits were filed, rural dwellers presented their own cases, they engaged in open discussions in an informal atmosphere, they negotiated settlements with the JP and their adversaries, and ultimately they witnessed the resolution of their cases quickly and at minimal cost.

To say that all citizens used the system of civil justice to defend their rights is, at first glance, to flirt with a platitude. After all, the answer is very nearly contained within the question, since the purpose of civil justice is to provide an objective, outside forum for the protection of rights, the fulfillment of contracts, and the restoration of proper relationships in society.

But the significance of revolutionary local civil justice becomes readily apparent when juxtaposed with seigneurial civil justice. To the inhabitants of rural Aunis and Saintonge prior to 1789, the purpose of civil justice was only too clear. First, justice appeared to be a source of income for the many professionals involved. From the attorney who encouraged people to press their claims in court to the clerk who wrote in exaggeratedly large letters to inflate the cost of a writ to the magistrate who expected generous *épices* for a judgment, the process of adjudication seemed inverted under the Old Regime, with litigants serving to line the pockets of legal magistrates. Furthermore, a lawsuit, rather than simply representing the desire to have one's rights restored, sometimes constituted an act of vindictiveness, since a plaintiff could, by filing a suit, require an enemy to invest in a quarrel an amount of time and money vastly disproportionate to the value of the object in question. Under such circumstances, the system of justice aggravated, rather than resolved, the disputes that plagued rural France. Finally, as rural inhabitants knew all too well, lords and other elites used the justice system as a form of social control, with the threat of a lawsuit often sufficing to enforce compliance with their will. As the people of Landraye contended, a lawsuit was "a declaration of war." Now, threatened lawsuits are not ipso facto a form of oppression; in fact, they are often justly employed to force payment of legitimate debts or to compel the fulfillment of other obligations. But when the means of defense are beyond most people or when plaintiffs gain enormous advantages through their wealth—by hiring

more qualified legal professionals or, more insidiously, by bribing officials—then a threatened lawsuit does more than protect one's rights.

The relative inaccessibility of civil justice under seigneurial tribunals
pointed to the necessity of other means of solving disputes, optimistically
through the informal mediation of a respected community member or even
the entire community itself, or, pessimistically, through violence. In both
cases, the state stood far removed from the rural community and the operation of these informal channels of justice. After 1789, the existence of an
accessible magistrate to whom parties entrusted the resolution of their conflicts signified the triumph of official justice and helped lay the groundwork
for the penetration of the state into rural areas. As a public, elected forum
to which rural dwellers willingly submitted their conflicts over rights and
contracts and where litigants experienced the reality of equality before the
law, the institution of the justice of the peace was a schoolhouse of modern
citizenship.[35]

---

35. G. Bossenga has pleaded for historians to examine how the Revolution contributed to the
formulation of a new conception of citizenship. See her review article, "Rights and Citizens in the
Old Regime," *French Historical Studies* 20 (Spring 1997): 217–43.

CHAPTER 7

The Enemies of Trials

Justices of the Peace and the Experiment in Mediation During the French Revolution

Voltaire once wrote, in a passage praising Holland's preference for mediation as a form of dispute resolution, "If the parties arrive with a barrister and an attorney, one has them [the practitioners] removed first of all, just as one takes the wood out of a fire that one wishes to extinguish."[1] True to the agenda of that indefatigable critic of Old Regime institutions, Voltaire's words implicitly heaped calumny on the French system of civil justice for granting a central role to lawyers, a group whose very existence required conflict and, in fact, whose power and wealth actually increased with the prolongation of each conflict. After 1789, revolutionary legislators would concur with Voltaire's assessment, making the reform of civil justice a crusade against chicanery, the crucial battles of which centered around the treatment of the legal professionals.[2]

Revolutionary lawmakers in Paris—themselves mostly legal professionals—were so convinced of the nefarious effects of the involvement of lawyers in disputes that they deemed their prohibition from minor rural conflicts essential to meeting the demands of constituents concerning civil justice. If revolutionaries agreed with the declaration of the legislator Portalis that "the two principal sources of trials, as with all the other troubles that afflict society, are ignorance and passion,"[3] then their animosity toward the legal professionals who preyed on those passions becomes understandable. As Portalis lamented, "Once a party has fallen into the hands of a practitioner, it can no longer escape. This agent will have an interest in rendering all conciliation impossible."[4] To avoid this scenario, revolutionary

---

1. Cited in Séligmann, *La justice en France pendant la Révolution*, 395.
2. On the treatment of the legal professionals during the French Revolution, see Woloch, *The New Regime*, 321–54.
3. *Le moniteur universel* 27, 4 nivôse IV, 76.
4. *Le moniteur universel* 27, 4 nivôse IV, 77.

legislators required parties in minor civil disputes to represent themselves before a justice of the peace; in other words, lawyers were prohibited from all cases before this new institution of justice in the first instance.

Yet perhaps the most intriguing manifestation of the revolutionary commitment to the battle against chicanery, and hence to fostering a different social climate in rural France, was the creation of the *bureau de paix et de conciliation*. No litigant regardless of the nature or value of a lawsuit could have a case heard before a district civil court without a prior attempt at mediation before a *bureau de paix*, composed of the JP and his assistants in rural cantons.[5] Thus, revolutionaries envisioned the JP as much a conciliator who convinced parties to reconcile their differences amicably as a magistrate who pronounced judgments for those conflicts that could not be resolved without recourse to the formal judicial system. The legislator Pastoret exclaimed in the Council of Five Hundred in the Year IV:

> The justice of the peace should be a mediator, a consoler, an arbiter. . . . Besides, the institution of the justice of the peace is the tutelary justice of the countryside. The peasant approaches without fear a magistrate whom he knows, whom he has elected; he puts his trust in the latter's wisdom and probity; he enjoys seeking the latter's counsel, in opening his heart to him, in receiving from him the comforts of beneficence and friendship. Let us add that bad faith hardly ever makes an appearance.[6]

Portalis echoed Pastoret's view that the JP was foremost a conciliator, and he even borrowed the imagery of paternalism from his colleague: "Conciliation is their natural attribute; it is the very essence of the institution. The function of a JP in his territory imitates perfectly the function and concern of a father in his family."[7] Similarly, the legislator Treilhard exclaimed that "the JP is an arbiter, a father rather than a judge: he ought to see his true

---

5. District courts adjudicated disputes that exceeded the jurisdiction of the justice of the peace (for example, cases involving real property or cases whose object exceeded one hundred livres) and also heard cases on appeal from the JPs' jurisdiction. *Bureaux de conciliation*, composed of six persons chosen by the municipal council and including at least two lawyers, also existed in each district capital. These *bureaux* mediated cases for which the litigants came from different cantons. They were abolished in 1796, leaving the JP from the plaintiff's canton responsible for mediating between parties.

6. *Le moniteur universel* 27, 25 frimaire IV, 6.

7. *Le moniteur universel* 27, 4 nivôse IV, 77.

glory less in pronouncing decisions between his children than in conciliating them."[8]

Not everyone, however, shared legislators' sanguine expectations for the *bureaux de paix*. In particular, a letter from the JP of Marennes, Fontenelle, to the Departmental Directory of Charente-Inférieure was a bucket of pragmatic cold water in the faces of revolutionary idealists. For cases whose value or nature was outside the jurisdiction of the justice of the peace, Fontenelle wondered why the law commanded parties to appear before this magistrate anyway:

> It seems that no cases can be brought to the district tribunals without having passed through the . . . *bureaux de paix*. At the same time the laws limit the jurisdiction of the JPs to fifty livres without appeal and to one hundred livres with appeal for matters strictly *personnelles*. And according to the instructions of the JPs' code it is expressly stated that everything that exceeds this jurisdiction must be carried to the district tribunals.
>
> It appears that there is a contradiction in these two points. An individual who is owed five hundred livres [a figure outside the JP's jurisdiction] or a *rente foncière ou constituée* [i.e., a case of real property, therefore outside the JP's jurisdiction] of fifty or one hundred livres, etc. has no need to be conciliated with his debtor; his payment is the sole issue. Since this sum exceeds the jurisdiction of the JPs, the creditor ought to be able to go directly to the district tribunal.
>
> Nevertheless, the law wants to subject him to the *bureau de conciliation*? This intermediary would appear useless.[9]

The Directory issued a terse and angry rebuttal arguing that the creditor was not in fact obligated to litigate before the district tribunal but did so only out of litigiosity or an excessive adherence to his rights. In doing so, Fontenelle's superiors displayed a conception fundamentally different from his regarding the role and efficacy of mediation in society. Whose view was

8. Cited in R. Perrot, *Institutions judiciaires* (Paris, 1992), 50.
9. ADCM L 865, 26 January 1791. Justices of the peace did not have juridiction over cases involving real property. For mobile property (*causes personnelles et mobilières*), the JP decided cases worth up to fifty livres without appeal and up to one hundred livres on appeal. Fontenelle's point is that the law required the hypothetical litigant to first go to the JP for mediation even though the case exceeded the jurisdiction of the JP. That was precisely the revolutionaries' intention: the JP served as a *judge* in the minor cases that fell within his jurisdiction and as a *mediator* in those cases that fell outside it.

justified? Could required mediation actually prevent trials and thereby abate social hostilities in rural France, or was a forced attempt at mediation a waste of time that threatened to make revolutionary civil justice as frustrating as that of the Old Regime?

Solving disputes without formal, adversarial litigation is of course an antediluvian social practice and occurs every day among families, friends, and neighbors. Often, informal dispute resolution has received an institutional basis, whether in the reforms of Solon of Athens or the law code of the Visigoths.[10] Although one leading French historian claims that "arbitration in civil cases was not a widespread practice among our ancestors,"[11] several other scholars attest to this practice in Old Regime France, and a cursory combing of the notarial archives of Charente-Inférieure reveals that conflicts were sometimes settled by mediation or arbitration.[12] Consistent with its desire to promote fraternity, the Revolution's emphasis on mediation and arbitration essentially institutionalized in official dispute resolution a practice familiar to rural inhabitants.

Despite this significant shift in the nature of official justice fostered by the French Revolution, the radical experiment in informal dispute resolution has received scant attention from historians.[13] The goal in this study,

---

10. See J.-J. Clère, "L'arbitrage révolutionnaire: Apogée et déclin d'une institution (1790–1806)," *Revue de l'arbitrage* (1981): 3–28.

11. Clère, "L'arbitrage révolutionnaire," 4.

12. S. Reinhardt's *Justice in the Sarladais*, J. Dewald's *Pont St. Pierre*, and N. Castan's *Justice et répression en Languedoc* all cite the existence of informal networks of dispute resolution. However, the efficacy of such networks is difficult to determine. Reinhardt states that 9 percent of 477 criminal cases before the royal courts in the Sarladais from 1770 to 1790 mentioned some *attempt* at prior mediation. Also, historians suggest that "popular justice" was growing less attractive and successful in the late eighteenth century. Reinhardt notes that people increasingly sought recourse before royal courts from 1770 to 1790; N. Castan argues that the declining role of lords and priests as trusted mediators in Old Regime France left justiciables without recourse to inexpensive conflict resolution and therefore more dissatisfied with the French system of justice on the eve of the Revolution; and Y. Castan states that traditional, extrajudicial forms of dispute settlement became less effective with the erosion of community solidarity in the late eighteenth century. See *Honnêteté et rélations sociales en Languedoc*, 56.

13. Both J. Bart's and J.-L. Debauve's admirable studies treat the *bureaux de paix*, albeit briefly and based on small statistical samples. See Bart, "La justice de paix du canton de Fontaine-Française," and Debauve, *La justice révolutionnaire dans le Morbihan*. Forced arbitration for family matters, conducted under the auspices of the *tribunal de famille*, has received the most attention from historians. See J. F. Traer, "The French Family Court," *History* 59 (June 1974): 211–28; J. Forcioli, *Une institution révolutionnaire: Le tribunal de famille de Caen* (Caen, 1932); M. Ferret, *Les tribunaux de famille dans Montpellier* (Montpellier, 1926); Phillips, *Family Breakdown in Late Eighteenth-Century France*. For the revolutionary emphasis on arbitration in general, see Clere, "L'arbitrage révolutionnaire." Perhaps

then, is to give what is effectively the first in-depth look at the workings of rural *bureaux de paix*. Since studies treating the institution and its impact are nearly nonexistent, the questions guiding this chapter will be basic. How did the system of mediation operate? What went on during its sessions? How did parties react to it? And ultimately, how well did conciliation work? Rather than constituting merely a minor figure who handled the petty affairs of country people, the JP was a public servant who, through the institution of the *bureau de paix,* touched on nearly every civil case in France. With proper mediating skills and the trust and respect of his fellow citizens, the JP did in fact stand in a position to alter the social climate of rural France.

The Theory of Mediation and Arbitration

Civil law defines the rights of members of society and prescribes their mutual obligations.[14] When someone's rights have been violated or a dispute arises over the failure to meet social obligations, the parties attempt to resolve the dispute through the judicial system. In an adversarial system, the opposing parties hire trained legal specialists to represent them. In turn, these specialists follow carefully defined rules of procedure and submit their clients' evidence in the hopes of scoring "points." In theory, the truth becomes clear in this process of following prescribed forms of presenting evidence, allowing a judge (or, outside of France, a civil jury) to decide who wins or loses a case. In other words, justice is a matter of ascertaining the truth concerning the purported violation of someone's rights and deciding who was in the right and who in the wrong.

The advantages of such a system are manifest, for it clearly specifies the rights and reciprocal obligations of members of society, facilitating the resolution of problems when they do occur. Furthermore, in societies that demand legal equality, the following of defined legal forms in the administration of justice stands as a bulwark against arbitrariness. In this sense, the

---

Woloch's *The New Regime*, 307–20, offers the most comprehensive view of informal dispute resolution in this period.

14. The following, general discussion borrows freely from the work of A. Bevan, *Alternative Dispute Resolution: A Lawyer's Guide to Mediation and Other Forms of Dispute Resolution* (London, 1992); and a number of articles: E. Durkheim, "Types of Law in Relation to Types of Social Solidarity"; M. Weber, "Rational and Irrational Administration of Justice"; T. Eckhoff, "The Mediator and the Judge"; and T. Kawashima, "Dispute Resolution in Japan"; all in Aubert, *Sociology of Law.*

judge is merely the organ of rational and objective "Law," guaranteeing litigants that the justice system has acted impartially in the adjudication of their conflicts.

Despite the theoretical impartiality of the adversarial system, the complexity of laws of procedure and evidence and the susceptibility of judges (or civil juries) to the persuasion of effective orators mean that in practice one party can often increase the likelihood that the "truth" is on its side by purchasing the services of a skilled lawyer. Thus, the adversarial form of conflict resolution potentially gives birth to offspring that devour the parents, since the important role of money, or more derogatively the propensity for chicanery, often mocks the claim that justice is blind. Moreover, even if the truth becomes clear, ensuring that justice has in fact been served in a case, the designation of a winner and a loser after an adversarial legal battle frequently precludes future relations among the litigants, who might be family members, neighbors, or commercial partners. Although the adversarial system can effectively police the rights of members of society, it often does so at the expense of harmonious social relations.

In contrast, the conciliation of informal dispute resolution declares no winner or loser in a case; indeed, conciliation avoids discussion of the parties' respective rights, concentrating instead on their common interests and the benefits of a peaceful settlement of the conflicts. As such, the preservation of social harmony in the French countryside was the desideratum guiding the mediation practiced in the revolutionary *bureaux de paix*. Through this focus on common ground as well as the avoidance of an assignment of right and blame, mediation allows for the future cooperation of the arguing sides. And unlike the adversarial system where their fates are in the control of judges and lawyers, parties dominate the process of mediation and are therefore guaranteed control over the settlement. A mediated agreement is one that the parties voluntarily regard as in their best interests (if not altogether fair) while a litigated case, besides being risky because the outcome is in the hands of others, can be a Pyrrhic victory in light of the expenses, time, and ruptured relations associated with it.

In addition to preserving important social relations and putting disputants in control of their own settlements, mediation offers distinct advantages in its procedural informality and the confidentiality of the proceedings. Because revolutionary legislation barred written testimony and lawyers from the *bureaux de paix* (although critics argued that legal professionals were working behind the scenes anyway), the process of mediation avoided the complex rules of procedure and the input of legal experts that render litigation so time-consuming and expensive. Likewise, mediation does not involve the public airing of grievances and therefore grants parties an important measure of privacy.

The practice of mediation, with its goal of harmonious relationships and its concomitant deemphasis on conflict, obviously appeals to all members of a society who have a stake in maintaining peace and order. Similarly, by solving problems through the principle of equity, or a natural sense of fairness, mediation brings a healthy dose of good sense to a process of dispute resolution that frequently suffers from the putative manipulation of legal conventions by trained professionals. Still, for a society educated in the language of rights and contracts, mediation can cause discomfort. A sense of equity might command a creditor to negotiate a settlement with a debtor who, through no fault of his or her own (a natural disaster that destroys crops, for example), cannot fulfill his or her obligations. But the creditor, through rights guaranteed by statute law, is entitled to full repayment. Thus, mediation's focus on common interests and equity can sometimes conflict with individual interests and rights.

On a more practical level, mediation can prove disadvantageous in dispute resolution because it guarantees no resolution at all; if the parties fail to conciliate their differences the conflict often reaches the courtroom. In this case, mediation only increases the time and money needed to terminate a dispute, which is plainly antithetical to its original purpose. By forcing all disputants to attempt to conciliate their differences in a *bureau de paix* before proceeding to formal litigation in a district tribunal, revolutionary legislation risked adding another obstacle to the resolution of civil conflicts.

Finally, arbitration, a practice midway between mediation and formal litigation, constituted another form of alternative dispute resolution followed in the cantonal *bureaux de paix* during the French Revolution. Arbitration shares with mediation the procedural flexibility, and hence speed and reduced costs (although arbitrators' services are sometimes expensive), associated with the minimization of the role of legal professionals. And because the parties themselves agree on the arbitrators who will decide the case, they often place more trust in the resolution process than in litigating before a judge. On the other hand, arbitration mirrors the adversarial system insofar as an outside party decides between the competing claims of the disputants and declares a winner and a loser. While it does not entirely share the social and moral benefits of mediation, arbitration is an attractive alternative for parties concerned about the time and cost of a court trial.

THE REVOLUTIONARY PRACTICE OF MEDIATION AND ARBITRATION

Most JPs acted as mediators on a fixed day per week, say on every Tuesday; at Marennes in the Year VI the JP, Ranson, convened the *bureau de paix* on the fifth, fifteenth, and twenty-fifth of every month.[15] Thus, when one party indicated an intention to file suit, the potential litigants received a summons to appear either before the *bureau de paix* on one of those dates if the issue fell in the jurisdiction of the district civil court or before the JP (acting as civil judge) on another date if the case belonged to his jurisdiction. Also, parties seeking conciliation could appear voluntarily at the *bureau de paix* and receive a free settlement regardless of the nature or value of litigation. Almost every conciliation, then, was one fewer case to reach the dockets of the district civil courts. At Marennes in the Year VI, Ranson successfully conciliated various cases, thereby preventing these disputes from reaching the district court. The issues involved were 500 francs over damages to salt marshes, 435 francs for various merchandise, the proprietorship of a house, the reduction in interest on a loan of 28,000 francs, 267 francs as income from one-quarter ownership of a mill, and so on.

On 17 ventôse in the Year III, André Doussin (on behalf of his son, who was ill) and several Abelin brothers appeared voluntarily before the *bureau de paix* of the canton of Marennes. Doussin claimed that trees bordering his son's side of a ditch were cut down by the Abelins. The latter rejoined that the trees were their property, since they were situated in the ditch, of which they were sole proprietors. In a move indicative of the style of justice practiced in rural France during the Revolution, the JP, "thinking that if [he] was at the location it might be possible to conciliate the parties," suggested that he and his *assesseurs* visit the site of contention. "At this point the Abelins proposed to the elder Doussin that, *in order to avoid all contestation,* his son cede his land to them, which Doussin accepted if they would pay twelve hundred livres and providing he could obtain his son's consent within twenty-four hours; the Abelins subsequently agreed to this, and we have sent the parties before the notary that they deem appropriate

15. ADCM L 864. These were large sums that greatly exceeded the JP's jurisdiction, the point being that these mediators often did prevent complicated cases from reaching district civil courts.

in order to draw up the contract."[16] This example shows the *bureau de paix* working as envisioned by its revolutionary creators. Although the willingness of the parties to find a settlement was the main thrust behind the resolution of the dispute, it seems likely that the mediating intercession of the JP and his willingness to be transported to the cite facilitated the process.

The crucial variable in the success of mediation is, of course, the parties' own motivation to reach a peaceful accord;[17] still, the existence of a trusted and respected third party is required in order to suggest potential solutions, to interject objectivity when passions arise, and to help overcome inevitable impasses. The records of the *bureaux de paix* of Charente-Inférieure give ample testimony to both the good faith of people seeking an alternative to formal litigation and to the useful services of the mediating JPs. At Ars-en-Ré, for example, the *cultivateurs* Verdon and Mounnier engaged in a property dispute quite representative of rural areas.[18] By a notarized contract from 1795, Verdon claimed to have acquired some land, including a garden, which Mounnier supposedly usurped. Mounnier admitted to working on the garden, but he was under the impression that it was included in the inheritance he had received from his parents, although he could not find the title. In order to avoid a lawsuit (which he would probably lose without a title to the property; did the JP make this clear to him during the conciliation session?), Mounnier promised to abandon the territory. Significantly, Verdon recognized the injustice posed by depriving Mounnier of the fruits of his labor, so he agreed to divide in half the garden's eventual harvest.

In another case from Ars-en-Ré, Francois Baudet and Jean Boisseau cited an adversary to appear before the *bureau de paix:*

> [Baudet and Boisseau] said that they gave four barrels of white wine to Jacques Guillon . . . in exchange for four bushels of wheat, which Guillon has refused to pay. And the said Guillon also appeared and confirmed the preceding information but observed that it was unfortunate for him to be obliged to pay the four bushels of wheat considering the

16. ADCM L 861. Emphasis added. *Assesseurs* were elected and unpaid assistants, two of whom normally assisted a JP in any given case.

17. For an overview of the variables determining the effectiveness of mediation, see K. Kressel and D. Pruitt, eds., *Mediation Research: The Process and Effectiveness of Third-Party Intervention* (San Francisco, 1989), especially 394–435.

18. ADCM L 793, 28 brumaire IV.

flooding and total loss of his building and the wine stored therein. Wanting nothing whatsoever to do with a trial, he desired to make some appropriate arrangements. After discussing the said arrangements, it is desired by the parties that: Guillon will be required to return within one month three barrels of quality white wine to the plaintiffs . . . who will abandon their claim to the fourth; furthermore, the promise of the payment of wheat will be annulled.[19]

What motivated Baudet and Boisseau to renounce their right to enforce Guillon's fulfillment of a legitimate contract? Were they guided by a sense of sympathy for his misfortunes? Were they friends or business partners for whom a harmonious settlement was necessary in order to ensure future friendship or commerce? Or were their motives less lofty, revolving not around concerns of equity, harmony, and sympathy but rather around the belief that the arrangement was better than the alternative, preferring the recoupment of three barrels within a month to the delayed repayment of four after a possibly long, expensive, and vexatious trial? Because of the strictures of confidentiality and minimizing paperwork, the records of the *bureaux de paix* often provide little insight into the motives of parties (the aforementioned motives are not mutually exclusive). But the important fact remains that through the *bureau de paix* the JP helped solve immediately and at minimal charge a potentially divisive problem in his rural canton.

Yet another example from Ars-en-Ré exhibits the amalgam of goodwill and pragmatism that frequently guided successful mediation. In this case, Alexis Raynaud brought Réné Berthommé (as the guardian of Entrope Berthommé) before the *bureau de paix,* signifying his intention to litigate over 130 livres for the increase in rent authorized by a contract from 1773. Berthommé recognized the legitimacy of Raynaud's claim but lamented that, because Entrope's endowment amounted to only forty livres per year, he was currently incapable of paying the 130 livres. Raynaud expressed satisfaction over the official acknowledgement of the debt (which would facilitate subsequent litigation if necessary) and exclaimed that "his charity persuaded him to await the fortunate moment when [Berthommé] will be able to pay in part or in full."[20]

Notwithstanding the charity and noble sentiments of parties, the ma-

19. ADCM L 792, 7 ventôse IV.
20. ADCM L 791, 1 July 1791.

jority of successfully mediated cases in rural Charente-Inférieure seem to have resulted from the desire to avoid a trial, whether "trop minutieux" or "trop dispendieux." On 25 frimaire Year IV in Gemozac, François Heard and Jean Tarin sparred acrimoniously over their mutual obligations. Heard requested nine bushels of grain for work he had performed on his adversary's behalf. Tarin, meanwhile, insisted that he owed Heard nothing, having executed their contract in its entirety; rather, Heard owed Tarin payment for the taxes on property that Tarin leased to him. The JP initially declared the failure of his efforts at mediating the parties, who persisted in their respective demands. However, after reminding Heard and Tarin of the likely fruits of their intransigence, the JP added: "Upon further reflection the parties, having considered that a *non conciliation* would subject them to an expensive trial, relaxed their claims toward one another."[21]

Although the pronounced desire among certain people to avoid formal litigation strikes one accustomed to a litigious culture as a breath of fresh air, critics of mediation contend that such a decision carries with it the price of the renunciation of rights. Again at Ars-en-Ré, the widow of Etienne Dervieux argued that, before his death, her husband had ceded half of a property to Pierre Bourgeois in return for 115 livres. Bourgeois acknowledged the veracity of Dervieux's claim but added that he had already paid one hundred livres of the amount. "Wishing to avoid and terminate all contestation with Bourgeois," Dervieux accepted the final fifteen-livre installment.[22] Shortly thereafter, she cited Jean Bourgeois before the *bureau de paix* for the return of two large barrels loaned by her husband at the previous harvest. Bourgeois replied that he had actually purchased the barrels from Etienne Dervieux for the price of forty-five livres. The widow expressed surprise at the news, but, after another explicit vow to avoid a court of law, declared her satisfaction with Bourgeois's oath that he had paid Dervieux for the barrels. Did Mme Dervieux renounce her rights as a legitimate creditor in these cases, or did she simply use the *bureau de paix* to compensate for her husband's incompetent bookkeeping, obtaining through it an inexpensive and quick updating of his accounts?

The preceding cases involved types of disputes that *bureaux de paix* were best able to mediate successfully: quarrels over relatively uncomplicated commercial conventions, disputes over unpaid debts, and the notoriously divisive arguments between neighbors over property. As such, it is

21. ADCM L 1436.2.
22. ADCM L 792, 29 thermidor II.

fair to argue that this revolutionary institution did contribute to an improved social climate in rural France by preventing the ebullition of animosity and recrimination stemming from minor affairs. On a more pragmatic level, each successful conciliation was potentially one less case crowding the dockets of district civil courts.

In addition to handling such cases, *bureaux de paix* could sometimes prove effective forums for the conciliation of two other important categories of rural disputes, the first of which was the ubiquitous verbal insult. The modern reader, confronted with the proliferation of cases of libel, slander, and verbal threats in the judicial archives, tends to attribute this to the pettiness or irrationality of the country dwellers of eighteenth-century France, whose insistence upon pursuing such quarrels through expensive legal channels represents the proverbial cutting off of the nose to spite the face. Yet it is crucial to recall that a person's honor was perhaps the most prized possession in the ancien régime, not only for its moral significance but also because a person's economic well-being frequently depended on others' perception of his or her upstanding character.[23] Thus, Pierre Bernard's appearance before the *bureau de paix* of Ars-en-Ré in order to demand reparations to the honor of his deceased wife, whom Véronique Caillard accused of being a habitual thief of beans, seems silly without an acknowledgment that both his social standing and his business concerns necessitated a reputation for honesty.[24] Caillard, pleading that she had only succumbed to a momentary fit of anger, promised not to repeat the slander and swore that Bernard's spouse had been a woman beyond reproach. Here, Bernard experienced satisfaction over the public avowal of his wife's (and his own) probity, while Caillard was able to admit her mistake and offer apologies without the investment of time and money that such cases of slander required under seigneurial justice.[25] The speedy and nearly cost-free resolutions of cases of verbal insults that abound in the records of the

23. On the significance of honor in Old Regime society, consult Y. Castan, *Honnêteté et rélations sociales en Languedoc*; Farge, *La vie fragile*; and Garrioch, *Neighborhood and Community in Paris*.

24. ADCM L 792, 27 germinal III. This seemingly minor affair appeared before the *bureau de paix* for one of two reasons. Either Bernard requested more than one hundred livres in damages, which placed the case in the jurisdiction of the district court, or the parties arrived voluntarily in search of the JP's mediation.

25. Under seigneurial justice, cases of slander and libel were subjected to such long and costly processes of adjudication that they often escalated into bitter affairs with major repercussions for a family, neighborhood, or village. See Chapter 2.

bureaux de paix highlight the stark contrasts between the administration of local justice under lords' courts and under the justices of the peace.[26]

The second additional category of disputes for which the *bureaux de paix* proved useful was the family quarrel. The involvement of *bureaux de paix* in family matters dated from the Year III, for prior to that time most civil suits concerning family members were settled by forced arbitration before *tribunaux de famille*.[27] The de facto abolition of this institution in 1795 meant that interfamily disputes now followed the path of all other civil litigation, the first step of which was the attempt at conciliation before a *bureau de paix*. If the JP's role was that of a restorer of harmony in the French countryside, few things could be of greater interest than preventing the conflagration of internecine struggles. The JP, as a benevolent yet disinterested mediator, could indeed embody the paternal role envisioned by its revolutionary creators.

Ideally, revolutionary legislators and rural JPs would have preferred family disputes to be solved in the same way as was the problem in the Bucheraud family in the Year IV. The conflict between Henry Bucheraud and his sons, Jacques and Pierre, stemmed from the division of property from the estate of Jeanne Sorignet, the wife of Henry and the mother of Jacques and Pierre—a type of dispute constituting one of the most common sources of litigation among rural inhabitants. Although the law authorized the sons to proceed with the execution of Sorignet's will, the JP persuaded them to consider their duties toward their father: "[Pierre and Jacques] realized the injustice committed by them in depriving a father in his old days of the property that helps him live . . . and wanting to give to him proof of the filial sentiments that animate them, they declare that they will not only abandon the property bequeathed by their mother but also

26. To be sure, district civil courts and the departmental criminal tribunal still judged many cases of slander, libel, and verbal threats, and Bernard could still go to court for damages if he wished to punish Caillard. The point here is that there was now a significant alternative available to Bernard.

27. Revolutionary laws required certain degrees of relatives (husbands and wives, parents and children, brothers and sisters, for example) engaged in disputes over certain issues (inheritances, divorce settlements, and so on) to arbitrate the case before a *tribunal de famille*. In theory, each party selected two arbitrators from among family or friends and agreed upon a fifth arbitrator in the event of a split decision. Clearly, the goal was to make families solve their own problems in an informal and confidential setting. In practice, parties selected lawyers instead of family members as arbitrators. Thermidorean legislators, wary of the threat to one's rights posed by *forced* arbitration, remained silent on the institution in the Constitution of the Year III and therefore issued its death warrant for all intents and purposes. See Traer, "The French Family Court."

renounce the division of *acquêts* [property jointly acquired by the parents]."[28] The Bucheraud brothers promised not to divide their inheritance until after their father's death. Henry, touched by the loving decency of his children, accepted their sacrifice only on the condition that he would not be a bother to them and finally swore to live with them "with the intelligence and the harmony appropriate for a family."

Perhaps the paramount reason for successful family conciliations was the desire for people to keep their arguments secret. At Gemozac, for example, M. Perreau arrived at the *bureau de paix* on behalf of his wife, Magdeline Richard, to demand three *pochées* of grain as indemnity for work that she had performed for her brother. François Richard verified that his sister had aided him but stated that his reciprocal assistance rendered three *pochées* too high a price for recompense; he offered to pay her six *boisseaux*. The siblings, "wanting to keep their business secret [*ne voulant point donner de connaissance à leur affaire*]," requested that the JP, Ollivaud, suggest an equitable solution and agreed to abide by it. After obtaining all the relevant information regarding the dispute, Ollivaud considered a payment of nine *boisseaux* a fair price. This case demonstrates not only the significant trust that parties exhibited toward the JP's intelligence and fairness but also the importance that some families attached to the confidentiality of their problems.

The obvious and beneficial opportunity for discretion guaranteed to families by the *bureaux de paix* is underscored by a peculiar case from Jonzac in the Year IV.[29] Here, François Laroche and Charles Barraud were conciliated over the problem that separated them: Laroche's wife, Marie Roux. After Laroche's serving eighteen months in the republican army, the joy that he felt over his homecoming to Jonzac was mitigated by his wife's pregnancy—evidently at the hands (so to speak) of Barraud, for whom Roux worked as a servant. In the interests of avoiding a public scandal, Laroche and Barraud—there is no sign of Roux's wishes or involvement in the settlement—accepted the following solution mediated by the JP: (1) Barraud will admit that he is the father of Roux's child; she will continue to stay with Barraud, who will be responsible for her upkeep, until fifteen days after she gives birth; (2) Barraud will nourish and raise the child as if from his own marriage; (3) Barraud will pay Laroche one thousand livres in *assignats* as damages; and (4) Barraud will desist from further activity

28. ADCM L 1435.2, canton of Gemozac, 5 ventôse IV.
29. ADCM L 1227, 13 vendémiaire IV.

with Roux. Apparently, Barraud's (and Roux's?) failure to observe the fourth clause brought him trouble, for Laroche's subsequent complaints about Barraud's continued debauchery resulted in a criminal investigation.

To parties unable to reach a mediated settlement yet desirous of a definitive decision in their dispute, JPs frequently suggested arbitration as an alternative to a formal lawsuit. Some JPs resorted to arbitration fairly soon after the inception of the institution of the justice of the peace in 1790—the JP of Jonzac settled seventeen cases through arbitration in the Year II[30]— but its increasing use dated from the Year III, when the abolition of the *tribunaux de famille* apparently brought the arbitration of family quarrels to the *bureaux de paix*. Furthermore, the degree to which JPs used arbitration was probably a reflection of the magistrates' personal preferences; Ventijol, the JP at Ars-en-Ré, was a skilled conciliator who very rarely employed arbitration, while the JP at Gemozac in the Year VI, Ollivaud, seems to have encouraged arbitration much more than mediation as a means of informal dispute resolution.

Ollivaud's talent for persuading parties to agree to arbitration stemmed from his understanding that the innumerable cases of rural property disputes benefited more from informal discussions on the spot than from adhering to complicated and expensive procedures in a court of law, since such arguments centered more on facts (easily ascertained at the site) than on points of law (argued by legal professionals before a judge). If parties agreed with Ollivaud that their case was well suited to arbitration, Ollivaud presided over the selection of arbitrators and then, significantly, convinced the disputants to renounce their right to appeal the arbitrators' decision. At that point, the arbitrators were free to gather the requisite information before rendering a decision.

In a case in which the parties selected Ollivaud and his *assesseurs* as the arbitrators, Marie Peronneau cited Jean Potet and Paul Birot before the *bureau de paix* for *troubles de jouissance de son possession* (the defendants habitually trespassed on her property and took wood while on the way to their fields).[31] The arbitrators, accompanied by a surveyor, promptly visited the location, where they asked neighbors about the argument, read the parties' respective property titles, did the surveying, placed appropriate boundaries between the properties, and oversaw the division of the dis-

---

30. ADCM L 826(2).
31. ADCM L 1435.2, canton of Gemozac, 6 floréal IV.

puted wood. In this efficient manner Ollivaud brought an end to the case on 4 prairial IV, less than one month after Peronneau's original complaint.

The cost of Peronneau's arbitration is not known, but in general the informality of the procedure—no written depositions, no costs involved in bringing witnesses to court, and so on—ensured that the expenses involved in arbitration remained lower than those of formal litigation. Pierre Cramich and François Porcq, engaged in a dispute over whether Porcq possessed the right to pass on Cramich's property with his wagons and livestock, expressed their understanding of the savings of time and money involved in arbitration when they transferred their lawsuit from the District Tribunal of Pons to arbitration under the JP of Jonzac.[32]

Arbitration also sometimes saved parties time and money by placing the dispute directly in the hands of people, whether technically trained experts or friends and neighbors knowledgeable about the quarrel, qualified to offer a judgment, thereby obviating the expensive involvement of attorneys. For example, Jean Roudier's case against Pierre Métraud for *légion d'outre moitié du juste prix* was correctly identified by Ollivaud as perfectly suited for arbitration, since Roudier and Métraud selected as arbitrators experts capable of determining the just value of property in 1786.[33] If the litigants had gone to court, their lawyers would have hired such expert witnesses anyway. Thus, by agreeing to arbitration, Roudier and Métraud circumvented the costly intervention of legal professionals.

Finally, as one might expect, many family arguments were settled by the path of arbitration in the *bureaux de paix*. In fact, this institution probably constituted an improvement over the *tribunaux de famille* for the resolution of family disputes, since it offered arbitration as an alternative to formal litigation but did not force this option on litigants concerned about their rights or absolutely unwilling to settle a problem amicably. At Gemozac, Marie Georjon, preferring solitude to living "incessantly at war," filed the following complaint and divorce request against her husband, Jean Potet: "[His] disposition is so incompatible with hers that it is no longer possible to remain in his company. He is so violent that he allows himself to give her angry blows, that it is nothing for him to overwhelm her with

32. ADCM L 826.2, 8 messidor II. The JP and his *assesseurs* called for a *transport* and rendered their decision on 12 messidor.

33. ADCM L 1435.2, canton of Gemozac (n.d.; Year IV?). French law permitted the annulment of contracts if the price was less than one-half of the "just" price. In this example, Roudier contended that his sale in 1786 of a minute slice of land to Métraud for thirty livres constituted such a case.

verbal outrages, that he strikes her in the most cruel fashion."[34] Potet, after blaming Georjon for their frequent animated "discussions," expressed his sadness over his wife's motion but vowed not to interfere if she persisted in her desire for a divorce. The JP's employment of "all our means of mediation to persuade Georjon to remain with her husband" exhibits the degree to which his paternal goal of preserving families might come at the expense of a woman's personal safety. Although Georjon rejected the attempts at conciliation, she did agree to subject the divorce settlement to arbitration.

Whom did parties choose to arbitrate their cases? The question is important because a contemporary criticism of revolutionary informal dispute resolution contended that, despite the effort to minimize the role of lawyers, legal professionals still dominated the dispute process by acting as arbitrators or by counseling clients behind the scenes of the *bureaux de paix*.[35] Although the infrequent mention of the names and occupations of arbitrators in the archives of Charente-Inférieure precludes a quantitative analysis, one can cautiously proffer the following information. First, parties did often choose neighbors and friends to arbitrate their disputes, but those neighbors and friends just as frequently renounced their commission. Second, despite the indisputably significant role played by legal professionals in arbitration, evidence suggests that litigants selected notaries and surveyors even more frequently, demonstrating a desire for technical expertise (especially in suits concerning property) over legal expertise. Finally, the recurring choice of the JP and his *assesseurs* as arbitrators highlights the trust that rural dwellers placed in these officials—a trust crucial to the success of informal dispute resolution and indicative of the revolutionary institution functioning as envisaged by the National Constituent Assembly that created it in 1790.

Despite the evidence demonstrating the efficacy of the *bureaux de paix* and the valuable services they rendered to rural inhabitants, this revolutionary institution was no panacea capable of terminating all quarrels amicably

---

34. ADCM L 1436.2, 6 fructidor IV.

35. According to E. Séligmann, the minister of justice in 1792 claimed that the *bureaux de paix* were not functioning as planned because of the *"ruse des practiciens"* (i.e., lawyers representing clients despite their prohibition from the *bureaux de paix*). The minister may have been referring to the district (urban) *bureaux*, abolished in 1796, more than the rural *bureaux*. Similarly, contemporaries complained, and modern research has corroborated the suspicion, that parties before the *tribunaux de famille* selected legal professionals as arbitrators more often than family members or friends, which conflicted with the spirit of the revolutionary conception of the institution. See Phillips, *Family Breakdown in Late Eighteenth-Century France*, especially 19–28.

before they reached a court of law (Table 23). The variables leading to a failure of conciliation are both myriad and notoriously difficult to isolate, but they generally fall under three large rubrics: the attitude and skill of the mediator, the attitude of the parties, and the nature of the disagreement.

The procedural simplicity and desire for celerity in dispensing justice leave the records from the *bureaux de paix* reticent regarding the JPs' mediating skills. While the reelection of JPs and their frequent selection as arbitrators might signify popular approbation of the conciliatory activities of some JPs, there exists evidence that other magistrates were less successful in, or unenthusiastic about, mediating between parties.[36] At Pons, for example, the justice of the peace successfully mediated only eight of eighty-six cases brought before the *bureau de paix* from February 1791 through September 1792 (Table 23). Of course, a 9 percent success rate failed to correspond to revolutionary expectations of altering rural social relations, but more seriously, it also condemned the *bureau de paix* at Pons as a burden on the time and money of most litigants. Was the JP, Gout, a poor mediator, possibly because as a former attorney he did not possess the proper disposition or share Parisian legislators' belief in the sanctity of the

TABLE 23   The Activity of Cantonal Bureaux de Paix

JP	Date	Not Conciliated	Conciliated	Agree to Arbitrate
Pons	2/91–9/92	78	8	—
Pons	Floréal II–frimaire III	20	10	—
Ars-Ré	3/91–mesidor II	41	60	—
Ars-Ré	Floréal IV–thermidor VI	7	20	—
Marennes	1791	24	10	—
Marennes	Vendémiaire II–fructidor III	26	10	—
Marennes	An VI	45	12	6
Gemozac	An VI	65	13	34
Cozes	An VI	78	20	14
Total		384	163	54

SOURCES: ADCM L 1464 and 1466, Pons; L 791–93, Ars-en-Ré; L 858, L 861, and L 864, Marennes; L 1435.2 and L 1436.2, Gemozac; L 1411.2, Cozes.

36. If the reelection of JPs signifies in part rural dwellers' satisfaction with these new magistrates, it is worth noting that forty-two of fifty-three JPs in Charente-Inférieure won reelection in 1792. I suspect that most of the eleven new JPs won open seats. For example, in the district of Saintes, six of nine incumbents were reelected. Two of the three new JPs won open seats, meaning that only one incumbent was unseated in Saintes. See *Ephémerides du département de la Charente-Inférieure.*

mediating mission? Or was Gout a victim of Pons's status as an important legal town in the Old Regime, which pitted his attempts at mediation against a swarm of attorneys who counseled clients about their rights and convinced them not to mediate?

Similarly, Fontenelle's letter to the Departmental Directory in 1791, already mentioned in this chapter's introduction, in which he questioned the efficacy of the *bureaux de paix* in conciliating certain cases (uncontested debts, for example) suggests that his efforts at mediation may have been halfhearted. The archival records, which contain numerous examples of payment schedules worked out and interest payments foregone after conciliatory sessions before the JP, seemingly justify the Directory's optimism about the potential of mediation as a form of dispute resolution. But the crucial point here is that Fontenelle's strictly legal interpretation of the case of the hypothetical creditor revealed an attitude that clashed with the Directory's view of the paternal conciliator. His objections to conciliation may have exposed him as an uninspired mediator, at least in the beginning of his tenure.[37]

Often, it made little difference whether or not the JP possessed the disposition of an effective conciliator, for the parties themselves expressed no willingness to find common ground. At times this unwillingness stemmed from a reluctance to back off of one's rights. At Pons in 1791, the former steward of the prieuré de St. Martin de Pons, Fleury, constrained the carpenter Libron to appear before the *bureau de paix* for exhibition of contracts and payment of seigneurial dues.[38] Libron admitted the legitimacy of the debt but, lacking the present means to repay Fleury, requested his creditor's continued forbearance. Fleury stated that he had already waited long enough and insisted on pursuing his lawful rights in a district court, a move that may have resulted in a foreclosure on Libron's property.

At other times the unwillingness to conciliate resulted from the parties' refusal to admit the existence of common ground, interpreting their dispute not as a misunderstanding whose solution lay in meeting halfway but rather as a matter of principle, of right and wrong. Witness, for example, the attitude of the notary Tourneur after an M. Pelisson cited him before the *bureau de paix* of Cozes, threatening to sue for damages and interests over the failure to produce a copy of an inventory that Pelisson needed in order

37. Table 23 gives the data for 1791 in the *town* of Marennes, whose JP was Marguard; Fontenelle was the JP of the *canton* of Marennes.
38. ADCM L 1457.1, 3 September 1791.

to claim an inheritance. Tourneur, rather than representing himself before the JP, sent the *fondé de pouvoir* (essentially a euphemism for a lawyer—technically forbidden to represent clients at the *bureaux de paix*—although it could signify any proxy) Verger to appear on his behalf. And instead of seeking grounds for reconciliation with Pelisson, Tourneur's proxy exclaimed in a contentious tone, "The demand of said Pelisson is an act of pure chicanery, the complete proof of which lies in the dishonest and unfaithful oral account on which it is based."[39] Not only did the disputants differ strongly about the facts of their case, which was itself a major obstacle to conciliation, but Tourneur's insistence on emphasizing the moral aspects of the conflict signified his desire to see an authorized judge declare the injustice of Pelisson's demand in a court of law. For parties stressing the legal, moral, or ideological sides of a conflict, slaking the thirst for justice brought greater pleasure than the gentler benefits of mediation.[40]

The final factor in the failure of mediation in the rural *bureaux de paix*, one closely related to the attitude of the parties, was the nature of the dispute. As was seen previously, when litigants disagreed strongly over the facts of their case, little recourse was left except to ascertain the truth in a civil court. Similarly, conflicts usually reached courts of law if they centered around the concept of justice or complicated legal issues. In addition, two specific types of cases stemming from the revolutionary situation itself proved troublesome for mediators. First, disputes over the payment of seigneurial dues were commonplace in the *bureaux de paix* but were rarely conciliated (and rarely paid even after a court decision), apparently as part of the peasant strategy to declare the illegitimacy of seigneurialism by refusing to pay even those dues authorized by revolutionary laws.[41] A large percentage of the failed conciliations at Pons in 1791 and 1792 reflected the obstinacy of peasants in the face of seigneurial obligations. Second, the abolition of the Maximum Law on 24 December 1794 as well as the precipitous devaluation of the *assignat* gave rise to mountains of disputed commercial contracts. At Ars-en-Ré, the merchant Bernard refused to be conciliated for five consecutive cases on 22 pluviôse III, since the repeal of

39. ADCM L 1411.2, 29 ventôse VI.
40. See T. Eckhoff, "The Mediator and the Judge," 180, in V. Aubert, *Sociology of Law*. Eckhoff calls mediation the "de-ideologization" of conflict.
41. See Luc, *Paysans et droits féodaux*. Although feudalism was putatively abolished after the Night of August 4, 1789, lords received indemnification for most seigneurial dues. In Charente-Inférieure, peasants simply refused to indemnify lords. The strategy eventually worked, as the National Convention subsequently abolished all seigneurial dues without indemnity on 13 July 1793.

the Maximum left him with the hope of reselling his goods at a higher price.[42] In Cozes, the law of 19 floréal VI, which permitted individuals to nullify sales made in *assignats* between January 1791 and floréal III, resulted in a slew of unconciliated cases as both parties insisted on the legitimacy of their claims.[43] Like the payment of seigneurial dues, these volatile problems of revolutionary social and economic policy frequently proved beyond the mediating skills of rural JPs. Their solution could not come in the fields of Aunis and Saintonge, but rather in the legislative chambers in Paris.

CONCLUSION

Table 23 shows the rates of conciliation for various cantons during the revolutionary decade. The figures range from a paltry 9 percent at Pons from February 1791 through September 1792 to a rather stunning 63 percent at Ars-en-Ré from 1791 through messidor II. To be sure, Ars-en-Ré's status as a relatively insulated island canton inflated the number of successful conciliations (just as Pons's status as a relatively important legal seat in both the Old Regime and during the Revolution may have deflated its success rate), since the problems of time and the inconvenience of travel associated with formal litigation were especially burdensome to the Rétais. Although few cantons could match the enthusiasm for conciliation exhibited by the people of Ars-en-Ré, few matched the pessimism of Pons.

In three cantons where records exist for the Year VI—Marennes, Gemozac, and Cozes—a total of 188 cases were not conciliated, 45 were successfully mediated, and 54 ended with agreements to arbitrate. This 34 percent success rate for informal dispute resolution appears far more representative than the figures for Ars-en-Ré or Pons, for the overall sample of 601 cases contained in Table 23 shows that 36 percent of cases brought before the *bureaux de paix* ended in conciliation or arbitration.[44] Of course,

42. ADCM L 792.
43. ADCM L 1411.2. Purchasers of property between 1791 and the Year III cited the legality of their purchases as well as their good faith. Was it their fault that the value of the *assignat* fell precipitously? Sellers, on the other hand, refused to conciliate while citing the authority of the law that allowed them to rescind sales.
44. In a rare study that analyzes more than just a handful of cases, L. Skorka found that 129 of 245 disputes (53 percent) were successfully conciliated in the canton of Auxerre (department of the Yonne) from 1790 to 1793. See "La création des justices de paix sous la Révolution," *Bulletin de la Société des Sciences naturelles et historiques de l'Yonne* 123 (1991): 71–72. Most other evidence about the

the interpretation of these figures is problematic. Simply stated, is the fact that roughly 36 percent of disputes were solved informally evidence of the success or failure of the revolutionary institution?

I have stressed in this study the success of the *bureaux de paix* in this region, in part for the very practical benefits they entailed, such as diminishing the dockets of district civil courts. Without one-third of disputes finding solutions through informal channels, the caseload of formal civil courts theoretically would have increased by 50 percent—an enormous weight on the judicial administration as well as a serious blow to the already strained finances of the French state. But perhaps the best evidence in support of the practical benefits of this revolutionary institution lies in their preservation in the Constitution of the Year VIII. Unlike the idealistic reformers of 1789 and the radicals of 1793 who championed mediation out of an ideological commitment to a new style of justice, Napoléon and the Brumairians kept the *bureaux de paix* simply because they were useful.[45]

But how can one gauge the psychological effects of a successful mediation in which the parties arrived at their own settlement? How can one measure the number of friendships or business relationships preserved because the parties avoided adversarial litigation? How many disputes did not degenerate into violent feuds, for many poor people a less expensive substitute for a formal lawsuit, because there now existed an inexpensive forum in which to air grievances and reconcile their differences?

The success of the *bureau de paix* is attributable in no small part to the fact that it institutionalized a peasant practice, or at least played on a popular desire, in the Old Regime. However, this should not obscure the significance and indeed improvements of the revolutionary creation, for revolutionary mediation was entirely free and it was carried out under the auspices of an official buttressed by state authority and community legitimacy.

Both the *cahiers* and the judicial records from Aunis and Saintonge testify to the large number of rural inhabitants who pleaded for the opportunity to settle problems without the acrimony and high stakes involved in a formal lawsuit. The *bureaux de paix et de conciliation* went a long way in

---

institution's efficacy is based on hearsay. For example, the legislator Portalis claimed that six thousand cases per year were successfully conciliated in Paris alone, but he was defending the institution during debates about its future in the year IV (see *Le moniteur universel* 27). I. Woloch assesses this "evidence" in *The New Regime*, 307–20.

45. In an important shift, however, subsequent laws granted lawyers the right to appear with their clients at these mediation sessions.

satisfying this important demand from rural constituents. At Ars-en-Ré between 1791 and the Year II, eighteen of nineteen disputes in which the parties appeared voluntarily at the *bureau de paix* were conciliated successfully—evidence of people's desire for a trusted conciliator.[46] If the revolutionary emphasis on mediation was no panacea capable of rendering formal litigation obsolete, it gave people wary of trials an important alternative to the hitherto existing options for solving disputes: litigate, do nothing, or take justice into one's own hands (through violence or private mediation). The existence of a popularly elected, mediating official in the countryside constituted a welcome addition to the administration of justice. In all likelihood it changed the way in which French people viewed and interacted with the nascent state, whose commitment to the satisfactory resolution of conflicts replaced the complacency of the Old Regime state in the face of a frequently predatory legal system.

46. ADCM L 792, 15 March 1791–22 messidor II. Not all voluntary appearances involved issues that fell in the jurisdiction of district civil courts, but this demonstrates that people desired conciliation even for relatively minor affairs. Otherwise they would have submitted their dispute to the *judgment* of the JP instead of his *mediation*.

CHAPTER 8

Whose Law and Whose Order?

The Justice of the Peace as a Police Officer

At first glance, the Revolution's impact on the maintenance of law and order in rural France seems difficult to assess at the local level because of a paucity of documents in the archives of the justice of the peace, the primary agent responsible for the charge in the countryside. But an investigation of the records of the departmental criminal tribunal illuminates the significance of that paucity, for it demonstrates that justices of the peace worked in close alliance with the departmental officials in the *chef-lieu* of Saintes and deposited the correspondence of their police activity there. Hence, the prevention, investigation, and prosecution of crime in France was marked by a considerable degree of cooperation between local and central authorities. The cooperation stands in contradistinction to the wrangling between royal and seigneurial officials in the Old Regime, especially prior to 1772, over who was to pursue and to prosecute crime, and over who was to pay for the pursuit and prosecution.

The French monarchy had responded to the vexing problems of criminal justice in rural areas by implementing the reforms of 1771–72, which sometimes relieved local seigneurial officials of the responsibility for prosecuting criminal matters but mostly relieved them of paying for prosecutions.[1] Later, Lamoignon's reforms of 1788 gave justiciables the right to take cases immediately to royal courts and placed such stringent conditions on the exercise of criminal justice by seigneurial courts as to render them potentially inactive.[2]

The revolutionaries built on the reforms of the Old Regime and in doing so left the adjudication of crime in the more learned and capable

---

1. Chapter 4 treats the crown's reforms aimed at improving criminal justice at the local level.

2. See J. Gallet, "Justice seigneuriale," in L. Bély, ed., *Dictionnaire de l'ancien régime* (Paris, 1996), 714–17.

hands of state magistrates. The revolutionary reorganization of criminal justice asked local judicial officials to serve as the eyes and ears of the state, to investigate criminal complaints, to document the results of their inquiries, and even to arrest suspects, but to hand over the prosecution to the judges of criminal tribunals located in the departmental *chef-lieu*. Importantly, not only did revolutionaries delineate a clear chain of command and list of responsibilities in criminal cases, but they also committed themselves to paying for their reforms, which removed the pecuniary impediments to law enforcement that had existed prior to 1789 even if it proved odious to French taxpayers. The reorganization of criminal justice, along with the determination to finance it, represented the bureaucratization of the maintenance of law and order in France. Although Tocqueville had long ago identified the growth of central authority as the desideratum of Old Regime monarchies, subsequent historians have demonstrated how this growth remained a goal more than fact.[3] To a significant degree, then, it was the French Revolution that laid the groundwork for the growth of the central government in the realm of repressive authority, thereby altering the relationship between the state and the inhabitants of rural Aunis and Saintonge.[4]

Rural dwellers, however, were ambivalent about their new relationship with the state, for although the growing repressive authority of the French government could increase the security of persons and property, it also brought thoroughness to the maintenance of order—a thoroughness resented by rural communities tolerant of some minor transgressions of the law or accustomed to dealing with them on their own, free of the intervention of state or seigneurial agents. In addition, the exigencies of revolution caused French authorities to vigorously enforce their new political values, which often clashed with the normal rhythms of rural life and the conservatism of rural culture. To many French, the Revolution introduced the state

3. Tocqueville, *The Old Regime and the French Revolution.*

4. Emphasis should be placed on the word *groundwork,* since many historians, particularly Eugen Weber in *Peasants into Frenchmen: The Modernization of Rural France, 1870–1914* (Stanford, 1976), have shown that the state's successful penetration of the countryside was a long process. It would be equally wrong to insist that no groundwork had been laid prior to the Revolution, as my discussion of the reforms of 1772 and 1788 points out. A main theme of S. Reinhardt's *Justice in the Sarladais* is that royal or official justice slowly but consistently encroached on the realm of popular justice from 1770 to 1790. For an important study of the state's growing reliance upon the military to assure law and order after 1797, consult H. Brown, "From Organic State to Security State: The War on Brigandage in France, 1797–1802," *The Journal of Modern History* 69 (December 1997): 661–95.

as a novel but more thorough oppressor of the rural populace, more rigorous in enforcing its political and economic values than the French monarchy or local seigneurs had ever been in imposing theirs.[5]

The justice of the peace was a crucial figure in the reorganization of France's repressive authority; indeed, he stood as the symbol of its triumphs and its failures. On the one hand, the JPs were diligent in their surveillance of society's interests and in maintaining order in the communities from which they came. On the other hand, they were agents of the state, expected to uphold the political values (for example, in forcing compliance with the revolutionary calendar) or the property laws (such as the continued payment of seigneurial dues until 1793) of Parisian lawmakers. As both insider and outsider in his repressive capacity vis-à-vis the rural community, the JP was an important bridge between the state and inhabitants of the countryside.

To continue the metaphor, the focus of this chapter is the construction of the bridge between state and rural society in the realm of law enforcement. Through a study of the institution of the justice of the peace, one can perceive both the solidity and the unsteadiness of the revolutionary creation. In addition, the assignment of police duties to justices of the peace had important and perhaps troubling implications for these officials, for by granting them significant repressive powers (to arrest, incarcerate, and inflict penalties), the revolutionary legislators threatened to undermine the image of the JP as a mediating conciliator, which was crucial to their acceptance by rural inhabitants.[6] Did the JP represent a disinterested, equitable conflict solver who promoted social harmony, or was he a symbol of the aggressive incursion of the state into rural society? The answer to this question is no small matter, since the way in which the JP was viewed could ultimately determine the success or failure of the institution on which so many hopes for the transformation of rural France rested.

5. This idea guides the important argument of T. G. A. Le Goff and D. Sutherland in "The Revolution and the Rural Community in Eighteenth-Century Brittany." The authors contend that the counterrevolution in Brittany can be explained as the rural communities' "violent political opposition to a regime harsher and more demanding, and yet more arbitrary and lacking in moral force, than the monarchy of the old regime had ever been" (p. 119). See also Sutherland, *The Chouans*.

6. This dilemma is also central to H. Brown's "From Organic Society to Security State." Brown notes that the Directory's legitimacy diminished because of its inability to combat problems of law and order (brigandage) in France. Yet the methods it adopted to bring law and order—increasing reliance on the military—were also detrimental to its legitimacy, because those methods contradicted so blatantly the revolutionary principles of individual liberty and the rule of law.

THE ORGANIZATION AND FUNCTIONS OF THE RURAL POLICE

Revolutionaries based their new system of criminal justice on two principles that distinguished it clearly from that of the Old Regime: trial by jury and the separation of police powers from the judiciary. "The jury," writes Bernard Schnapper, "more than a creation of the Revolution, was its symbol,"[7] for it protected the liberties of individual citizens and stood as a bulwark against despotism. Indeed, the jury exemplified the Revolution's commitment to the ideal of popular sovereignty. If the people made law through its representatives, it dispensed justice through its juries.[8] The distinction between the police and the judiciary was, in the view of legislators, as indispensible to the preservation of liberty as were jury trials. Although a vigorous police was necessary in France, now a "free" country where lawbreaking constituted a breach of the social contract, it was imperative to separate the pursuit of crime from adjudication in order to prevent a dangerous concentration of power, so prejudicial to the rights of the accused but one exercised by magistrats prior to 1789.[9]

The separation of police powers from judicial duties had important implications for justices of the peace, for revolutionaries made them the primary agents responsible for police activity in the French countryside. Reacting to the inadequacy of the *maréchaussée* and seigneurial officials in the realm of rural law enforcement, which offered malefactors a significant degree of impunity, legislators insisted on the necessity of ensuring the presence of an official of order close to each local community. The JP was an obvious candidate for the responsibility of investigating crime, "which requires only sane judgment and the love of order, natural to the good inhabitants of the countryside."[10] If JPs embodied for rural dwellers impartial civil magistrates who strove to bring social harmony to the communities from which they came, then would they not also be active, elected enforcers of those laws that guaranteed social order? Furthermore, the selection of JPs as officials of the *police de sûreté* placed a police agent in each canton while obviating a duplicate law enforcement bureaucracy and hence a mas-

---

7. B. Schnapper, "Le jury criminel," in Badinter, *Une autre justice*, 149–70. For a detailed study of French juries in action and of a revolutionary criminal tribunal in general, see R. Allen, "The Criminal Court of the Côte d'Or, 1792–1811," (Ph.D. diss., Columbia University, 1991).

8. Schnapper, "Le jury criminel," in Badinter, *Une autre justice*, 153.

9. See especially the speech of Thouret concerning the *police de sûreté* and the commitment to trial by jury, *Septième discours . . . séance du 28 décembre 1790* (Paris, 1790).

10. Thouret, *Huitième discours . . . séance du 28 décembre 1790* (Paris, 1790), 4.

sive source of funding. In other words, since JPs were already on the state payroll, it was financially and administratively convenient to assign them local police duties.

After basing their new system of criminal justice on these two principles, revolutionaries identified four separate categories of transgressions and hence four categories of police activity: *la police constitutionelle* for crimes against the state, *la police de sûreté* for the repression of crime, *la police correctionnelle* for misdemeanors that did not merit "une peine afflictive et infamante,"[11] and *la police municipale* for the maintenance of local order. Importantly, they assigned JPs a significant role in the *police de sûreté*, making these local agents responsible for the the pursuit and investigation of crimes in their cantons. After accumulating the information surrounding a crime and perhaps issuing an arrest warrant for the incarceration of a suspect—a stunning amount of power for local officials devoid of any professional education[12]—the JP forwarded his findings to an *accusateur public* who decided whether to go forward with an indictment. If he sought an indictment, the *accusateur public* presented the case to a *jury d'accusation*. If the jury granted the indictment, the case was tried before the *tribunal criminel* located in the department's capital, whereas the case was dismissed if the *jury d'accusation* concluded that there was insufficient evidence for a prosecution. Legal transgressions deemed insufficiently serious could be sent before a lower tribunal that judged *correctionnellement*.

In their role as judicial police officers, JPs were crucial components of France's new criminal justice system. If a major problem of Old Regime criminal justice was the reluctance of local officials (whether royal or seigneurial) to actively pursue and investigate misconduct, then the success of its reformation depended to a large degree on the willingness of JPs to act on complaints or even rumors of crime and their competence in investigative work. Was it too much to ask of these unarmed, untrained magistrates? After all, there were few financial incentives to reward such willingness, and the work could be downright dangerous in the face of violent individuals or powerful bands of criminals operating in rural cantons.[13]

11. Séligmann, *La justice en France pendant la Révolution*, 1:450.

12. See Debauve, *La justice révolutionnaire dans le Morbihan*, 324.

13. Lawmakers in Paris, realizing that the suppression of crime required force, allowed JPs to call the National Guard to make arrests and to help in tracking suspects. To avoid the abuses of the *maréchaussée*, lawmakers required JPs, and not the National Guard, to sign and present arrest warrants. On the other hand, the role of the National Guard in police work was to offset the timidity of unarmed JPs as well as their potential partiality to their families and villages. See Thouret, *Huitième discours . . . séance du 28 décembre, 1790*, 8–9.

In addition to their important work in the suppression of serious crimes against persons and properties, JPs, as members of the *police correctionnelle*, were largely responsible for maintaining order in their cantons by prosecuting those transgressions of the law that fell between crimes and police contraventions. Composed in rural areas of the JP and two of his *assesseurs*, the *police correctionnelle* passed judgment on the following misdemeanors after a complaint by a private party or by the *procureur* of the commune of the injured party:[14] (1) transgressions of morality (for example, "outrages à la pudeur des femmes," "excitation à la débauche"); (2) the disruption of worship; (3) verbal insults and violence toward persons (including involuntary manslaughter); (4) troubling public tranquility through illegal mendicancy,[15] vagabondage, or incitement to riot; (5) attacks on property, whether by damage, larceny, simple theft, swindling, or the opening of a gambling house. The penalties imposed by the *police correctionnelle* ranged from fines of up to three thousand livres (and ten thousand for some cases of recidivism) and imprisonment for up to two years.

The Directory later limited the jurisdiction of the *police correctionnelle* to misdeanors for which the punishment did not exceed three days in prison or the value of three days of labor. For misdemeanors worthy of between three days and two years in prison, the Directory created *tribunaux correctionnels* at the level of the *arrondissement*. A *tribunal correctionnel* consisted of the president (who was a judge from a civil tribunal), a commissioner named by the Directory, a clerk, and the two justices of the peace whose cantons fell within the *arrondissement*. The power to judge the misdemeanors that most frequently upset the rural social order as well as the redoubtable power to incarcerate malefactors for up to two years highlight the JPs' central role in maintaining law and order in the countryside. As such, it is clear why the success of revolutionary criminal justice hinged on the issue of whether the JP was perceived by his constituents as a member of the local community or as an "outsider."

To summarize the revolutionary reorganization of the rural police, it is instructive to examine the procedure that JPs followed in criminal matters. Either the injured party, the *procureur de la commune*, or the latter's substitute confronted the JP with a criminal complaint or a suspect caught in

14. The law of 19 July 1791 defined the jurisdiction and procedure of the *police correctionnelle*. *Archives parlementaires*, 28:429–33.

15. Illegal mendicancy included "menacing or violent begging," begging with arms, begging at night, begging with two or more persons, or begging with false infirmities.

flagrante delicto. The JP proceeded to investigate, interrogating the suspect and taking depositions from witnesses. Based on his judgment of the evidence, the JP released the suspect if he thought him or her innocent, or he issued an arrest warrant for the suspect and sent the *procès-verbal* to the *accusateur public* if sufficient evidence existed to justify criminal prosecution. If the *jury d'accusation* decided that a transgression was a misdemeanor meriting judgment by the *police correctionnelle,* the JP and two *assesseurs* determined the suspect's fate (until the Directory, after which time a misdemeanor might be judged by either a *tribunal correctionnel* or the *police correctionnelle,* depending on the seriousness of the infraction). Sessions of the *police correctionnelle* were held in public, and the defense had the right to employ a legal advisor. Procedure before the tribunal was quite simple, as both parties questioned the suspect and the witnesses and submitted conclusions; the decision, if not immediate, came during the following session at the latest. Appealed decisions went to the district tribunals, which judged these cases definitively.

THE GROWING TENTACLES OF RURAL LAW ENFORCEMENT

According to several witnesses of the hamlet of Jazennes, François Rivault fired his rifle at another citizen on 14 October 1793, leaving that unfortunate man perilously close to death. Upon hearing the news, the citizens of the municipality of Jazennes immediately informed the JP of Pons and impressed upon him the need to "investigate [the matter] in fulfillment of the charge of [his] office."[16] The JP quickly complied by issuing to the commander of the National Guard a warrant for Rivault's arrest. The JP questioned witnesses about the event and interrogated Rivault once the National Guard had succeeded in placing him in custody. Deciding that the shooting was neither an accident nor an act of self-defense, the JP ordered Rivault's imprisonment and forwarded the case file to the *jury d'accusation* of Pons, which would ultimately determine whether Rivault would be tried in criminal court.[17]

In the canton of Cozes in the Year VI, a *garde-champêtre* sighted twenty-one individuals harvesting grapes in violation of the commune's *ban de vendange.* Informed of this harvest of grapes outside the days specified

16. ADCM L 1474 (letter of commune of Jazennes to JP of Pons), 15 October 1793.
17. I was unable to follow Rivault's case to its conclusion.

by the communal authorities, the *procureur* of the commune decided to prosecute the twenty-one people before the *police correctionnelle*. The JP heard the testimony of the ranger and the commune's agent as well as the numerous defendants, whose defense was that the grapes were ready for harvesting and that, in any case, they were not responsible for their transgression, each having been led into error by others. Citing the laws of 24 August 1791, 22 September 1791, and 28 September 1791 concerning the rural police (demonstrating the JP's familiarity with a body of law, which contradicts the image of them as simple—or ignorant—cultivators), the JP found the defendants guilty and fined them a modest three francs, payable to the nation.[18] In a similar type of case, the *procureur* of Ars-en-Ré successfully prosecuted 10 people before the *police correctionnelle* for failure to keep clean the path in front of their houses; they all received fines of two francs.[19]

The preceding examples highlight the existence of a network of agents—*gardes-champêtre*, bailiffs, municpal agents, JPs, national guardsmen, magistrates of departmental criminal courts—who worked in close cooperation to ensure the upkeep of local order and to police rural society. The clear existence of this network as well as its rather smooth and cooperative functioning stand as the most striking features of the archives of the local police after 1789 and emphasize the differences with rural criminal justice in the Old Regime. Each commune and each canton now had its authorities to watch over the local community, to report antisocial or criminal behavior, and to prosecute and punish transgressors.

Even if the highly questionable assertion is advanced that a similar network existed prior to the Revolution, it has already been shown in Chapter 4 that there still existed powerful disincentives to pursuing crime. Foremost among those disincentives for both private parties and public officials was the high cost surrounding criminal cases. After 1791, no longer did injured parties refuse to demand justice for fear that they would be burdened with the expenses of a criminal investigation or trial. No longer were there seigneurs who dissuaded their agents from fulfilling the duties of criminal justice out of concerns for the high costs borne by lords. No longer did magistrates prosecute selectively, choosing to pursue cases where they stood to receive payment for their troubles—those with known (and usually financially solvent) defendants. Instead, private parties, knowing that minor affairs no longer resulted in interminable and expensive trials,

18. ADCM L 1411.3, canton of Cozes, 1 vendémiaire VI.
19. ADCM L 788, canton of Ars-en-Ré, 25 messidor VII.

brought complaints to the attention of salaried officials who neither gained nor lost financially by investigating or prosecuting a crime. The payment of salaries to the officials of justice itself equaled a revolution in criminal justice and was perhaps the greatest blow to the disincentives to pursuing crime that existed prior to 1789.

At the local level during the Old Regime, financial concerns rendered the duty of maintaining local order anathema to lords. As Nicole Castan contends, seigneurial justices were "almost completely lacking in a police force worthy of its name,"[20] meaning that officials were unable or unwilling to offer justice in the cases that most affected local communities: *délits ruraux*, verbal arguments, and violent quarrels.[21] Into the vacuum created by the unwillingness of lords to police the realm of *délits ruraux* stepped the parties themselves, whose exercise of the functions of justice practically guaranteed the escalation of minor affairs and the creation of long-standing feuds.[22] In the absence of a public force willing to, and capable of, maintaining order, villagers often took justice into their own hands.[23]

Given the consequences of the absence of seigneurial justices from the realm of local law and order, the activity of JPs in this area of law enforcement takes on a heightened significance. Two important items stand out in the minutes of the *police correctionnelle* registers: first, the willingness of private parties to lodge complaints with official agents of justice; second, the zeal with which officials carried out their duties of maintaining law and order, witnessed in speedy adjudication, rigorous enforcement of local police decrees, and a high number of cases brought by the *procureurs* of communes. Together, the combination of a public willing to seek justice

20. N. Castan, *Justice et répression en Languedoc*, 56.

21. A *délit rural* was a misdemeanor relating to rural property, such as hindering a public path, taking one's livestock onto the property of another, harvesting illegally, and so on.

22. In such cases I part ways with several scholars such as S. Reinhardt and M. Greenshield who see violence as an expression of a self-regulating community or of an "organic" community. Of course, private violence was ubiquitous and often did express community sentiments, for example when directed against outside brigands. On the types of community in the Old Regime, see Bouton, *The Flour War*, 163–222. Yet J. Dewald rightly notes in *Pont St. Pierre* that the "community" was a complex and shifting web of alliances and that community regulation of affairs often meant that the most powerful villagers got their way. J. P. Jessenne underscores this point in "Le pouvoir des fermiers." In the cases discussed here, the resort to "ritualized, measured violence," prior to 1789 looks less like popular justice than vigilanteeism and the right of the strongest. Such violence resulted not only from a culture attached to certain conceptions of honor but also because other paths of justice were closed.

23. N. Castan, *Justice et répression en Languedoc*, 64.

through official channels and a police force that took its duties seriously exemplify the revolutionary changes in local criminal justice.

The register of the *police correctionnelle* of Cozes for the Year VI, to take but one example, shows that private parties and local officials combined to preserve order in the French countryside by prosecuting numerous cases of *délits ruraux*. Nineteen of the twenty-two cases decided by the JP in that year involved rural misdemeanors, demonstrating the degree to which quarrels over property dominated conflicts in rural areas. Of those twenty-two cases, eight were initiated by communal *procureurs*, whose motives were to ensure that citizens recognized harvest dates and kept their animals off the property of others. To a large extent, the preservation of social peace among denizens of rural Aunis and Saintonge depended on recognizing property boundaries and keeping cattle, sheep, and horses from straying onto the property of neighbors. That JPs and community agents proved vigilant in policing those boundaries and the laws that guided the rhythms of rural life contributed significantly to the preservation of peace.[24]

Perhaps Table 24 provides the best overview of the activity of the rural police during the French Revolution. The sixty-five entries in the register of the *police correctionnelle* from Marennes in the Year VI depict not only a JP intent on maintaining law and order in his commune, but also private citizens willing to bring their complaints to constituted officials. The sixty-five entries—thirty for *délits ruraux*, twenty-four for such police contraventions as working on the *décadi* or plying a trade without certification, and eleven for cases of slander and verbal threats of violence—include thirty-eight initiated by private citizens. Given the propensity for the JP to mete out minor fines payable to the nation rather than large damage payments to plaintiffs, the impetus behind complaints by private individuals was not so much financial gain as it was a desire to see their claims vindicated through official channels. Rural dwellers viewed the *police correctionnelle* as an inexpensive, quick, and, more important, legitimate venue for airing

---

24. One might be inclined to argue that the peace was in some sense unjust because the preservation of property rights (and JPs certainly protected the rights of property) came at the expense of the unpropertied who sought to raise livestock on the property of others (which is possible under less vigilant authorities). However, the evidence does not support the idea that the preservation of peace primarily entailed the squeezing of an already marginalized group. The vast majority of cases involving rural misdemeanors pit one *cultivateur* against another and stem from the overcrowding and fragmentation of property in rural areas. Thus, I think it is more important to view the preservation of peace in terms of the changing dynamics between rural society and the state (in which rural inhabitants gradually accept the state's intervention in local conflicts) than to emphasize the dynamics of class at work here (in which peace means the protection of "bourgeois" property rights at the expense of inhabitants whose link to the land is tenuous).

their grievances. In light of the probably justified reluctance of people to file criminal complaints with seigneurial officials during the Old Regime, the relative trust and expectations of action exhibited when those same people brought grievances to the JP highlight the changing attitudes of members of the rural society toward the French state.

A case from Marennes in the Year VI serves as an example of the changes (or improvement, in this instance) in rural criminal justice under the justices of the peace. Several individuals filed charges against Jacques Coindriaud, "accused of obscene acts of bestiality." The complaint itself was significant, for the parties sought no damages but only hoped to point out a public menace—an action that may have been prohibitively expensive in a seigneurial jurisdiction. Instead of prosecuting Coindriaud and inflicting a severe, physical punishment for such a morally heinous crime, Marenne's JP convened a family council composed of Coindriaud's brother-in-law, an uncle, and four cousins. The JP told the council of the charges against their kinsman and read the depositions of witnesses. Following are the results of the family members' deliberations with the JP:

> After a closed session, [it was determined] that Coindriaud had use of his reason until age seventeen but has been without it for the past eight years, that his madness causes him to chase after girls and even after animals, that he would behave violently if he were not prevented from doing so, that his condition becomes more alarming with the various phases of the moon, and that he has escaped many times despite the surveillance of everyone.
>
> Considering that it is their [the family's] duty and also in the interest of society to prevent Coindriaud from roaming, that the law holds them responsible for the acts that he might commit, but that they can do nothing without being authorized by the law, Pacquet, brother-in-law, was named guardian in order to present himself before the court with the goal of seeking Coindriaud's detention.[25]

Under the Old Regime, not only is it unlikely that a private party would have filed a potentially financially disastrous complaint against Condriaud, but it is also quite possible that the seigneurial authorities would have neglected the case.[26] If a lord's (or parish clergyman's) sense of morality de-

---

25. ADCM L 849, 30 pluviôse VI.

26. The zeal of officials in pursuing crime varied according to the financial concerns of lords. As the example from St. Martin de Ré in Chapter 4 makes clear, lords did not hesitate to instruct their judicial officials to avoid prosecutions, even for cases of manslaughter, if an investigation and trial threatened to be expensive.

TABLE 24   Police Activity by the Justice of the Peace of
Marennes, an VI

Item	Issue	Result/Activity
1	DR (damage to vines)	Plaintiff to prove
2	P (sale of grain on road)	NG
3	P (horse's contagious disease)	Experts called—kill animal
4	DR (grapes taken)	G—confiscate grapes, give to poor
5	IV	G—fine of one day's work for nation
6	DR (animals on property of others)	G—3 fr. to nation, 21 fr. damages
7	DR (damages to public path)	G—repair within 24 hours
8	DR (animals on property of others)	G—3 fr. to nation, 3 fr. damages
9	IV	G—3 fr. to nation, *reparations d'honneur*
10	DR (animals on property of others)	G—3 fr. to nation
11	DR (trees cut)	G—3 fr. to nation, 3 fr. damages
12	DR (damages to prop. by animals)	Postponed
13	DR (damages to prop. by animals)	Postponed
14	P (patente)	Prosecutor to prove
15	P (patente)	NG
16	P (patente)	G—fined 1/10 value of patente
17	P (patente)	G—fined 1/10 value of patente
18	P (patente)	G—fined 1/10 value of patente
19	P (patente)	G—fined 1/10 value of patente
20	P (patente)	G—fined 1/10 value of patente
21	P (patente)	G—fined 1/10 value of patente
22	DR (animals on cultivable property)	G—3 fr. to nation, 3 days of work as damages
23	Continuation of #12	G—3 fr. to nation, 24 hours prison
24	DR (damage by dogs)	G—3 fr. to nation, 6 fr. damages
25	Continuation of #13	G—3 fr. to nation, 24 hours prison
26	DR (animals in vines of others)	G—3 fr. to nation, 3 days of work as damages
27	DR (animals in vines)	G—3 fr. to nation
28	IV (over missing grain)	NG—admonition to live as good neighbors
29	IV (debt)	Plaintiff to prove
30	DR (animals on salt marshes)	G—3 fr. to nation
31	P (patente)	G—fined 1/10 value of patente
32	Continuation of #29	G—3 days prison
33	DR (animals on property)	G—3 fr. to nation
34	DR (animals in vines)	G—3 fr. to nation
35	IV	NG
36	P (charge of bestiality)	No prosecution—insanity
37	DR (animals on property)	G—3 fr. to nation
38	DR (animals on property)	G—3 fr. to nation
39	IV	Mutual; 2 days prison/1 day for plaintiff
40	IV	Mutual; 1 day prison each
41	IV (accusation of theft)	G—3 fr. to nation; *reparations d'honneur*
42	P (*loi sur logement militaire*)	Not in jurisdiction of *police correctionnelle*
43	DR (alteration of course of water)	Plaintiff to prove
44	Continuation of #43	G—3 fr. to nation; 45 fr. damages; repairs
45	DR (animals on property)	G—3 fr. to nation; 10 fr. damages

46	DR (animals in salt marshes)	G—3 fr. to nation; 2 fr. damages
47	P (sale of goods outside fixed place)	12 defendants G—1 fr. to nation each
48	IV (accusation of theft)	G—3 days prison
49	DR/IV (picking fruit/insults)	G—3 fr. to nation
50	DR (horses on property)	G—3 fr. to nation
51	P (hindering public path)	G—recidivist 2 days prison; others 1 fr. fine
52	DR (animals on property)	G—3 fr. to nation; 4 fr. damages
53	P (dung heap disturbs neighbors)	Plaintiffs to prove
54	Continuation of #53	G—1 fr. to nation; remove heap
55	P (dancing on Sunday)	G—3 days prison
56	DR (entry into garden/taking prunes)	G—3 days prison
57	P (playing illegal game, *quilles*)	G—2 fr.to nation each defendant
58	IV	Plaintiff to prove
59	P (playing *quilles*)	G—1 fr. to nation each defendant
60	P (working on *décadi*)	Postponed
61	P (working on *décadi*)	G—1 fr. to nation
62	DR (horses on property)	G—3 fr. to nation
63	P (working on *décadi*)	G—2 fr. to nation
64	DR (animals on property)	G—3 fr. to nation; 3 fr. damages
65	P (working on *décadi*)	G—1 fr. to nation each defendant

SOURCE: ADCM L 849.

LEGEND: P—Police contravention; DR—*Délit rural*; IV—*Injures verbales*; G—Guilty; NG—Not guilty.

manded Condriaud's prosecution, then a lengthy proceeding ensuring the payment of ample wages to the judicial personnel would have ensued. If convicted, Condriaud's punishment would have been corporal and severe. What is striking under the JP of Marennes is how quickly he proposed a solution that protected rural society from a potentially violent person while recognizing the best interests of a family. This combination of the JPs' seriousness about preventing disruptions in the countryside and respect for the concerns of their constituents and neighbors shows the revolutionary institution at its best and points to the beneficial aspects of the growing tentacles of rural law enforcement.

TENSIONS BETWEEN THE RURAL COMMUNITY AND LOCAL POLICE

The justice of the peace was both a representative of the state and a member of a local community. Insofar as a respected member of the community imposed values shared by both the state and rural inhabitants, the JP stood as an important link between the central authority and the local community.[27] Hence, the institution of the justice of the peace worked extremely well, thereby helping legitimate the state in the eyes of its citizens, when the values it strove for coincided with those of rural constituencies: quick and inexpensive justice, protecting property from damages by neighbors, defusing verbal arguments before they escalated into violent feuds. But the state also expected its functionaries to carry out its will even when its policies clashed with the sentiments of large segments of the citizenry. And it is here that the JPs' police powers became problematic, because by carrying out revolutionary social and economic policies the JP risked being identified as an outsider, as someone granted the authority to enforce unpopular laws just as surely as the *procureur fiscal* had enforced the hated laws governing seigneurialism. The perception of the JP as an intrusive, coercive outsider who imposed order threatened to undermine the revolutionaries' vision of their creation: that of a member of the community who was granted authority by his fellow citizens and who restored harmony to rural social relations.

One example of the JP standing as a representative of an outside, state power rather than as a member of a rural community was when Parisian legislators requested that peasants continue to pay seigneurial dues even after the celebrated "abolition of feudalism" of 4 August 1789. So unpopular and illegitimate were seigneurial dues in the eyes of rural producers that they agitated incessantly over the issue until the final abolition of such dues without indemnity in 1793.[28] The JP, who in civil cases sided with former seigneurs demanding payments of dues and who in criminal matters arrested and prosecuted antiseigneurial agitators, often provoked the wrath of his constituents in such actions. At St. Genis in the district of Pons, the *procureur syndic* wrote to the JP denouncing the activities of Andre Médion, the former mayor of Mônac. "I denounce to you, Monsieur, this individual and ask that you act against him through the path indicated by law and take him into your hands. . . . It is time to have the guilty punished and to stop a course already too advanced. I count on your zeal and your patriotism in this matter."[29] The prosecutor referred to the wave of antiseigneurial

---

27. As M. Banton writes, "The policeman obtains public cooperation, and enjoys public esteem, because he enforces standards accepted by the community." See "Law Enforcement and Social Control," in Aubert, *Sociology of Law*, 129.

28. See J. Markoff on the continuation and efficacy of rural violence regarding the continued payment of seigneurial dues. "Violence, Emancipation, and Democracy: The Countryside and the French Revolution," *American Historical Review* 100 (April 1995): 360–86.

29. ADCM L 1057 and 1059, District of Pons, 24 August 1792. The existence of forged documents announcing the suppression of seigneurial dues was widespread during this time.

activity in the vicinity of St. Genis, supposedly precipitated by Médion's assertion that the Legislative Assembly had abolished the payment of dues. The JP, accompanied by three members of the gendarmerie, descended upon St. Genis, where they discovered Médion posting announcements on the parish church proclaiming the suppression of the *agriers*. After the JP ordered Médion's arrest, a number of armed people converged threateningly on the authorities. Several shots were fired, and the authorities prudently retreated without seizing Médion. After calling for reinforcements, the JP returned to St. Genis and arrested Médion, along with nine people accused of rioting during his previous visit.

In a very similar case from St. Nazaire, the JP of Soubise, Jean-Joseph Bourgeois, ordered the arrest of seventeen people for *attroupement*. These individuals physically threatened members of the gendarmerie who had received Bourgeois's instructions to seize Joseph Gibaud for publishing false decrees about the abolition of seigneurial harvest dues.[30] Such struggles between local authorities and people intent on not paying seigneurial dues also plagued St. Vaize, Varaize, and other communes, but these examples suffice to demonstrate the tension between JPs and rural dwellers when the former enforced the wildly unpopular economic policies of Parisian legislators. Lawmakers had not envisioned their peacemakers as the rifle targets of irate peasants.

The JPs' police work in imposing the revolutionary laws of the Maximum was another area that risked provoking the ire of rural inhabitants. In particular, the enforcement of revolutionary laws on the grain trade entangled JPs in a bitter battle between producers who resented forced requisitions and artifically low prices and consumers who, staring in the face of indigence during the harsh economic climate, constantly accused authorities of laxity in provisioning local markets—a laxity that could mean starvation.

At Mirambeau on 26 September 1793, the *procureur de la commune,* Jagoult, brought Papon, miller, and Fourchaud, cultivator, before the *police correctionnelle* for refusing to obey the commune's grain requisition.[31] Citing the Law of 12 September, granting communes the right to require cultivators and proprietors to bring grain to market, the JP ordered the confiscation of Papon's and Fourchaud's grain and made them pay the court costs. The register of Mirambeau's *police correctionnelle* from 1793 through the

---

30. ADCM L 1059, canton of Soubise, August 1792.
31. ADCM L 874 (2).

Year II deals almost exclusively with issues of grain; the JP ordered eight confiscations in September and October alone, which could not have made producers enamored of him. In an extreme display of the power invested in him to control the local populace, the JP sentenced the miller Antoine Voltière to ten years in irons (and the confiscation of his flour) for an illegal commerce in flour.[32] According to witnesses, Voltière loaded his cart with flour at 4 A.M. and hid it at his daughter's house in order to minimize the amount of produce he would have to bring to the legal market from his mill.

If the preceding actions of the JPs were met with approbation by rural consumers, other actions by JPs and local officials could just as easily stir the animosity of hungry crowds. Again at Mirambeau in the Year II, authorities posted guards at the grain storage building "in order to ensure a tranquil distribution."[33] For the saddle maker and onetime communal officer Michel Véal, the appearance of armed guards at the gates of the *minage* could only signal the existence of a conspiracy between local officials and grain monopolists intent on making fortunes while patriotic citizens starved. Insisting that the sale of grain should take place in public, Véal yelled to the assembled, anxious crowd to take the *minage* by force, and he even authorized the action as a municipal officer (which he no longer was). The JP ordered the arrest and detention of Véal and sent him before the District Tribunal of Pons for incitement to riot and interfering with the commerce of foodstuffs.

The final area of revolutionary policy that brought JPs into conflict with many of their constituents was the enforcement of the revolutionary calendar. Unlike the installation of the metric system, which gave France a much needed standardization of weights and measures, the "rationalization" of the calendar seemed like nothing but political harrassment by a revolutionary elite wishing to marginalize religious traditions.[34] In their insistence that local officials force recognition of the new calendar, Parisian lawmakers pushed JPs into a political service that pitted them directly against the vast majority of French people, who resented the disruption of antediluvian rhythms of work and rest. When the municipal administration

---

32. ADCM L 874 (2), canton of Mirambeau, 19 October 1793. The Law of 12 September authorized the *police correctionnelle* to impose sentences of up to ten years in cases of the illegal commerce in grain. The law also encouraged denunciations by granting accusers one-half of the grain confiscated. The other half went to the commune.

33. ADCM L 874 (2), 23 brumaire II.

34. On the republican calendar, see Woloch, *The New Regime*.

of Marennes complained to the JP that laws on the *décadi* "hadn't produced the desired effect," the JP went into action and vigorously pursued transgressors of the following laws: no working on the *décadi* (the tenth, or rest, day in the republican calendar); no opening of workshops or stores on the *décadi;* inns and cabarets were closed to all except travelers on Sundays of the old calendar; no *jeu de quilles* (a game of chance) on Sundays.[35] One day after the municipal officers' complaint, the JP arrested six people for violating laws on the revolutionary calendar. One woman, the citizen Delage, spent three days in prison for serving wine and allowing people to dance on a Sunday.

Occasionally, rigorous enforcement of unpopular laws precipitated violent quarrels between JPs and their constituents. At Gemozac in the Year VIII, the JP, Ollivaud, and his assessors had just found four defendants (Fillaud, Bouyer, Talbot, and Blanchard) guilty of working on the *décadi*—a relatively minor transgression that normally merited a small fine. But just as the tribunal issued its sentence, the defendants caused a commotion and demanded to be heard. Ollivaud reported, "They were in the wrong, that they owe obedience and submission to the law, that instead of listening to our paternal observations, they carried themselves violently and responded with disrespectful words toward the tribunal."[36] Before the sergeant could remove the defendants from the courtroom, they gestured violently and struck furniture with their sticks, claiming that it was time for a second Vendée and warning Ollivaud that he would not always be justice of the peace, that he would not always be able to protect himself with the mantle of his authority. Ollivaud had the four arrested and incarcerated, and the tribunal at Saintes found them guilty of "outrages and disobedience" toward constituted officials; they received prison sentences ranging from five to eight days.

Clearly, then, in pursuing too enthusiastically controversial aspects of revolutionary social, political, and economic policy, the JP risked drifting from his mission of bringing harmony to rural social relations. It may be recalled from Chapter 7 that Ollivaud was a skilled mediator who succeeded in defusing many arguments between civil parties. What were the repercussions of his active enforcement of unpopular laws on the *décadi?* Did he not lose the confidence of some members of his community? Did his role as a police officer, someone with the redoubtable authority to de-

35. ADCM L 849, canton of Marennes, 4 thermidor VI.
36. ADCM L 1190 (6), canton of Gemozac, 25 vendémiaire VIII.

prive people of their liberty, alter the way constituents perceived him? Whereas his authority had once come from his status as a respected and freely elected member of the community, did it now come from his position as an agent of the state, capable of invoking the state's monopoly on the means of violence to enforce compliance with the law?[37]

Several contemporary observers of local justice did in fact vehemently oppose the assignment of police powers to JPs while stressing the incompatibility of the roles of mediator and police officer. One such observer, Antoine Collin, railed in particular against the JPs' power to issue arrest warrants. "The liberty of a man finds itself prey to the capriciousness or the arbitrariness of a single justice of the peace. . . . His [the JP's] will alone will suffice to throw at him [the accused], not a *lettre de cachet*, but a *mandat d'arrêt*, which differs only in name. . . . How is it possible that, next to the Declaration of Rights, there exists an article so barbarous and so destructive of the principles of liberty?"[38] Especially threatening to Collin was the JPs' power to issue fines and imprison putative wrongdoers for outrageous or menacing words or gestures toward public functionaries, including members of the National Guard or even a JP. Such power to interpret and censure words and actions constituted a veritable inquisition to Collin. In addition to pointing out the excess of power envisaged, Collin warned of the JPs' neglect of their primary functions. "The justice of the peace, who should be the neighborhood's tutelary angel,"[39] would be too busy, too agitated from criminal pursuits, to adjudicate and conciliate civil matters with the spirit of calm and sang-froid necessary for the function. Collin had voted for a conciliator to bring social harmony, but in the absence of this conciliator (who would be occupied with police matters) Collin foresaw an increase in social conflict, the ebullition of minor quarrels, and a rise in vigilanteeism—in short, a return to the problems caused by the poor administration of local justice under the Old Regime.

Whereas Collin predicted dire effects of the JPs' police powers, a mem-

---

37. Of course, when JPs acted as civil judges they also had the power to invoke the forces of violence by ordering compliance with their decisions. But civil decisions are a restoration of things to their proper relationship. As police officers and criminal judges, JPs used the means of violence in a punitive and repressive sense, often by depriving citizens of their personal liberty. As such, the invocation of the forces of violence in penal law is qualitatively different from the invocation in civil law. See V. Aubert's introduction to *Sociology of Law*, 12.

38. A. Collin, *Réflexions sur quelques articles du Code de police correctionnelle* . . . (Paris, 1792), 4–5.

39. Collin, *Réflexions*, 18.

ber of the *corps législatif* claimed to have actually observed a decrease in the JPs' popularity, which altered peoples' perception of, and interaction with, the new state authorities. Referring to the 1791 laws that granted JPs duties in police matters and criminal justice, Antoine Bergier wrote: "They [JPs] began to be feared. . . . [These laws] succeeded in denaturing the pacifist character of the institution when they made JPs the primary ministers in criminal actions. JPs especially lost their popularity when the terrifying power to issue arrest warrants put the liberty of citizens at the mercy of their arbitrary wills."[40] Fillaud, Bouyer, Talbot, and Blanchard, sent to jail for expressing displeasure with the JP's decision to fine them for working on the *décadi*, would not have quarreled with this assertion. Bergier argued that JPs' involvement in criminal matters led to an unhealthy negligence of their primary functions. Ultimately, he warned, people would lose confidence in their new institutions.

Although the enforcement of certain aspects of revolutionary policy always won a JP some support—enforcing the Maximum pleased consumers, enforcement of the new calendar pleased zealous republicans, and so on—the danger to the institution lay in the public's perception of the JP as too deeply enmeshed in the political quarrels of the central government. When political tides turned (and they repeatedly did during the Revolution), there would be scores to settle, and instead of being seen as a conciliator who had stood outside the fray of political struggles, the JP could be perceived as someone who had done the dirty work of a discredited regime.

Nowhere was this risk more evident than at La Flotte on the Ile de Ré, renamed Isle Républicaine during the Revolution's radical phase. After a visit in 1793 from the representative-on-mission Lequinio, La Flotte's *comité de surveillance* became radicalized and engaged in a whirlwind of activity: frequent denunciations and orders of arrest of suspected citizens. The JP, Barabé, acted as the right hand of the committee, circulating with the National Guard and placing judicial seals on the papers and property of suspects; he placed seven such seals at the request of the *comité de surveillance* from 6 brumaire to 2 frimaire.[41] By brumaire III, this committee had been suppressed and replaced by a conservative *société populaire*, which

40. A. Bergier, *Traité-manuel du dernier état des justices de paix, au 30 floréal an X* (Paris, an X), 2–3. Bergier's lengthy work argued for more training for JPs, stricter requirements, higher pay, and so on, in order to attract more qualified personnel to the position.

41. ADCM L 807, canton of La Flotte. In brumaire II the JP changed in La Flotte and the *comité de surveillance* became very active in the canton. This suggests that Lequinio had purged the JP and the committee, although I was unable to find direct evidence of this.

asked the prosecutor (*agent national*), Petit, to press charges against Barb-
aré for *soustration d'un enfant hors de mariage*.[42] Petit admonished the Popular Society for its scandalous proceedings since its inception, and he
defended Barabé as an honest and sacrificing official who had a "sacred
right to the esteem of everyone." Several members of the Popular Society
then shifted their attack to Petit, whom they accused of being a liar and an
oppressor of patriots, of malversation, and of granting himself a *certificat de
civisme*. Petit's response was to cite the merchant, Jacques Margotteau, before the *police correctionnelle* for slander. Since Barabé would preside over
the case before the *police correctionnelle*, Margotteau immediately demanded
Barabé's recusation and claimed that "the said justice of the peace was
chased from the *société populaire* and does not have the public's confidence."
Convinced that Margotteau's defamatory recusation would hinder his capacity to effectively exercise his public functions, Barabé sued him for thirty
thousand livres in damages. Clearly, then, Barabé's police activity on behalf
of a zealous *comité de surveillance* resulted in his loss of some of the public's
confidence and esteem. Instead of acting as a peacemaker who stood outside the quarrels of his constituents in order to adjudicate them fairly, Barabé joined the fray of political debates. As someone with the power to
arrest and imprison persons, Barabé could be seen as doing the bidding of
an unpopular, resented central authority. Was he a state agent or a community member?

CONCLUSION

Did the assignment of police duties and an important role in criminal justice to JPs undermine the popularity of the institution—a popularity based
on the successful reorganization of civil justice? The answer remains am-
biguous. On the one hand, many of the problems of law and order under
seigneurial justice, which combined to create nothing less than a "judicial
crisis,"[43] diminished when JPs assumed responsibility for local order: there
were few financial disincentives to pursuing crimes, and JPs acted quickly
and authoritatively to protect persons and property in their localities. A
case from Royan in the Year VI demonstrates the smooth functioning of

42. ADCM L 808, canton of La Flotte, brumaire III. I was unable to follow the conclusion of
this case to the district court.
43. Hufton, "Le paysan et la loi en France au XVIIIe siècle," 697.

the rural police and exemplifies what the revolutionaries envisaged when making JPs responsible for law and order. After investigating the death of Jean Bonnaud, the JP, Bednarski, declared to the director of the jury of Marennes that Bonnaud had committed suicide in a fit of frenzy. He wrote: "Hearing the mother and the brother-in-law was only a complement to my conscience, which declares them not guilty [in Bonnaud's death]. This is also the public opinion. But I would not have feared finding myself in opposition to it [public opinion] if I had had the least suspicion or if their morality had been less known to me."[44] Here was a public servant sensitive to, but not dominated by, public opinion. As a member of his community, he knew the family well, including its upstanding character and Bonnaud's bouts of rage, and was therefore able to protect society's interests while avoiding an intrusive and accusatory stance toward a family. In this example, Bednarski was an effective bridge between the state and a rural community.

On the other hand, the creation of an effective system of law and order meant that agents of the state settled matters that communities had once dealt with themselves in light of the inability of authorities to penetrate rural areas.[45] In addition, it meant that those agents had important repressive powers, in theory to force compliance with laws, but that sometimes proved oppressive or arbitrary. In a case from Charentes in 1793, the JP, François Rousseau, arrested and imprisoned Pierre Averon on suspicion of operating a monopoly on wine after a denunciation by three citizens.[46] After Rousseau had forwarded the dossier to the *jury d'accusation,* the district tribunal decreed the immediate release of Averon as the definitive judgment in the case. In its decision, the tribunal cited many anomolies in the JP's investigation, the most egregious of which included insufficient evidence to issue an arrest warrant, the fact that Averon's actions did not fall under the laws on monopoly, Rousseau's failure to acknowledge Averon's challenge of the witnesses, and Rousseau's failure to

44. ADCM L 1151 (25), district tribunal of Marennes, 2 messidor VI.

45. See the excellent study by J. Dewald, *Pont St. Pierre,* on the way communities regulated their own affairs. Dewald demonstrates how authorities exercised only limited control over villages elites, whose power enabled them to impose their own settlements in community matters. Thus, to say that communities regulated their own affairs does not mean that the community was a homogeneous or democratic organism without its own internal divisions and power structure. Rather, it simply means that the regulation of affairs occurred often without the intervention of state or seigneurial agents.

46. ADCM L 591, District Tribunal of Rochefort, 4 September 1793.

call Averon's witness (the only person present at the time Averon sold his wine). Whether malice or incompetence guided Rousseau in his investigation, it mattered little to Averon, deprived of his liberty in a dank cell and wondering if he might not end up at the guillotine. Averon's predicament was not unique: as Table 25 shows, at least eleven out of twenty-eight arrests by JPs in the district of Rochefort from 1793 to Year II did not lead to prosecution by the criminal tribunal; fully seven cases were dismissed completely.

That rural dwellers reacted with ambiguity toward the JP in his capacity as the keeper of local law and order should come as no surprise, for the JP was, by definition, both a member of his community and an official of the state. In all times and localities, when state policy reflects the wishes of its constituents, then those constituents accept state authority as legitimate. Thus, when the revolutionary reorganization of criminal justice rendered justice inexpensive and gave rural areas active agents who worked hard to ensure the security of people and property, then this reorganization helped legitimate the nascent state in the eyes of inhabitants of the French countryside. But the controversial policies of the revolutionary state often clashed with the desires of large segments of the rural population, and the forced compliance with such policies threatened to paint local authorities as the foot soldiers of an alien and illegitimate entity.

The ambiguity of the people of Aunis and Saintonge toward the new organization of criminal justice lends support to an important argument advanced by Olwen Hufton. She contends that rural France in the Old Regime had two contradictory goals: more efficacious justice but without an abusive bureaucracy.[47] In this chapter I have demonstrated how the creation of the justice of the peace and the reorganization of criminal justice after 1789 contributed significantly to the first goal, for there is no doubt that the Revolution inaugurated an efficacious system of local criminal justice. But the efficacious administration of justice entails external organs—

47. Hufton, "Le paysan et la loi en France au XVIIIe siècle," 697. Since the seigneurial police and *maréchaussée* were "completely discounted as an efficacious mechanism capable of protecting law and order," denizens of the countryside obviously craved more effective criminal justice, especially when confronted with bands and brigands from outside their communities. On the other hand, Hufton asserts, communities wished to be left alone in the affairs that concerned them: how to handle their own poor, what to do with a local petty thief, and so on. Despite his Foucauldian approach that lends an ominous air to the rise of the "security state," H. Brown recognizes that many French actively desired better law enforcement. See "From Organic "Society to Security State," 689–92.

TABLE 25   Cases Sent by Justice of the Peace (JP) to the Jury
d'Accusation, District of Rochefort

Item	Origin of JP	Issue	Decision of Jury
1	Rochefort (V)	*Propos inciviques*	Accusation too vague; accused freed but still suspect (has émigré brother)
2	Rochefort (C)	Violence	Accusation registered (no accompanying decision)
3	Surgères	?	Accusation registered
4	Charentes	?	Accusation registered
5	Surgères	Mendicancy and vagabondage	1 suspect freed (has passport); 2d suspect sent to *police correctionnelle*
6	Rochefort (V)	?	Accusation registered
7	Surgères	Theft of horse	To be prosecuted
8	Charentes	Monopoly on wine	No basis for prosecution
9	Rochefort (V)	Violence with stick	?
10	Rochefort (V)	False witness	Sent to *police correctionnelle*
11	Charente	Accomplice to murder	To be prosecuted
12	Rochefort (V)	?	?
13	Rochefort (V)	*Agiotage* ("vive le roi")	To be prosecuted
14	Rochefort (V)	*Propos inciviques*	Sent to *police correctionnelle*
15	Rochefort (V)	*Propos inciviques* (recruitment)	Sent to Rev. Tribunal in Paris
16	Rochefort (V)	*Propos inciviques*	To be prosecuted
17	Ciré	Theft	To be prosecuted
18	Rochefort (V)	Speculation in assignats	To be prosecuted
19	Rochefort (V)	Theft	To be prosecuted
20	Rochefort (C)	False witness by communal officer	Sent to *police correctionnelle*
21	Surgères	Attempted murder	To be prosecuted
22	Rochefort (V)	*Propos inciviques*	No basis for prosecution
23	Rochefort (V)	Theft	To be prosecuted
24	Rochefort (V)	Libel toward communal officer	No basis for prosecution
25	Rochefort (V)	*Propos inciviques*	No basis for prosecution
26	Rochefort (V)	Theft	To be prosecuted
27	Rochefort (V)	*Propos inciviques*	No basis for prosecution
28	Rochefort (V)	Abuse of confidence by official	Sent to *police correctionnelle*

Actions:

No basis for prosecution	7	Prosecution by *police correctionnelle*	4
Prosecution by Rev. Tribunal	1	Prosecution by criminal tribunal	10
Unknown	6		

SOURCE: ADCM L 591, district of Rochefort, 4 April 1793–16 messidor II. Rochefort (V) stands for Rochefort ville, while Rochefort (C) signals the canton of Rochefort.

? = Data not available.

numerous and vigilant agents, and the threat of violence—for the application of the law.[48] Was this price too high?

Perhaps the most crucial point about the revolutionary reorganization of local criminal justice is that it contributed to the ultimate success of "official justice." In his work on Old Regime justice, Steven Reinhardt posits the existence of three competing systems of justice: popular justice, in which communities and individuals regulated their own affairs through private vengeance, unofficial arbitration, and informal collective sanctions; seigneurial justice, a semiofficial system of justice in which the lord and seigneurial agents strove to maintain the social hierarchy; and royal or official justice, in which state agents sought to enforce the king's law.[49] It is shown in this chapter how, by abolishing seigneurial justice and creating an efficient (albeit sometimes oppressive) system of local law and order, the Revolution contributed to the ultimate triumph of official justice, in which official magistrates enforced the laws of a central authority. Rural society now submitted its conflicts to JPs or witnessed the rapid (if uninvited) involvement of these officials in their affairs. That this was partially by consensus and partially by imposition from above makes little difference; the relationship between the state and rural society was in the process of being altered. The process was slow and often difficult, but in the realm of justice the revolutionary state realized the long-standing goal of French monarchies—to penetrate rural areas.

---

48. Hufton, "Le paysan et la loi en France au XVIIIe siècle," 697.
49. Reinhardt, *Justice in the Sarladais*, xvii.

REFLECTIONS

In his erudite and popular book *Citizens,* Simon Schama summarizes a main current of recent revisionist thought on the French Revolution in the following passage: "The drastic social changes imputed to the Revolution seem less clear-cut or actually not apparent at all. . . . The modernization of French society and institutions seem to have been anticipated by the reform of the 'old regime.' "[1] Such revisionist thought not only seeks to minimize the historical significance of the French Revolution, but in doing so it also portrays the events from 1789 to 1815 as essentially a political drama—and an unfortunately bloody and illiberal one.[2] Undeniably, revi-

---

1. S. Schama, *Citizens: A Chronicle of the French Revolution* (New York, 1989), xiv. W. Doyle gives a history of revisionism in *Origins of the French Revolution,* 2d ed. (Oxford, 1990).

2. "Revisionists" or "post-revisionists" tend to eschew social history, resulting in the present triumph of "political culture" in French Revolutionary historiography. The most ambitious interpretations of the Revolution as the result of dynamics in political culture are Furet and Ozouf, *A Critical Dictionary of the French Revolution;* K. Baker, *Inventing the French Revolution* (Cambridge, 1990); and K. Baker and C. Lucas, eds., *The French Revolution and the Creation of Modern Political Culture,* 4 vols. (Oxford, 1987–94). For an illuminating look at Furet's thought, see M. Kristofferson, "An Antitotalitarian History of the French Revolution: François Furet's *Penser la Révolution française* in the Intellectual Politics of the Late 1970s," *French Historical Studies* 22 (Fall 1999): 557–611. Some recent scholarship shows increasing signs of discontent with the neglect of social issues in the French Revolution. See not only C. Jones, "Bourgeois Revolution Revivified," in C. Lucas, ed., *Rewriting the French Revolution* (Oxford, 1991); but also Markoff, *The Abolition of Feudalism;* T. Tackett, *Becoming a Revolutionary: The Deputies of the French National Assembly and the Emergence of a Revolutionary Culture (1789–1790)* (Princeton, 1996), and J-P. Gross, *Fair Shares for All: Jacobin Egalitarianism in Practice* (Cambridge, 1997). J. Censer reviews the current state of the field in "Social Twists and Linguistic Turns: Revolutionary Historiography a Decade after the Bicentennial," *French Historical Studies* 22 (Winter 1999): 139–67. See also S. Desan, "What's After Political Culture? Recent French Revolutionary Historiography." *French Historical Studies* 23 (Winter 2000): 163–196. Rather than wishing to return to the halcyon days prior to the "linguistic turn" and the concomitant rise of political culture, I only suggest that the triumph or rejection of revolutionary political culture must be understood in terms of peoples' social experience. The Revolution was not merely logomachy; its

sionist historiography has rescued historical understanding from the overly schematic, Marxist-Jacobin view of the Revolution as the triumph of the bourgeoisie, and it should also be applauded for counseling a cautious approach to the revolutionaries' rhetoric about making a complete break with the past. However, the revisionists' denial of important social changes attributable to the Revolution and their portrayal of the modernization of Old Regime society and institutions may be as overly-schematic as the views they challenged. It is revealed in this study how, in the realm of local justice, the French Revolution did in many ways effect a marked break with the past that resulted in portentous changes for rural society and its relations with the state.

The promised abolition of seigneurial justice on the Night of August 4 doomed an institution that, far from being moribund on the eve of the Revolution, was a Doric pillar of the inegalitarian social hierarchy in France. Even as the villagers of Varaize blamed their *seigneurs* for their fragile existence—"We have also observed that the extreme misery into which we are plunged is a natural and evident result of the tyranny that Sieur Amelot and his wife have exercised"—they also recognized the importance of seigneurial justice in allowing the Amelots to exploit their tenants: "The [hypothetical] veteran, who found in his courage the force to fight enemies of *la patrie,* finds no protection against fraud in the bosom of the tribunals to which his fear and his ignorance have brought him; he is ruined."[3] To revisionist historians who depict an eighteenth-century society already colonized by "bourgeois" values (the importance of wealth, talent, and public service), the testimony of the people of Varaize should serve as a cautionary reminder of the persistence of seigneurialism and the important function fulfilled by the privilege of seigneurial justice in a polity distinguished by legal and social inequality.

The abolition of seigneurial courts signified the death warrant for a system of justice whose frequent though not universal maladministration is a recurring theme of this study. The operation of a semiprivate judicial

---

values, policies, and institutions had implications for the time, property, and social relations of the French. For a different view of how to understand discursive triumphs, see J. Smith, "No More Language Games: Words, Belief, and the Political Culture of Early Modern France," *American Historical Review* 102 (December 1997): 1413–40.

3. ADCM L 739, 3 October 1790. The people of Varaize denounced "the maxim, as barbarous as it is noxious, that imperiously ordered that all lands be subject to seigneurial rights," and they accused the Amelots of "deeds so criminal that they deserve all the severity of justice." The antiseigneurial activity in Varaize is first discussed in the introduction to Chapter 3.

system removed from the oversight of a central authority had serious repercussions for rural society. In civil matters, procedural formalities and opportunities for fraud meant that, in words perhaps best expressed by the district *cahier* of Saujon, "So many monstrous legal actions are formed that ruin parties or prevent a rapprochement . . . or a reconciliation."[4] Ruin or irreconciliation: such was the potentially unenviable predicament of a litigant before a lord's tribunal. Ironically, seigneurial courts contributed to the predicament for which they in theory ought to have been the *solution*. In criminal matters, seigneurial agents' derogation of duty left a void in the maintenance of law and order into which stepped the parties themselves, kin groups, or some other unofficial arbiter. But the absence of officials whose exercise of authority was perceived as legitimate by rural dwellers fueled the endemic violence and prevalence of revenge that were hallmarks of Old Regime French society.[5]

The Revolution was not merely destructive. Institutionalizing the peasant practice of informal mediation and building upon the crown's own reforms of criminal justice in 1772, it created a new system of local justice with the goal of profoundly altering rural social relations as well as the relationship between state and society. The institution of the justice of the peace did in fact bring expedited civil justice to denizens of the French countryside, a change that introduced judicial agents as providers of a crucial service rather than as exploiters of social tensions. Faced with the opportunity to submit their quarrels to trusted and elected officials, the people of Aunis and Saintonge changed their behavioral patterns in conflicts and came to accept the primacy of the state in the resolution of disputes. Similarly, the justice of the peace proved efficacious in the maintenance of law and order in their cantons. Responding to the Department's inquiry into local morale, the cantonal administrators of Néré in 1798 attested to the improvements in the maintenance of order in a passage discussing the justice of the peace: "Few infractions are committed, and the activity exerted to repress them assures all citizens of the tranquility that they ought to enjoy."[6]

In the second half of this study I have stressed the themes of the pene-

4. ADCM C 26obis.
5. As Nicole Castan argues, the justice of tight-knit groups signals the "absence of arbitral power, whether public or not, capable of maintaining order and terminating disputes." See *Justice et répression en Languedoc,* 64.
6. ADCM L 158, brumaire VII.

tration of the state into rural France, the maintenance of local order, and expedited civil justice. But to these irrefragable conclusions might one add a fourth, that of the contribution to social harmony? Did the Revolution's commitment to a new style of adjudication and its promise of expeditious justice result in less acrimonious relations among people of the French countryside? Although I have been able to document significant behavioral shifts among rural inhabitants that followed changes in the system of local justice, one can only infer the psychological shifts associated with that changing behavior. But it would be difficult to quarrel with the commentator on local justice Camille Billion, who, thirty-five years after the inauguration of the justices of the peace, testified to the importance of the institution to rural social relations: "This institution, through its useful and moral aim [and] by the success that it has obtained, has become a habit, a social need. . . . *Let's go to the justice of the peace' is today an appeal to order, an invocation to reason.*"[7] Lasting until 1958, when it was replaced by a *juge d'instance,* the justice of the peace was woven into the fabric of rural France.

To defend against claims of scholarly myopia, I point out that this study shows only how the reorganization of local justice contributed to the state's attainment of legitimacy in the eyes of rural inhabitants, not that it inaugurated a completely harmonious relationship between the French state and rural society. After all, there existed ample reasons for the outright hostility of rural dwellers toward the state—conscription and the disruption of religious practices, for example—and still others such as the land settlement resulting in the ambivalence of peasants toward the central authority.[8] On the issue of representativeness, that *bête noire* of scholars of France, I must alas claim agnosticism, in the absence of comparable studies.[9] But above all, I hope to have demonstrated how, in the realm of local justice in southwest France, the French Revolution was indeed a revolution.

7. C. Billion, *Des Juges de paix en France, ce qu'ils sont, ce qu'ils devraient être* (Lyon, 1824), 1. Billion's emphasis.

8. On the subject of how peasants gained and lost by revolutionary policies, see Jones, *The Peasantry in the French Revolution,* especially chap. 8, "The Balance Sheet."

9. Clearly, my conclusions about justices of the peace would not hold for any region of intense counterrevolutionary activity. See, for example, Le Goff and Sutherland, "The Revolution and the Rural Community in Eighteenth-Century Brittany." Despite the body of literature cited throughout this study and that surveyed by J. Markoff in *The Abolition of Feudalism,* 111–18, there is still a need for systematic studies of the social impact of the practice of seigneurial justice and especially civil justice. For example, in D. Sutherland's study, *The Chouans,* he states that seigneurial courts "provided quick, cheap, and, for the most part, impartial justice," largely because lords fulfilled their paternalistic roles as guardians of the peace in rural communities (183). This may indeed be true, but little evidence

The reader may recall the anecdote about the elderly Rochelois whose comment that "there wasn't any [justice]" during the French Revolution introduced this study. In retelling the story, I obviously tried to suggest how popular and even scholarly consciousness pertaining to revolutionary justice is dominated by images of the guillotine. But my acquaintance's comment earned him an unanticipated and probably unwelcome lecture from an American graduate student about that other image of revolutionary justice: the justice of the peace. At least I bought him a pastis.

---

in support of the assertion is offered, which is an important omission, since it contradicts Giffard's major study of Brittany's seigneurial courts in which he denounces the poor quality of local justice (in truth, Giffard's own conclusions are mostly assertions based on his reading of the *cahiers*). And might shortcomings in seigneurial justice have contributed to the antiseigneurial activities that afflicted fully one-third of western *bailliages?* See Markoff, *The Abolition of Fedualism,* 346.

The following costs were incurred in a case pitting the fiscal procurator of Archaic against L'houmeau for illegal hunting. The court convicted the defendant, fined him one hundred livres, and ordered him to pay these expenses.

		Cost		
ITEM		LIVRES	SOLS	DENIERS
1.	Plainte au procureur fiscal (PF)	0	13	4
2.	Notre ordonnance au bas	0	16	0
3.	Nos droits de la déposition de 11 témoins dans l'information et continuation (12 s./témoin)	12	6	0
4.	Notre soit communiqué au PF	0	8	0
5.	Conclusions du PF tandante au décret	0	12	0
6.	Au greffier la moitié de notre droit compris le papier	3	14	0
7.	La taxe des journées de 11 témoins	14	14	0
8.	Nos droits du décret	0	16	0
9.	L'expédition au greffier	1	0	0
10.	Raports d'assignations données à 11 témoins compris le controlle et papier	9	4	0
11.	Raport d'assignation du décret à l'accuzé compris le controlle et papier	1	2	6
12.	Droits de l'interrogatoire de l'accuzé sur le décret	1	0	0
13.	Compris le soit communiqué au greffier	0	8	0
14.	Requête à nous presentée par ledit PF tandante au règlement à l'extraordinaire	0	13	4
15.	Notre appointement au bas	0	8	0
16.	Requis à notre appointement de règlement extraordinaire au PF	1	10	0
17.	Nos droits	0	5	0
18.	Expédition au greffier compris papier	0	14	0
19.	La signiffication audit PF	0	6	0
20.	Raports des assignations données à 11 témoins compris le controlle et papier aux fins du récollement et leurs dépositions et confrontations à l'accuzé	8	9	0
21.	Autre raport de signiffication dud. appointement avec	1	7	6

ITEM		COST		
		LIVRES	SOLS	DENIERS
	assignation devant nous audit accuzé aux fins de son récollement et confrontation aux témoins			
22.	Nos droits du récollement de 10 témoins	4	2	6
23.	Le greffier compris le papier	2	5	3
24.	Taxe des journées des témoins au récollement	10	6	0
25.	Nos droits du récollement de l'accuzé	0	7	6
26.	Notre soit communiqué	0	8	0
27.	Au greffier compris le papier	0	5	9
28.	La confrontation de 10 témoins à l'accuzé pour nos droits (4 s./témoin)	12	0	0
29.	Au greffier compris le papier	6	8	0
30.	Conclusions deffinitive au PF, suivant ses épices	18	0	0
31.	Interrogatoire dernier le bareau, pour nos droits	1	12	0
32.	Au greffier compris le papier	0	18	0
33.	Assignation audit accuzé aux fins dudit interrogatoire compris le controlle	1	7	6
TOTAL COSTS		112	13	2

SOURCE: ADCM B 2695, Marquisat d'Archaic, 2 January 1767.

Supplicates humbly Marie Comté, duly authorized by Jean Pillet her stepfather, saying that she remained for five years as a servant in the household of Simon at the place of Les Plantes in the parish of Jonzac, where she had the misfortune to make the acquaintance of Pierre Phelipeaux fils, a miller at Corvert.

The said Comté, scarcely twenty-one years old—issued from parents whose probity, despite a far from lofty condition, has always recommended them in the neighboring parishes and has earned them the esteem of nearly everyone—but at this tender age and without experience, when the heart is more susceptible to the impressions of love than the rules of right reason, or rather outside the state of reasoning altogether, could only hear at first while trembling the said Phelipeaux, who, encouraged by the timidity of this girl, did not hesitate to offer the most insinuating and flattering discourses, who forced her to listen to how she had broken his heart and that he had conceived for her the most tender fondness and the most sincere attachment.

Phelipeaux served at the side of several individuals at Les Plantes; never did one see a miller more exact and vigilant in satisfying the demands of his trade; he visited them often. It doesn't take a great effort of the imagination to penetrate the source of his vigilance; one understands easily that his interest in his work (which is not ordinary for people of his status) had less to do with it than the pernicious design he had formed to abuse the simplicity of this girl and to ravish what she held most dear.

In effect, after having visited her for a very long time and offering a thousand promises of his simulacrum of affection, without convincing her and without conducting her to the goal that he desired, he attempted to seduce her with the false promises of a legitimate marriage. Perseverence, frequent visits, attention, compliments, protestations, oaths—nothing was spared for the purpose of persuading her.

In the name of nuptials her young heart, so sensitive to the truth, felt itself moved, was perhaps flattered (for one can't deny that this sweet name, far from displeasing, is ordinarily full of charm for the fair sex)—she didn't doubt that one day he must ravish her. From this moment she gave him a more favorable ear, and she had confidence in his honor and his probity. His continual flattering, his innumerable compliments, his little gestures of caring, his oft-repeated oaths, and his mouth always full of honey permitted her no doubt about the sincerity of his love. Persuasion glided into her heart, and she had in him a blind confidence.

Phelipeaux, not content to see her so disposed to be the source of his future felicity, pursued still more arduously the execution of his abominable project. He used all his efforts to persuade her that to wait for the ceremonies of the Church would defer for too long a time the moment of their happiness; that perhaps there might be some obstacles to their marriage and that to guard against all inconveniences, they must circumvent the rights of the Church and work in concert to hasten the fortunate instant which would render them happy.

Wise and virtuous, the young Comté resisted like another Lucretia these infamous propositions. She rejected them with indignation; she repelled their author with a hitherto unknown anger; she rose brusquely in order to flee. But Phelipeaux recognized, or at least feigned to recognize, his fault and . . . stopped her. He offered his excuses and promised to be more reserved, and his false tears succeeded in convincing her of his repentence, for the tears of a lover are powerful intercessors with a girl whose heart is already wounded! She gladly pardoned him and consented to remain with him, never imagining that there would be still greater danger for her.

Even the imposter and the traitor Phelipeaux, who based the success of his pernicious enterprise less on the force of his discourses and more on his excesses and violence, would not have dared to return to the offensive. But her pardon, far from retaining him within the boundaries of decency, only augmented his audacity. He delivered to her on the battlefield, not one, but a thousand new assaults that she resisted with the courage of a heroine. She rejected him with all her energies and tried many times, but in vain, to escape from him. What can a weak girl do against the violence and the excesses of a robust and vigorous man such as the infamous Phelipeaux? The reproaches, the tears, the cries of the young Comté, the sole defenses remaining for her, ought to have put a brake to the brutality of his passion, but it only became more violent and frenzied. Finally, exhausted and outside herself, she succumbed to the power of her cruel ravisher. It would be useless to expose to the eyes of the judge what happened if the scene had not become entirely tragic. . . .

From this fatal moment this young girl, totally beside herself, thrust into the abyss of the darkest chagrin, subject to the most profound sadness, nourished in her heart the fruit of the excesses and violence of the perfidious Phelipeaux. The execution of his design put an end to his visits and his love, and she asked him several times not to lose sight of the oaths that he had reiterated so often, to be faithful to his word, to repair through a legitimate marriage the honor that he had desecrated.

The traitor! The imposter! The liar! He had never made her promises; he had never spoken to her! He even carried the affrontery so far as to say that he didn't know her! What could have made the poor girl believe that the constantly reiterated promises of marriage, affirmed by what is most sacred in religion, and accompanied by the most enchanting speeches, would serve as a prelude to the darkest treason and the most execrable perjury? Was there ever a more odious crime or one more deserving of all the rigor and severity of justice?

This is a crime of *rapt* in which violence played as large a role as seduction, and the vengeance of this crime interests the entire public. The Roman laws did not distinguish between *rapt de violence* and *rapt de séduction*, condemning equally to death those convicted. . . . But since these laws appeared too severe, penalties of death were often enough commuted to payments of damages and interest. [Such payments] couldn't be too great to punish Phelipeaux and to indemnify the supplicant for the wrong done to her honor. . . .

This considered, Monsieur, if it pleases your grace, give the supplicant permission to file a suit and to declare herself, under the authorization of Jean Pillet her stepfather, civil party in a case investigated by the *procureur fiscal*.

Source: ADCM B 3076 (1771), Comté de Jonzac.

BIBLIOGRAPHY

MANUSCRIPT SOURCES

Archives Départementales de Charente-Maritime (ADCM)

Série B: Justice
This series contains the records for Old Regime justice. Although there is (sometimes)
chronological order to the records for seigneurial justices, thematic order is quite rare.
Thus, a carton may contain any or all of the following: (1) registers of civil audiences; (2)
registers of *juridiction gracieuse;* (3) correspondence; (4) registers of criminal matters; (5)
registers of seigneurial matters; (6) registers of sentences (both civil and criminal); (7)
police registers. I consulted a broad range of approximately 275 cartons in series B for this
study. Instead of enumerating every carton, I offer the following list to indicate those
justices researched in most detail and to note other cartons of special interest.

B3076–88	Jonzac, 1771–88: audiences civiles et criminelles
B2362–67	Jonzac, 1769–90: audiences civiles et criminelles
B2368	Jonzac, 1772–74: police
B2357	Jonzac, 1750: audiences criminelles
B3090	Jonzac, 1727–78: registres civiles
B3329–42	Marennes, 1770–88: audiences civiles, criminelles, et extraordinaires
B2134	Ars, Loix, et Les Portes en Ré, 1749–51: audiences
B2144–55	Ars, Loix, et Les Portes en Ré, 1765–90: audiences
B5562–63	Varaize, 1785–90: registres
B2280–81	Cônac, 1774–86: audiences civiles
B2809–12	Brizambourg, 1782–90: registres civiles et criminelles
B2432–37	St. Seurin d'Uzet, 1773–90: registres civiles et criminelles
B2474–77	Fouras, 1775–90: registres civiles et criminelles
B2063	Pons, 1757–66: audiences civiles et criminelles
B2065	Pons, 1773–79: audiences civiles et criminelles
B2076	Pons, 1729–66: jugements
B2080	Pons, 1766–69: jugements
B3861	Pons, 1758–70: police
B2524	Archaic, 1759–65: affaires du marquisat
B2695–99	Archaic, 1769–90: procédures
B2793	Benon, 1672–90: registre criminel
B3232	Marans, 1747–65: audiences extraordinaires
B3254	Marans, 1775–85: registre de consignation d'épices

B2403   Montendre, 1780–82: affaires du marquisat
B2096   Croix-Chapeau, 1773–90: audiences
B5041   Présidial de Saintes, 1775–93: appels
B5552   Tonnay-Boutonne, 1766–87: affaires criminelles
B5553   Tonnay-Boutonne, 1766–87: état des frais de justice
   B2   La sénéchaussée de St. Jean d'Angély en Xaintonge
   B3   Présidial de Saintes, les juridictions qui y ressortissent

Série L: Révolution

This series contains the documents of the justices of the peace until 1800, after which date they are found in series U (not yet classified in the departmental archives in La Rochelle). Like the records for seigneurial justice, the cartons for justices of the peace have some semblance of chronological order while varying considerably in terms of their content, which might include one or more of the following: (1) civil judgments; (2) minutes of JPs' civil, police, and voluntary activities; (3) registers of *police correctionnelle;* (4) registers of *bureaux de conciliation;* (5) *juridiction gracieuse;* (6) correspondence. Again, the following list of cartons is only a representative sample of the approximately three hundred consulted in series L and is meant to indicate those areas studied in most detail as well as to specify cartons of particular interest.

   L1463   Pons, 1791–92: jugements
   L1464   Pons, an II–an VIII: tutelles, curatelles, déliberations de famille
   L1465   Pons, 1791–92: bureau de conciliation
   L1466   Pons, an II–an III: bureau de conciliation
   L1467   Pons, an III–an XI: bureau de conciliation
   L1469   Pons, 1792–an VI: minutes
   L1470   Pons, an VII–VIII: minutes
   L1471   Pons, an IX–an X: minutes
   L1472   Pons, 1792–93: police correctionnelle
   L1473   Pons, an V–an X: minutes de police
   L1474   Pons, an VII: affaire de Bouyer, extorsion de signature
   L1745   Pons, an II: correspondence
L1425–30   Gemozac, 1790–an X: jugements
L1431–33   Gemozac, various years: curatelles, baux judiciaires, apposition de scellés
   L1434   Gemozac, 1791–an II: audiences du bureau de conciliation
   L1435   Gemozac, an III–an V: affaires conciliées
   L1436   Gemozac, an II–an VI: affaires non-conciliées
L1438–41   Gemozac, 1790–an VII: minutes des jugements et procès-verbaux
   L894   La Rochelle (canton), 1791: minutes des actes
   L832   Marans, 1791–an II: audiences
   L837   Marans, 1791–an IV: repertoires
 L823–26   Jonzac, 1790–an II: audiences et jugements

L827–28   Jonzac, 1791–an VII: jugements volontaires, actes diverses
L829   Jonzac, 1792–an III: police correctionnelle
L1227   Jonzac, an IV–an V: simple police
L479–84   Marennes (canton), 1791–an IV: audiences des affaires ordinaires
L842–44   Marennes (canton), 1790–93: jugements
L858   Marennes (canton), 1791: bureau de conciliation
L861   Marennes (canton), an II–an III: bureau de conciliation
L787   Ars-en-Ré, 1791–93: jugements
L788   Ars-en-Ré, an III–an VII: jugements
L791   Ars-en-Re, 1791–an II: bureau de conciliation
L792   Ars-en-Ré, an IV: bureau de conciliation
L794   Ars-en-Ré, an VI–an X: bureau de conciliation
L1523–26   Port d'Envaux, 1791–93: minutes
L1532–33   Port d'Envaux, 1790–an III: minutes des affaires extrajudiciaires
L1538–39   Port d'Envaux, an IV–an IX: police judiciaire
L1411.1   Cozes, an VI: minutes des actes
L1384   Elections des JPs
L 697   Elections des JPs (district de Saintes)
L147   Troubles à Varaize
L158   Administrations cantonales sur la situation politique et morale
L1338   Installation des JPs
L495   Serments des JPs
L1173   Procès du JP de Jarrie
L185   Frais de justice
L479–84   District de Marennes, 1791–an IV: appels des JPs
L199   Traitement des corps judiciaires
L591   District de Rochefort, 1793–an III: affaires criminelles, procès-verbaux des JPs

Série C: Administration

C177   Intendance: justice et police; état des crimes et délits, 1671–1787
C178   Intendance: justice, correspondence
C179   Sénéchaussées de Saintes et St. Jean d'Angély—leur composition
C260   Cahiers: clergé et 3e état de Saintes
C260bis   Cahiers: Saintes
C262bis   Cahiers: siège royal de Rochefort
C263   Cahiers: Beauvais, Brie sur Matha
C263bis   Cahiers: Saint-Jean d'Angély
C267   Cahiers: La Rochelle

Série E: Notaires

E342   Chaland, correspondence avec notaire

E404   Galliffet, vente de moyenne justice
E487   Depont des Granges, registres de correspondence
E7   Commanderie de Bourgneuf, 1786: terrier général
E2919–21 Bodin, notaire de Pons

Série J: Familles

1J361   Matha: justice
4J1820 Mesnac et Chazotte: justice
4J963   Papiers Jean Lalère, ancien JP
4J1245 Papiers Ranson de La Rochelle
4J1303 Papiers Rougier, notaire et procureur de Chaux, 1739–42
4J1514 Seigneurie de Montguyon
4J1523 Riguer, membre de l'Assemblée à JP de Montlieu
4J3212 Duburg, justice de Mirambeau, 1770–78
1J116   Mémoire des habitants de La Jarne contre M. le seigneur de Ronflac

Bibliothèque Municipale de La Rochelle

539 Folio 14   Liste des sénéchaux de Saintonge
539 Folio 69   Etat des paroisses de l'élection de La Rochelle
539 Folio 121   Lettre de Louis XV réunissant à son domaine la haute justice de l'Ile de Ré
539 Folio 88   Lettre de Foucault sénéchal de Ré sur les juridictions de l'île
603 Folio 189   Petit livret de recettes de la seigneurie de Cheusses, 1759–90
502 Folio 32   Titres et papiers concernant la terre d'Aigrefeuille
503 Folio 33   Terrier général d'Aigrefeuille
663 Folio 14   Lettres des fermiers des droits de l'île de Ré

Bibliothèque Nationale—Collection Joly de Fleury

1384–85 St. Martin de Ré: correspondence, 1775–84
1084   Lettres du procureur général aux officiers judiciaires
1093   Correspondence avec intendants
2153   Mémoire d'Aguesseau sur les juridictions inférieures
2155   Liste des justices du ressort du Parlement de Paris
2160   Sièges subalternes. Receuil de mémoires sur leur fonctions, compétence
2202   Règlements de frais de justice
2423   Droit et administration. Collection de dossiers des juges seigneuriaux
2426   Droit et administration. Officiers des justices seigneuriales

Archives Nationales

D XIV 2   Comité des Droits Féodaux: Charente-Inférieure

NEWSPAPERS

Journal de la Saintonge et d'Angoumois
Journal spécial des justices de paix
Courrier de l'armée des côtes de La Rochelle, publié par les citoyens Richard, Chardieu, Bourlotte,
     Tureau, et Tallien, représentants du peuple . . .
Réimpression de l'ancien Moniteur

PRINTED PRIMARY SOURCES

Archives parlementaires de 1787 à 1860. Receuil complet des débats législatifs et politiques des
     chambres françaises. Première série, 1787–99. 92 vols. (Paris, 1862–1980).
Avoyne de Chantereyne, V. *Essai sur la réforme des lois civiles* (Paris, 1790).
Begon, M. "Mémoire sur la généralité de La Rochelle." *Revue de Saintonge et Aunis* 2
     (1875).
Bergier, A. *Traité-manuel du dernier état des justices de paix, au 30 floréal an X* (Paris, an
     X).
Billion, C. *Des Juges de paix en France, ce qu'ils sonts, ce qu'ils devraient être* (Lyon, 1824).
Boncerf, P-F. *Les inconvéniens des droits féodaux* (London, 1776).
Boucher d'Argis, A.-J. *Cahier d'un magistrat du Châtelet de Paris, sur les justices seigneuriales*
     et l'administration de la justice dans les campagnes (Paris, 1789).
Bucquet, L.-J.-B. *Discours . . . sur cette question: "Quels seraient les moyens de rendre la justice*
     en France avec le plus de célérité et le moins de frais possibles?" . . . (Beauvais, 1789).
Bulletin des loix (revolutionary period).
Collin, A. *Réflexions sur quelques articles du Code de police correctionnelle . . .* (Paris 1792).
Dagar, C. *Dictionnaire de droit et de pratique civil, commercial, criminel et judiciaire . . .*
     (Paris, 1804–5).
Delamare, N. *Traité de police.* 4 vols. (Paris, 1705–38).
Duport, A.-J.-F. *Principes fondamentaux de la police et de la justice, présentés au nom du*
     comité de constitution (Paris, 1790).
———. *Principes et plans sur l'établissement de l'ordre judiciaire . . . 29 mars 1790* (Paris,
     1790).
Ephémérides du département de la Charente-Inférieure (La Rochelle, 1792).
Essai sur les privilèges (Paris, 1789).
Fouqueau de Pussy. *Idées sur l'administration de la Justice dans les petites villes et bourgs de*
     France pour déterminer la suppression des juridictions seigneuriales (Paris, 1789).
Idées d'un citoyen sur la réforme de l'administration de la justice en France (n.p., 1788).
Isambert, F-A., et al., eds. *Receuil général des anciennes lois françaises depuis l'an 420 jusqu'à*
     la Révolution de 1789. 29 vols. (Paris, 1821–33).

Jacquet, P. *Traité des justices de seigneur, et des droits en dépendent conformément à la Jurisprudence actuelle des différents Tribunaux du Royaume* (Paris, 1764).

Loyseau, C. de. *Discours de l'abus des justices de villages* (Paris, 1604).

Mémoire à nosseigneurs de l'Assemblée nationale sur les juges de paix et sur la défense des pauvres en matière criminelle (n.p., n.d.).

Metman, C. *Essai sur le notariat, ou ce qu'il devraient être dans le nouveau système judiciaire. Ouvrage lu à la Société des Amis de la Constitution* (Paris, 1790).

Observations sur les justices de paix (n.p., 1810).

Pétion de Villeneuve, J. *Fragments d'un ouvrage sur les lois civiles et l'administration de la justice en France* (Paris, 1789).

Poix de Fréminville. *Dictionnaire de police* (Paris, 1756).

———. *Pratique universelle pour la rénovation des terriers et des droits seigneuriaux*, 5 vols. (Paris, 1752–57).

Renauldon, J. *Traité historique et pratique des droits seigneuriaux . . .* (Paris, 1765).

Ricard, M. *Observations sur les juges de paix* (Paris, n.d.).

Roy, J. *Le crime des suppôts de justice* (n.p., 1789).

Sagnac, P., and P. Caron, eds. *Les Comités des droits féodaux et de léglislation et l'abolition du régime seigneurial* (Paris, 1907).

Sanois, Comte de. *Aux Etats-généraux sur la nécéssité d'une réforme dans l'Ordre juridique* (Paris, 1789).

Talon, A-D. *Simplifications des procédures et réduction des frais de justice* (Paris, 1790).

Thorillon, A-J. *Réflexions sommaires sur les attributions et l'organisation des justices de paix, et sur les moyens de ne plus les détourner du but de leur institution* (Paris, an X).

Valin, R.-J. *Nouveau commentaire sur la coutume de La Rochelle et du pays d'Aunis*. 3 vols. (La Rochelle, 1756).

Vivien de Goubert, A.-P.-J.-B. *Exposé de différents abus dans l'administration de la justice, moyens certains de les extirper* (Paris, 1790).

Young, A. *Travels in France*. Edited by J. Kaplow (Garden City, N.Y., 1969).

SECONDARY SOURCES

L'abolition de la féodalité dans le monde occidental. Toulouse, 12–16 novembre, 1968 (Paris, 1971).

Agulhon, M. *La République au village: Les populations du Var de la Révolution à la Deuxième République* (Paris 1979).

Allen, R. "The Criminal Courts of the Côte d'Or, 1792–1811" (Ph.D. diss., Columbia University, 1991).

Andrews, R. "The Justices of the Peace of Revolutionary Paris, September 1792–November 1794 (Frimaire Year III)." *Past and Present* 52 (August 1971): 56–105.

———. *Law, Magistracy, and Crime in Old Regime Paris, 1735–1789*. Vol. 1: *The System of Criminal Justice* (Cambridge, 1994).

Aubert, V., ed. *Sociology of Law* (Baltimore, 1969).

Aubin, G. "La seigneurie de bordelais d'après la pratique notariale (1715–1789)" (Thèse de doctorat, Université de Rouen, 1981).

Aubin, R. *L'organisation judiciaire d'après les cahiers de 1789* (Paris, 1928).

Audiat, L. "Evêché et chapitre de Saintes, documents (IIII–1785)." *Archéologie historique de la Saintonge* 10 (1882).
Augustin, J.-M. *La Révolution française en Haut-Poitou et pays charentais* (Toulouse, 1989).
Badinter, R., ed. *Une autre justice: Contributions à l'histoire de la justice sous la Révolution française* (Paris, 1989).
Baker, K. *Inventing the French Revolution* (Cambridge, 1990).
Baker, K., and C. Lucas, eds. *The French Revolution and the Creation of Modern Political Culture*, 4 vols. (Oxford, 1987–94).
Bar, C. *A History of Continental Criminal Law* (Boston, 1916).
Bart, J. "La justice de paix du canton de Fontaine-Française à l'époque révolutionnaire." *Mémoires de la Société pour l'histoire du droit et des institutions des anciens pays bourgognons* 26 (1965).
———. *La Révolution française en Bourgogne* (Dijon, 1996).
Bastier, J. *La féodalité au siècle des lumières dans la région de Toulouse (1730–1790)* (Paris, 1975).
Bataillon, J.-H. *Les justices seigneuriales du bailliage de Pontoise à la fin de l'ancien régime* (Paris, 1942).
Beattie, J. *Crime and the Courts in England, 1660–1800* (Oxford, 1986).
Beik, W. *Absolutism and Society in Seventeenth-Century France: State Power and Provincial Aristocracy in Languedoc* (Cambridge, 1988).
———. *Urban Protest in Seventeenth-Century France: The Culture of Retribution* (Cambridge, 1997).
Bell, D. *Lawyers and Citizens: The Making of a Political Elite in Old Regime France* (Oxford, 1994).
Berland, A. "Les débuts de J. Roux et la Révolution en Angoumois et en Saintonge" (D.E.S., Poitiers, 1965).
Berlanstein, L. *The Barristers of Toulouse in the Eighteenth Century (1740–1793)* (Baltimore, 1975).
Bernard, D. *La justice de paix du canton de Cleder Cap Sizun, 1790–1800* (Quimper, 1933).
Bernard-Griffiths, S., et al., eds. *Révolution française et vandalisme révolutionnaire* (Paris, 1992).
Besnier, R. "Le problème des justices seigneuriales en Normandie." *Revue historique du droit* (1933).
Bevan, A. *Alternative Dispute Resolution: A Lawyer's Guide to Mediation and Other Forms of Dispute Resolution* (London, 1992).
Bleton-Rouget, A. "L'infrajudiciaire institutionalisée: Les justices de paix des cantons ruraux de district de Dijon pendant la Révolution." In B. Garnot, ed., *L'infrajudiciaire du Moyen Age à l'époque contemporaine. Actes du colloque de Dijon, 5–6 octobre 1996* (Dijon, 1996).
Bloch, M. *French Rural History: An Essay in Its Basic Characteristics.* Translated by J. Sondheimer (Berkeley, 1966).
Bois, P. *Paysans de l'Ouest: Des structures économiques et sociales aux options politiques depuis l'époque révolutionnaire dans la Sarthe.* Abridged ed. (Paris, 1971).
Bossenga, G. *The Politics of Privilege: Old Regime and Revolution in Lille* (Cambridge, 1991).
———. "Rights and Citizenship in the Old Regime." *French Historical Studies* 20 (Spring 1997): 217–43.

Boucher, P., ed. *La Révolution de la justice: Des lois du roi au droit moderne* (Paris, 1989).
Bouguet, D. "La sociabilité conflictuelle dans le canton de Loches, d'après les archives de la justice de paix (1790–an III)." *Histoire moderne et contemporaine* 1, no. 2 (1986).
Bourbeau, M. O. *Théorie de la procédure civile.* Vol. 7: *De la justice de paix* (Poitiers, 1863).
Bouswema, W. "Lawyers and Early Modern Culture." *American Historical Review* 78, no. 2 (1973): 235–65.
Bouton, C. *The Flour War: Gender, Class, and Community in Late Ancien Régime French Society* (University Park, Pa., 1993).
Brémond d'Ars, M. de. *Pièces pour servir à l'histoire de Saintonge et d'Aunis* (Saintes, 1863).
Brennan, T. "Police and Private Order in Old Regime France." *Criminal Justice Review* 13 (1988): 1–20.
———. *Public Drinking and Popular Society in Eighteenth-Century Paris* (Princeton, 1988).
Brissaud, J. *A History of French Private Law* (Boston, 1912).
Brown, H. "From Organic Society to Security State: The War on Brigandage in France, 1797–1802." *Journal of Modern History* 69 (December 1997): 661–95.
Calhoun, C. *Social Theory and the Politics of Identity* (Oxford, 1994).
Cameron, I. *Crime and Repression in the Auvergne and the Guyenne, 1720–1790* (Cambridge, 1981).
———. "The Police of Eighteenth-Century France." *European Studies Review* 7 (1977).
Carey, J. *Judicial Reform in France Before the Revolution* (Cambridge, Mass., 1981).
Castan, N. *Justice et répression en Languedoc à l'époque des Lumières* (Paris, 1980).
Castan, Y. *Honnêteté et relations sociales en Languedoc, 1715–1780* (Paris, 1974).
Castan, Y., and Y.-M Bercé, eds. *Les archives du délit: Empreintes de société. Colloque Archives judiciaires et histoire sociale, les 24 et 25 mars 1988 à l'Institut d'histoire moderne et contemporaine* (Toulouse, 1990).
Cavignac, J. "Troubles municipaux à Saint-Jean d'Angély au début de la Révolution." *Receuil de la Société d'archéologie et d'histoire de Charente-Maritime* (1973–74): 257–67.
Cazenave, J. "Justice et répression à Belpach pendant la Révolution." *Bulletin de la société d'études scientifiques de l'Aube,* 85 (1985): 139–48.
Censer, J. "Social Twists and Linguistic Turns: Revolutionary Historiography a Decade After the Bicentennial." *French Historical Studies* 22 (Winter 1999): 139–67.
Charbonnier, P. *Une autre France, la seigneurie rurale en basse Auvergne du XIVe et XVIe siècle.* 2 vols. (Clermont-Ferrand, 1980).
Chartier, R. *The Cultural Origins of the French Revolution.* Translated by L. Cochrane (Durham, N.C., 1991).
Chastel, A., ed. *Le château, la chasse, et la forêt* (Bordeaux, 1990).
Chaussinand-Nogaret, G. *The French Nobility in the Eighteenth Century: From Feudalism to Enlightenment.* Translated by W. Doyle (Cambridge, 1985).
Christian, T., et al., eds. *Expanding Horizons: Theory and Research in Dispute Resolution* (Washington, D.C., 1989).
Church, W. "The Decline of French Jurists as Political Theorists." *French Historical Studies* 5 (1967): 1–40.
Clark, J. *La Rochelle and the Atlantic Economy During the Eighteenth Century* (Baltimore, 1981).
Clère, J.-J. *Les paysans de la Haute-Marne et la Révolution française: Recherches sur les structures foncières de la communauté villageoise* (Paris, 1988).

———. "L'arbitrage révolutionnaire: Apogée et déclin d'une institution (1790–1806)." *Revue de l'arbitrage* (1981).

Cobb, R. *The Police and the People: French Popular Protest, 1789–1820* (Oxford, 1970).

Collins, J. *The State in Early Modern France* (Cambridge, 1995).

Combier, A. *Les justices seigneuriales du bailliage de Vermandois sous l'ancien régime* (Paris, 1897).

Coppolani, J. *Les élections en France à l'époque napoléonienne* (Paris, 1980).

Coquard, C., and Durand-Coquard, D. "Société rurale et Révolution: L'apport des actes de deux justices de paix de l'Allier (1791–fin de l'an VI)" (Ph.D. diss., Université de Bourgogne, 1998).

Dangibeaud, C. "Un fief en Saintonge, la Maison de la Madeleine à Cognac." *Archéologie historique de la Saintonge* 28 (1899): 17–214.

———. "Saintes en 1778, notes de Le Berton, lieutenant général de la sénéchaussée de Saintonge et présidial de Saintes." *Archéologie historique de la Saintonge* 7 (1880): 433–43.

Darnton, R. *The Forbidden Best-Sellers of Pre-Revolutionary France* (New York, 1996).

———. *The Literary Underground of the Old Regime* (Cambridge, Mass., 1982).

David, P. *Un port de l'Océan pendant la Révolution: La Rochelle et son district, 1791–1795* (La Rochelle, 1938).

Davis, J. *Conflict and Control: Law and Order in Nineteenth-Century Italy* (Atlantic Highlands, N.J., 1988).

Dawson, P. *Provincial Magistrates and Revolutionary Politics in France, 1789–1795* (Cambridge, Mass., 1972).

Dawson, P., et al., eds. *The French Revolution and the Meaning of Citizenship* (Westport, Conn., 1993).

Debauve, J.-L. *La justice révolutionnaire dans le Morbihan, 1790–1795* (Paris, 1965).

Delayant, L. *Histoire du département de la Charente-Inférieure* (La Rochelle, 1872).

Desan, S. "Reconstituting the Social After the Terror: Family, Law, and Property in Popular Politics." *Past and Present* 164 (1999): 81–121.

———. "'War Between Brothers and Sisters': Inheritance Law and Gender Politics in Revolutionary France." *French Historical Studies* 20, no. 4 (1997): 597–634.

———. "What's After Political Culture? Recent French Revolutionary Historiography." *French Historical Studies* 23 (Winter 2000): 163–196.

Deveau, J-M. *Atlas de la région Poitou-Charentes* (Poitiers, 1964).

———. *Histoire de l'Aunis et de la Saintonge* (Paris, 1974).

Dewald, J. *Pont St. Pierre 1389–1789: Lordship, Community, and Capitalism in Early Modern France* (Berkeley, 1987).

Dontenwill, S. *Une seigneurie sous l'ancien régime: "L'Etoile" en Brionnais du XVIe au XVIIIe siècle (1575–1778)* (Raônne, 1973).

Doyle, W. *Origins of the French Revolution*. 2d ed. (Oxford, 1980).

Duby, G., and A. Wallon, eds. *Histoire de la France rurale*, 4 vols. (Paris, 1975–76).

Esmein, A. *Histoire de la procédure criminelle en France et spécialement de la procédure inquisitoire depuis la XIIIe siècle jusqu'à nos jours* (Paris, 1882).

Estaintot, R. de. *Recherches sur les hautes justices féodales existantes dans les limites du département de la Seine-Inférieure* (Rouen, 1892).

Even, P. "Assistance et charité à La Rochelle au XVIII siècle" (Thèse de l'école de Chartres, 1980).

Fairchilds, C. *Domestic Enemies: Servants and Their Masters in Old Regime France*
    (Baltimore, 1984).
Farge, A. *La vie fragile: Pouvoirs et solidarités à Paris au XVIIIe siècle* (Paris, 1986).
Ferchaud, L. *Saujon le Gua (1789–An III): La Révolution dans deux cantons ruraux* (Saujon,
    1988).
Ferret, M. *Les Tribunaux de famille dans Montpellier* (Montpellier, 1926).
Fitzsimmons, M. *The Remaking of France: The National Assembly and the Constitution of
    1791* (Cambridge, 1994).
Forcioli, J. *Une Institution révolutionnaire: Le Tribunal de famille de Caen* (Caen, 1932).
Forrest, A. *Conscripts and Deserters: The Army and French Society During the Revolution
    and Empire* (New York, 1989).
———. *The Revolution in Provincial France: Aquitaine, 1789–1799* (Oxford, 1996).
Forrest, A., and P. Jones, eds. *Reshaping France: Town, Country and Region During the
    French Revolution* (Manchester, 1991).
Forster, R. *The House of Saulx-Tavanes: Versailles and Burgundy, 1700–1830* (Baltimore,
    1971).
———. *Merchants, Landlords, Magistrates: The Depont Family in Eighteenth-Century
    France* (Baltimore, 1980).
———. *The Nobility of Toulouse in the Eighteenth Century: A Social and Economic Study*
    (Baltimore, 1960).
Foucault, M. *Discipline and Punish: The Birth of the Prison*. Translated by A. Sheridan
    (New York, 1979).
Furet, F., and M. Ozouf, eds. *A Critical Dictionary of the French Revolution*. Translated by
    A. Goldhammer (New York, 1989).
Gallet, J. "Justice seigneuriale." In L. Bély, ed., *Dictionnaire de l'ancien régime* (Paris, 1996).
Garrioch, D. *Neighborhood and Community in Eighteenth-Century Paris* (New York, 1986).
Gatrell, V. et al. *Crime and the Law: The Social History of Crime in Western Europe Since
    1500* (London, 1980).
Gauthier, F. *La voie paysanne dans la Révolution française: L'exemple picard* (Paris, 1977).
Giffard, A. *La justice seigneuriale en Bretagne aux XVIIe et XVIIIe siècles* (Paris, 1902).
Gilard, K. "La criminalité dan le ressort du présidial de Saintes, 1770–1790." *Revue de la
    Saintonge et d'Aunis*, 19 (1993): 71–90.
Giraud, E. *L'oeuvre d'organisation judiciaire de l'Assemblée constituante* (Paris, 1921).
Godechot, J. *Les institutions de la France sous la Révolution et l'Empire* (Paris, 1951).
Goubert, P. *Beauvais et le Beauvaisis de 1600 à 1730: Contribution à l'histoire sociale de la
    France du XVIIe siècle* (Paris, 1960).
———. *The French Peasantry in the Seventeenth Century*. Translated by I. Patterson
    (Cambridge, 1986).
———. "Le paysan et la terre: Seigneurie, tenure, exploitation." In F. Braudel and C.
    Labrousse, eds., *Histoire économique et sociale de la France*. Vol. 2: *Des derniers temps
    de l'âge seigneurial aux préludes de l'âge industriel 1660–1789* (Paris, 1970).
Gourdon, D. "Criminalité et déliquance rurales en Aunis, 1750–1765" (Maîtrise, Paris X,
    1978).
Greenshield, M. *An Economy of Violence in Early Modern France: Crime and Justice in the
    Haute-Auvergne, 1587–1664* (University Park, Pa., 1994).
Gresset, M. *Gens de justices à Besançon: De la conquête par Louis XIV à la Révolution
    française, 1674–1789* (Paris, 1978).

Grivel, A. *La justice dans le district de Montpellier en 1790–1791* (Montpellier, 1928).

Gross, J. P. *Fair Shares for All: Jacobin Egalitarianism in Practice* (Cambridge, 1997).

Guéniffey, P. *Le nombre et la raison: La Révolution française et les élections* (Paris, 1993).

Guérin, E.-J. "Les comités révolutionnaires à Saintes (1793–1795)." *Bulletin de la Société des Archéologistes historiques de la Saintonge* (1916): 9–25, 92–105.

———. *Les justices de paix de Saintes depuis 1790* (La Rochelle, 1915).

———. "Un procès devant le juge de paix du canton de Saintes pendant la Révolution." *Revue de la Saintonge et d'Aunis* 39 (1914).

Guillaume, E. *Justice seigneuriale et vie quotidienne dans la vallée du Mont-Dore au XVIIIe siècle* (Clermont-Ferrand, 1992).

Gutton, J-P. *Villages du Lyonnais sous la Monarchie (XVIe–XVIIIe siècles)* (Lyon, 1978).

———. *La société et les pauvres: L'exemple de la généralité de Lyon, 1534–1789* (Paris, 1970).

———. *Domestiques et serviteurs dans la France de l'ancien régime* (Paris, 1981).

Hamada, M. "Une seigneurie et sa justice en Beaujolais aux XVIIe et XVIIIe siècles: Saint-Lager (Rhône)" (Thèse 3e cycle, Lyon II, 1984).

Hay, D., et al., eds. *Albion's Fatal Tree: Crime and Society in Eighteenth-Century England* (London, 1975).

Henry, P. *Crime, justice, et société dans la principauté de Neufchâtel au XVIIIe siècle (1707–1806)* (Neufchâtel, 1984).

Herbert, S. *The Fall of Feudalism in France* (London, 1921).

Hufton, O. "Attitudes Towards Authority in Eighteenth-Century Languedoc." *Social History* 3 (1978).

———. "Le paysan et la loi en France au XVIIIe siècle." *Annales: Economies, sociétés, civilisations* 38 (1983): 679–701.

———. *The Poor of Eighteenth-Century France, 1750–1789* (Oxford, 1974).

———. *The Prospect Before Her: A History of Women in Western Europe* (New York, 1996).

Hunt, D. "Peasant Politics in the French Revolution." *Social History* 9 (1984): 277–97.

Hunt, L. *The Family Romance of the French Revolution* (Berkeley, 1992).

———. *Politics, Culture, and Class in the French Revolution* (Berkeley, 1984).

Jeanvrot, V. *Les juges de paix élus sous la Révolution* (Saintes, 1883).

Jessenne, J. *Pouvoir au village et Révolution: Artois, 1760–1848* (Lille, 1987).

———. "Le pouvoir des fermiers dans les villages d'Artois (1770–1848)." *Annales: Economies, sociétés, civilisations* 38 (1983).

Jones, C. "Bourgeois Revolution Revivified." In C. Lucas, ed., *Rewriting the French Revolution* (Oxford, 1991).

Jones, P. *The Peasantry in the French Revolution* (Cambridge, 1988).

———. *Politics and Rural Society: The Southern Massif Central, c. 1750–1800* (Cambridge, 1985).

Jousmet, R. "Fermiers et métayers d'Aunis, 1750–1789" (Thèse de doctorat, Université de Rennes, 1989).

Julien-Labruyère, F. *Paysans charentais: Histoire des campagnes d'Aunis, Saintonge et Bas Angoumois.* 2 vols. (La Rochelle, 1982).

Kagan, R. *Lawsuits and Litigants in Castile, 1500–1700* (Chapel Hill, 1981).

Kaiser, C. "The Deflation in the Volume of Litigation at Paris in the Eighteenth Century and the Waning of the Old Judicial Order." *European Studies Review* 10 (1980): 309–36.

Kaplan, S. "Réflexions su la police du monde de travail, 1700–1815." *Revue historique* 26 (1979): 17–28.

Kressel, K., and D. Pruitt, eds. *Mediation Research: The Process and Effectiveness of Third-Party Intervention* (San Francisco, 1989).

Kwass, M. "A Kingdom of Taxpayers: State Formation, Privilege, and Political Culture in Eighteenth-Century France." *Journal of Modern History* 70 (June 1998): 295–339.

Landau, N. *The Justices of the Peace, 1679–1760* (Berkeley, 1984).

Laveau, C. *Le monde rochelais des Bourbons à Bonaparte* (La Rochelle, 1988).

Lebigre, A. *Les grands jours d'Auvergne: Désordes et répression au XVIIe siècle* (Paris, 1976).

———. *La justice du Roi: La Vie judiciaire dans l'ancienne France* (Paris, 1988).

Lefebvre, G. *Les paysans du Nord pendant la Révolution française* (Lille, 1924).

Le Goff, T. *Vannes and Its Region: A Study of Town and Country in Eighteenth-Century France* (Oxford, 1981).

Le Goff, T., and D. Sutherland. "The Revolution and the Rural Community in Eighteenth-Century Brittany." *Past and Present* 62 (1974): 96–119.

Legoux, L. "Les Tribunaux de district en Ille et Vilaine, 1790–1795" (Thèse de doctorat, Université de Rennes, 1912).

Lemarchand, G. "La féodalité et la Révolution française: Seigneurs et communauté paysanne (1780–1799)." *Annales historiques de la Révolution française,* 52 (1980): 536–58.

Lemercier, P. *Les justices seigneuriales de la région Parisienne de 1580 à 1789* (Paris, 1933).

Lemonnier, P. *Etude historique de Rochefort-sur-Mer, 1789–1802* (La Rochelle, 1901).

———. "L'impôt sur le revenu à Rochefort-sur-Mer (1789–1793)." *Bulletin de la Société des archéologistes historiques de la Saintonge* (1908): 5–29.

———. "Le Tribunal révolutionnaire de Rochefort." *Bulletin de la Société des archéologistes historiques de la Saintonge* (1910–12).

Le Roy Ladurie, E. "Révoltes et contestations rurales en France de 1675 à 1788." *Annales: Economies, sociétés, civilisations* (1974): 6–22.

Leymarie, D. "Les redevances foncières seigneuriales en Haute-Auvergne." *Annales historiques de la Révolution française* 40 (1968): 299–380.

Luc, J-N. *Paysans et droits féodaux en Charente-Inférieure pendant la Révolution française* (Paris, 1984).

———. "Les révoltes paysannes de Varaize et des villages voisins en 1790." *Receuil de la société d'histoire de la Charente-Maritime* 25 (1973–74).

———., ed. *La Charente-Maritime, l'Aunis et la Saintonge des origines à nos jours* (St. Jean d'Angély, 1981).

Lucas, C., ed. *Reshaping France: Town, Country, and Region During the French Revolution* (New York, 1991).

Mackrell, J. *The Attack on "Feudalism" in Eighteenth-Century France* (London, 1973).

McManners, J. *The French Revolution and the Church* (New York, 1969).

Maltbie, H. "Crime and the Local Community in France (Drôme), 1770–1820" (Ph.D. diss., Oxford University, 1980).

Marion, M. *Dictionnaire des institutions de la France depuis 1715* (Paris, 1969).

———. *La Garde des Sceaux Lamoignon et la réforme judiciaire de 1788* (Paris, 1905).

Markoff, J. *The Abolition of Feudalism: Peasants, Lords, and Legislators in the French Revolution* (University Park, Pa., 1996).

————. "Violence, Emancipation, and Democracy: The Countryside and the French Revolution." *American Historical Review,* 100 (April 1995).

Markoff, J., and G. Shapiro. *Revolutionary Demands: A Content Analysis of the Cahiers de Doléance of 1789* (Stanford, 1998).

Massé, P. *Varennes et ses maîtres, un domaine de l'ancien régime à la Monarchie de Juillet (1779–1842)* (Paris, 1956).

Massiou, D. *Histoire politique, civile et religieuse de la Saintonge et de l'Aunis.* 6 vols. (Paris, 1836–38).

Merryman, J. *The Civil Law Tradition* (Stanford, 1969).

Mesnard, A. *Histoire de Saint-Jean d'Angély sous la Révolution et l'époque contemporaine* (Paris, 1910).

Métairie, G. *Le monde des juges de paix de Paris, (1790–1838)* (Paris, 1994).

Millot, J. *L'abolition des droits féodaux dans le département du Doubs et la région Comtoise* (Besançon, 1941).

Mousnier, R. *The Institutions of France Under the Absolute Monarchy, 1598–1789.* Translated by B. Pierce. 2 vols. (Chicago, 1979, 1984).

Muchembled, R. *L'invention de l'homme moderne: Sensibilités, moeurs et comportements collectifs sous l'ancien régime* (Paris, 1988).

————. *La violence au village* (Paris, 1989).

Muir, E. *Mad Blood Stirring: Vendetta and Factions in Friuli during the Renaissance* (Baltimore, 1993).

Palmer, S. *Police and Protest in England and Ireland, 1780–1850* (Cambridge, 1988).

Parker, D. *Class and State in Ancien Régime France* (New York, 1996).

Peret, J. "Seigneurs et seigneuries en Gâtine poitevine: Le duché de la Meillaraye, XVIIe–XVIIIe siècles." *Mémoires de la Société des antiquaires de l'Ouest,* 13 (1974–76): 357–77.

Perrot, E. *Les cas royaux: Origine et développement de la théorie au XIIIe et XIVe siècles* (Paris, 1910).

Perrot, R., *Institutions judiciaires* (Paris, 1992).

Phillips, R. *Family Breakdown in Late Eighteenth-Century France: Divorce in Rouen, 1792–1803* (Oxford, 1980).

Pinasseau, J. *L'Emigration militaire: Emigrés de Saintonge, Angoumois et Aunis dans le corps de troupe de l'émigration française, 1791–1814* (Paris, 1974).

Poitrineau, A. "Aspects de la crise des justices seigneuriales dans l'Auvergne du XVIIIe siècle." *Revue historique du Droit français et étranger* 39 (1961): 552–70.

————. *Ils travaillaient la France: Métiers et mentalités du XVIe au XIX siècle* (Paris, 1992).

————. *La vie rurale en basse Auvergne au XVIIIe siècle (1726–1789)* (Paris, 1965).

Postel, N. "Les soulèvements populaires en Aunis et en Saintonge, Poitou et Angoumois, 1483–1787" (D.E.S., La Sorbonne, 1966).

Proust, A. *Archives de l'Ouest, receuil de documents concernant la Révolution, 1789–1800.* Série A: *Opérations électorales de 1789.* 2 vols. (Poitiers, 1867–68).

Queguiner, J-P. "Violence à La Rochelle et dans son district (1790–1799)" (D.E.A., Université de Poitiers, 1981).

Ramsay, C. *The Ideology of the Great Fear: The Soissonnais in 1789* (Baltimore, 1992).

Ratour, A. *Géographie humaine et aménagement en Haute Saintonge* (Poitiers, 1979).

Redfield, R. *Peasant Society and Culture* (Chicago, 1956).

Reinhardt, S. "Crime and Royal Justice in *Ancien Régime* France: Modes of Analysis." *Journal of Interdisciplinary History* 13, no. 3 (1983): 437–60.

———. *Justice in the Sarladais, 1770–1790* (Baton Rouge, 1991).

Reinhardt, S., and E. Cawthon, eds. *Essays on the French Revolution: Paris and the Provinces* (College Station, Tex., 1992).

La Révolution et l'ordre juridique privé: Rationalité ou scandale? Actes du colloque d'Orléans 11–13 septembre 1986 (Paris, 1986).

Reveilland, E. *Histoire politique et parlementaire des départements de la Charente et de la Charente-Inférieure de 1789 à 1830* (St. Jean d'Angély, 1911).

Riollot, J. *Le droit de prévention des juges royaux sur les juges seigneuriaux* (Paris, 1931).

Robert, J. *L'arbitrage: Droit interne, droit international privé* (Paris, 1983).

Robin, R. "Fief et seigneurie dans le droit et l'idéologie juridique à la fin du XVIIIe siècle." *Annales historiques de la Révolution française* 43 (1971): 554–602.

Root, H. *Peasants and King in Burgundy: Agrarian Foundations of French Absolutism* (Berkeley, 1987).

Royer, J-P. *Histoire de la justice en France: De la monarchie absolue à la République* (Paris, 1995).

———. *La société judiciaire depuis le XVIIIe siècle* (Paris, 1979).

Ruff, J. *Crime, Justice, and Public Order in Old Regime France: The Sénéchaussées of Libourne and Bazas, 1696–1789* (London, 1984).

Sabean, D. *Power in the Blood: Popular Culture and Village Discourse in Early Modern Germany* (New York, 1984).

Sagnac, P. *La législation civile de la Révolution française* (Paris, 1898).

Sagnac, P., and M. Bruchet, eds. *L'abolition des droits seigneuriaux en Savoie (1761–1793)* (Annecy, 1908).

Saint-Jacob, P. de, *Les paysans de la Bourgogne du Nord au dernier siècle de l'ancien régime* (Paris, 1960).

Sautel, G. *Une juridiction municipale de police sous l'ancien régime: Le bureau de police d'Aix-en-Provence* (Paris, 1946).

Schama, S. *Citizens: A Chronicle of the French Revolution* (New York, 1989).

Schnapper, B. *La diffusion en France des nouvelles conceptions pénales dans la dernière décennie de l'ancien régime* (Paris, 1986).

———. "Pour une géographie des mentalités judiciaires: La litigiosité en France au XIX siècle." *Annales: Economies, sociétés, civilisations* 2 (1979): 399–419.

Schneider, Z. "The Village and the State: Justice and the Local Courts in Normandy, 1670–1740" (Ph.D. diss., Georgetown University, 1997).

Schwartz, R. *Policing the Poor in Eighteenth-Century France* (Chapel Hill, 1988).

Scott, J. *Weapons of the Weak: Everyday Forms of Peasant Resistance* (New Haven, 1985).

Seguin, M. *Jonzac au XVIIIe et XVIIIe siècles* (St. Jean d'Angély, 1983).

Séligmann, E. *La justice en France pendant la Révolution.* 2 vols. (Paris, 1901, 1913).

Shapiro, B. *Revolutionary Justice in Paris, 1789–90* (Cambridge, 1993).

Smith, J. "No More Language Games: Words, Belief, and the Political Culture of Early Modern France." *American Historical Review* 102 (December 1997): 1413–40.

Soboul, A., ed. *Contributions à l'histoire paysans de la Révolution française* (Paris, 1977).

Soman, A. "Deviance and Criminal Justice in Western Europe, 1300–1800: An Essay in Structure." *Criminal Justice History* 1 (1980): 3–28.

Sutherland, D. *The Chouans: The Social Origins of Popular Counter-Revolution in Upper Brittany, 1770–1796* (Oxford, 1982).
———. *France, 1789–1815: Revolution and Counterrevolution* (Oxford, 1986).
Tackett, T. *Becoming a Revolutionary: The Deputies of the French National Assembly and the Emergence of a Revolutionary Culture (1789–90)* (Princeton, 1996).
Tapie, V. "Les officiers seigneuriaux dans la société provinciale du XVIIe siècle." *Dix-septième siècle* 42–43 (1959).
Taylor, G. "Revolutionary and Nonrevolutionary Content in the *Cahiers* of 1789: An Interim Report." *French Historical Studies* 7 (1972): 479–502.
Ten Raa, C. "De Oorsprong Van De Kantonrechter (Les origines du juge de paix en France ainsi que celles du Kantonrechter en Hollande)" (Ph.D. diss., University of Rotterdam, 1970).
Thompson, E. P. "The Moral Economy of the English Crowd in the Eighteenth Century." *Past and Present* 50 (1971).
———. *Whigs and Hunters: The Origin of the Black Act* (New York, 1975).
Timbal, P. *Droit romain et ancien droit français* (Paris, 1960).
Tocqueville, A. de. *The Old Regime and the French Revolution.* Translated by S. Gilbert (Garden City, N.Y., 1955).
Torlais, J. *Le journal d'un bourgeois rochelais pendant la Révolution* (La Rochelle, 1941).
Tournerie, J.-A. *Recherches sur la crise judiciaire en province à la fin de l'ancien régime: Le Présidial de Tours de 1740 à 1790* (Tours, 1975).
Traer, J. "The French Family Court." *History* 59 (1974): 211–28.
Uglow, S., *Policing Liberal Society* (Oxford, 1988).
Valin, C. "Recherces sur La Rochelle, ville frontière au cours de la crise révolutionnaire, 1790–an III" 2 vols. (Thèse de doctorat, Université de Rouen, 1994).
Vardi, L. "Peasants and the Law: A Village Appeals to the French Royal Council, 1768–1791." *Social History* 13 (1988): 295–318.
Vaux de Foletier, F. de. *Histoire d'Aunis et de Saintonge* (Paris, 1929).
Villard, P. *Les justices seigneuriales dans la Marche* (Paris, 1969).
Vincenti, A. *Le Tribunal du département du Vaucluse, de l'an IV à l'an VIII* (Aix-en-Provence, 1928).
Vovelle, M. *La découverte de la politique: Géopolitique de la Révolution française* (Paris, 1993).
———. *The Revolution Against the Church: From Reason to the Supreme Being.* Translated by A. Jose (Cambridge, 1991).
———. *Ville et campagne au 18e siècle: Chartres et la Beauce* (Paris, 1980).
———., ed. *La Rochelle, ville frontière. Actes du Colloque des 28–29 avril 1989* (La Rochelle, 1989).
Weber, E. *Peasants into Frenchmen: The Modernization of Rural France, 1870–1914* (Stanford, 1976).
Weber, M. *Economy and Society* (New York, 1968).
Wells, C. *Law and Citizenship in Early Modern France* (Baltimore, 1995).
Wiesner, M. *Women and Gender in Early Modern Europe* (Cambridge, 1993).
Williams, A. *The Police of Paris, 1718–1789* (Baton Rouge, 1979).
Woloch, I. *The New Regime: Transformations of the French Civic Order, 1789–1820s* (New York, 1994).